GREAT SCOTT!

GREAT SCOTT!

The Best of
Jay Scott's Movie Reviews

Edited by Karen York

M&S

Canadian Cataloguing in Publication Data
Scott, Jay
Great Scott! : the best of Jay Scott's
movie reviews

Includes index.
ISBN 0-7710-3365-6

1. Motion pictures – Reviews.   I. Title.

PN1995.S36 1994   791.43'75   C94-930492-1

The publishers acknowledge the support of the
Canada Council, the Ontario Ministry of Culture,
Tourism and Recreation, and the Ontario Arts Council
for their publishing program.

Typeset by M&S
Printed and bound in Canada. The paper used in
this book is acid-free.

McClelland & Stewart Inc.
The Canadian Publishers
481 University Avenue
Toronto, Ontario
M5G 2E9

1 2 3 4 5   98 97 96 95 94

Contents

Foreword

Jay Scott was the writing hero of the *Globe and Mail* newsroom from the day he started producing film reviews in 1977. He was the writer others hoped to become, and, over time, many others did grow into better writers because of his example and proximity.

Jay Scott wrote brilliantly about film because he loved the medium and knew it intimately. He wrote brilliantly because he had a fine mind, a wicked sense of humour and a playful confidence in the language that generated vibrant prose. He wrote brilliantly because he wrote bravely, expressing his convictions without compromise, revealing himself without indulgence. He wrote brilliantly because he distinguished empathy from sentimentality, in other people's work as well as his own. And always, he wrote with the intent of the artist and the pleasure of the reader in mind.

This collection of his reviews and features for the *Globe and Mail* documents and illuminates sixteen years of filmmaking in the world, and well illustrates the scope and power of Jay Scott's mind and spirit. It was selected after his untimely death in July 1993 by his long-time editor, Karen York – her hand as important in shaping this anthology as it was in shaping the work of which it is comprised. Proceeds from the sale of this book will be directed to research into AIDS, in memory of Jay Scott.

We are proud that Jay Scott was among us, was one of us. We are delighted that, in collaboration with McClelland & Stewart, his work will now reach a wider audience across the generations.

William Thorsell
Editor in Chief
The Globe and Mail

Introduction

He was a newspaper reporter who transformed himself into a virtuoso critic, and did it among people who often cast a cool eye on such grand ambitions. Newspapers, for the most part, want it fast and plain, and while he was always fast, Jay Scott was never plain. For all his lightheartedness, he cared about films and about his own writing. That produced certain difficulties, since editors often think it's silly to take movies seriously and even sillier for a newspaper writer to cultivate an individual style. Moviemakers, for their part, seldom encourage the emergence of good critics, since most of them are egomaniacally committed to the belief that a critic's sole function is to praise them as often as possible. And there are readers beyond number who regard a movie reviewer not as a writer but as a kind of taste-tester, a consumer guide who shouldn't bother the public with ideas. Taken together, these forces can discourage just about anyone who brings a free-flying imagination to the job of writing about popular culture.

Yet once in a while, someone like Scott moves so far beyond the arthritic routines of journalism that reading him feels something like watching a first-class athlete, one of those people who create excitement just by their presence. At the top of his form, in the 1980s, he recalled earlier stars of the culture pages, like Kenneth Tynan of the London *Observer* in the 1950s and Pauline Kael of *The New Yorker* in the 1970s. Like them, he put on a spectacular show and loved to be talked about: he generated excitement about his subject by first of all making himself exciting. Critics shape the context in which artists reach their public, and Scott did as much as anyone to create a sophisticated audience for film. In a sense, the audience found itself through Scott. By becoming a centre of discourse, he helped moviegoers in Toronto to make connections among themselves and form an articulate community.

Scott's ambitions set him apart from most journalists. He was reluctant to say much about what a critic should do, but his writing makes it clear that he was aiming for something grander than everyday newspaper work. His appetite for subject matter was insatiable: he wanted to write, with verve and intimacy, about art, sex, literature, food, politics, fashion and anything else that fell under his watchful eye. He had another ambition, still larger: he wanted to be himself rather than a standard-issue journalist. In what the critic Jacques Barzun called "the great American tradition of the judicious eccentric," Scott was determined to make his own kind of noise. He wanted to be in print what he was in life: a witty, curious, irony-loving, leather-clad homosexual who rode his motorcycle (always at judicious speed) through the streets of Toronto. He wanted to think his own odd thoughts, make his own outlandish connections, and tell us about them. Astonishingly, he succeeded in doing most of these things, so that his life, while far shorter than it should have been, was its own kind of triumph.

He was born Jeffrey Scott Beaven in Lincoln, Nebraska, on October 4, 1949. He attributed his addiction to movies (in a slow week he saw about five of them) to his Seventh-Day Adventist parents, who forbade moviegoing during his childhood. When he was sixteen and the family was living in Albuquerque, New Mexico, his parents divorced. Shortly after, his father committed suicide. The following year Scott enrolled in an experimental liberal arts college, and not long after that he was at the University of New Mexico, studying acting while editing the arts section of the college paper. He married and moved to Toronto, where he worked on a construction-trade paper, the *Daily Commercial News*. This first attempt at immigration was a failure: potential employers apparently assumed he had little to offer. Back in New Mexico, on the *Albuquerque Journal* in 1972, he began covering movies and occasionally art, along with the usual police and courts stories that fall to young reporters. His career was nicely under way, but he continued to dream of a radical change. By answering an ad, he found a job as an arts journalist at the Calgary *Albertan,* a paper he had never read in a city he had never seen.

There, as in Albuquerque, he was Scott Beaven. That was the name I saw on a clipping in 1975, when I was a judge of the criticism category for the National Newspaper Awards. He reviewed, in his idea of cowboy language, "*The Alberta Cowboy Show . . .* by this theatre company from Toronto what calls themselves Theatre Passe Muraille and what came to Alberta to live with cowboys and what did this play 'bout cowboys. . . . I couldn't tell if those young folks was makin' fun of us or tryin' to understand us. . . ." It wasn't brilliant, but I thought it easily the best among the entries, and my fellow judges agreed. Scott Beaven, only a few months in Canada, won a National Newspaper Award, his first of three. His picture, with long seventies hair flowing down the side of his face, appeared in the program of the awards dinner in Toronto. Then, as far as I knew, he vanished from the face of the earth.

Four or five years later, long after I became one of Jay Scott's admiring readers, I learned the fate of Scott Beaven. He had been hired by *The Globe and Mail* in November 1977. Having never liked his last name, he decided that this was the time to change it: a new name for a new job. He was twenty-eight, a talented, hard-working young man who also happened to be lucky. In joining the *Globe,* he not only came to the right place, he came at the right time. Ten years earlier, in 1967, Toronto was far less attractive to someone writing about movies, if only because there were far fewer films being shown or made. Ten years before that, in 1957, some local newspaper editors didn't even believe they needed a full-time movie critic. But in the late seventies, Toronto was as ready for Jay Scott as he was for it, and they happily embraced each other.

Every year, in early autumn, thousands of Torontonians watch movies from morning to midnight for ten days, spilling out into the streets and cafés and creating their own *Cinema Paradiso* along Bloor Street. We have lived with this event for so long that it's been absorbed by the city and taken for granted. But the Festival of Festivals was a wonderful gift to Scott, and so was the fact that Toronto in his time became a place to make movies, either by masquerading as an American city or (less often) by producing Canadian films.

Scott didn't make Toronto a great moviegoing city (well before he got here, the papers were running stories about our local passion for films), nor did he help the festival get started. The third festival, in 1978, was the first one he covered for the *Globe*. And yet he became central to Toronto's image of itself as a movie town. He was, for instance, crucial to the Carlton Cinema, where his reviews of exotic films (including, sometimes, exotic Canadian films) appeared on the walls so often that his face became part of the decor. It's still hard to imagine the Carlton without him. Scott and the festival were made for each other, both of them committed to contradictory passions: for movies as a global art form, and for Hollywood-type stardom.

From his perch at the *Globe*, Scott watched two transformations in the culture of movies, one of them deadening and the other exciting. The depressing news came from Hollywood: 1977, the year he arrived in Toronto, also brought *Star Wars* and a new era. Movie producers, far more than in the past, began looking for the formula that would not just make them rich but would drown them in money. Their search for the titanic hit became a kind of collective madness, which everyone in Hollywood deplored even as they succumbed to it. *Star Wars* was the dividing line, the dawn of machine-made products with stereotyped characters in expensive settings. By 1985, Scott was writing that "the ineptitude, cowardice, and greed of the Hollywood studios" had just about killed movies. But something much more encouraging was also happening. Sophisticated moviegoers were welcoming films from the far corners of China or Finland or Africa. Scott made himself into a kind of ambassador from these national cinemas, interpreting them to Canada. Again, he and the festival meshed.

Helga Stephenson, Scott's close friend and, until 1994, the director of the Festival of Festivals, recently summed up his attitude to the films that he liked: "When Jay discovered something, he wanted the whole world to share it, like a kid bringing home a prize: Look what I found." He was an impresario of opinion who understood that searching for little-known talent was his duty. By 1981, he was a force in the film world, and not only in Toronto. "*Diva* is the classic case," according to Stephenson. It was a bizarre French thriller that failed when it first appeared in France. At the Festival of Festivals, "Jay jumped all over it," Stephenson remembers. "He could turn up the heat on a film. He knew how to fill a theatre." The day of its North American première, Scott's review in the *Globe* called it "the most impressive debut from a French director since Godard's *Breathless*... 21 years ago." Within a few days, the same distributors who had earlier rejected it were signing a contract for North American rights. *Diva* turned into one of the great art-house hits and soon became a success in Europe, too.

Scott's energy was prodigious. For years, he saw every Canadian feature made; he played a large role in the careers of directors ranging from Denys Arcand (*Jesus of Montreal*) to Atom Egoyan (*Family Viewing*). He became a valued regular contributor to *Canadian Art* magazine, wrote a breezy column on books for *Chatelaine*, and for TVOntario chose international films that he introduced with easy grace. In the 1980s he went back to his old home, Albuquerque, to gather information for *Changing Woman: The Life and Art of Helen Hardin* (1989), a biography of a Pueblo Indian artist whose modern paintings reflect the themes of her culture. In 1988 he set to work on a biography of the Canadian filmmaker Norman Jewison, which may have been Scott's only major career mistake. Jewison's films have been consistently middlebrow and mainstream, not at all the sort of work that most excited Scott. (At his death only a part of the book was written.)

For a while Jay Scott seemed to be everywhere. And then, a couple of years ago, he began to appear in the *Globe* rather less, and people who followed his work but didn't know him began to worry. It was the kind of worrying that has become painfully familiar to everyone in the arts.

Oscar Wilde said that criticism is a form of autobiography, and that was certainly true of Jay Scott: he wrote the story of his life between the lines of his reviews. Sometime around 1980, he and his wife broke up and the fact that he was gay became widely known. Helga Stephenson remembers a farewell party at a gay disco in Toronto for another film critic who was moving to New York. Scott showed up in leather and began sashaying around the floor with Craig Russell, the female impersonator. Stephenson says, "I thought, well, there's a new era at the *Globe.*"

Scott's careful readers noticed. Clearly, a gay sensibility was speaking to us through our morning paper. He became the first prominent journalist in Canada to absorb and project the self-confidence created by the gay liberation movement. When he described the German film-maker Rainer Werner Fassbinder, for instance, Scott adopted an insider's easy tone: Fassbinder, he said, "constantly wore clumps of keys clipped to his left hip, a signal to all gays that he was a homosexual who took a dominant sexual role, and a signal to gays in his own S&M subculture that he was a sadist, or 'top'." And yet in 1985, the same year he published that passage in *Midnight Madness,* a book of his articles, Scott asked Ian Pearson, who was writing an article about him for *Saturday Night,* not to mention his sexual orientation. He feared it might endanger the career of his companion, a schoolteacher. It was a transition period, when a new frankness coexisted alongside the old uneasiness.

For a while, through the late seventies and early eighties, many homosexuals were so exuberant, so delighted with their new freedoms, that some people suggested that homophobia was nothing more than envy of the sexual liberty that gays enjoyed. That period was, of course, poignantly brief. It ended with the arrival of AIDS, when a dark ash of dread fell over homosexual life. Jay's lover, Gene Corboy, fell ill. He died in 1989. That year, reviewing *Torch Song Trilogy,* the movie version of a New York play written by Harvey Fierstein before the AIDS epidemic, Scott called it "a period piece perched on the brink of the abyss."

Scott himself tested HIV-positive about seven years ago, and within the last two years grew thin and weak. He kept writing, although at a slower pace. He seldom spoke of his illness and refused to acknowledge that at certain times he couldn't work. He wanted his suffering to be private, which for the most part it was. His death on July 30 [1993], at the age of forty-three, came as a surprise to many of his friends and readers. They had counted on seeing a lot more of him.

What startled me about his work when it began appearing regularly in the *Globe* was the swarm of proper nouns that buzzed through just about every piece he wrote. In 1981, reviewing in four paragraphs a remake of *The Postman Always Rings Twice*, Scott managed to mention Luchino Visconti, Albert Camus, Edward Hopper, Ingmar Bergman, a dress from I. Magnin, and eight other movies. That habit looked at first like name-dropping, but as it became woven into his style, Scott's purpose became clearer. He was outlining a context, drawing a kind of cultural grid on which a film could be placed. He played with voices and forms (sometimes he wrote a whole review as a series of rhetorical questions) but he wrote his best pieces in a brilliant mélange of far-reaching analogies, learned references and hip vernacular. While he was anxious to share his enthusiasms with a wide public, he wanted to reach that public in his own way, without writing directly to it. In 1983, he told a student journalist: "I tend to write for three or four of my closest friends; if they like it, that's praise enough." That's an unlikely confession from a journalist, and many an editor would call it élitist. But it worked for Scott: it gave the best of his writing the intimacy of an overheard conversation. He didn't always come through clearly, but that's a hazard of eavesdropping. It seems unlikely, for instance, that even his three or four closest friends understood what he meant when, on August 20 last year, he described a character in a new Canadian movie as an "ithyphallic virgin" (apparently the fellow's penis was erect). Nor did his friends necessarily pick up every reference when, in one brief passage of a piece about the Havana film festival, he referred to Meyer Lansky, Carmen Miranda, Disney, De Mille, *The Godfather II*, "A hugely fat diva with the face of

Pontiac and the voice of Birgit Nilsson on a bad night," and "A male singer with the flat-featured, smiley face of Don Ho . . ."

A *Globe* colleague, Rick Groen, argued in an obituary that Scott placed his sometimes arcane analogies in a context that made them clear. And if they weren't, well then, "You could look it up later – the reader, like the watcher, had responsibilities too," as Groen said. Scott trusted his readers, and his editors trusted him. He didn't think everything had to be explained. Overexplaining was a temptation to be ordinary, a fate he wanted to avoid and usually did.

Much of journalism, alas, is dead on arrival. Henry James wrote a piece in 1891 describing the reason: often there isn't enough living material to fill the pages. A publication, he said, is like a train that leaves at a certain hour but only if every seat is occupied. On this imaginary train there aren't always enough passengers, so dummies have to be manufactured. "A stuffed mannikin is thrust into the empty seat, where it makes a creditable figure till the end of the journey. It looks sufficiently like a passenger, and you know it is not one only when you perceive that it neither says anything nor gets out."

Jay Scott so arranged his life that he was always among the living passengers and always had something to say. In the 1980s, he wrote, "I knew, and I thought every journalist . . . knew, that although he or she might be unique, replacement was clearly possible." Not in this case.

Robert Fulford
Toronto Life
October 1993

Interiors

Written and directed by Woody Allen
Starring Diane Keaton, Geraldine Page and E. G. Marshall

Tragedian: Get serious. We're going to discuss Woody Allen's *Interiors*.

Comic: Oh ho. You mean the movie in which he has betrayed his audience, you mean the phony Ingmar Bergman film, you mean the most wretchedly self-indulgent, hysterically pretentious bit of bilge since *The Trial of Billy Jack*.

Trag: I mean the well-modulated study of affluent angst –

Com: Annie Angst; or, Take the Ennui and Run.

Trag: – which gives us three sisters – Diane Keaton, as an awesomely unhappy poetess; Kristin Griffith, as a moderately unhappy movie actress; Marybeth Hurt, who hurts – and their two unhappy parents, Geraldine Page and E. G. Marshall, and E. G.'s new lease on life, Maureen Stapleton, of whom Hurt says, "She's a vulgarian!"

Com: From Vulgary?

Trag: Desist. You sound like the old Woody Allen.

Com: God go with him. Wherever he is.

Trag: You really didn't like *Interiors*? You must admit that it's ambitious, and a step –

Com: – backward.

Trag: – sideways, at least. It's nicely photographed by Gordon Willis in beiges and pale pinks –

Com: The colours of a cosmeticized corpse.

Trag: – and it has a number of special performances, especially from Geraldine Page and E. G. Marshall.

Com: Granted. The performers are excellent. They make excellent corpses. It's too bad they have to say lines such as: "I can't seem to shake the implication of dying – it's terrifying. The intimacy of death embarrasses me"; "I feel a real need to express something but I don't know what it is or how to express it"; "She's a perfect example of form without content."

Trag: Enough already.

Com: Not quite. There's the topper: "In the face of death, life loses meaning. Write it down." What do you do with lines like that?

Trag: Squirm. No, seriously, Woody Allen is not speaking through his characters, he's speaking about them. The point is that they're clichéd and self-pitying and overarticulate. Earlier, you said Bergman. Not so. It looks like Altman's *Three Women*, but the real influence on this film is the Edward Albee of *A Delicate Balance* – suburban alienation, the breakdown of the family, the perils of loneliness and of togetherness and *Who's Afraid of Virginia Woolf?* The Maureen Stapleton character, who wears red while everyone else wears grey and beige, and has some good lines, such as "You'll live to be a hundred if you give up all the things that make you want to" and "You only live once, but once is enough if you play it right" is like a nice Martha; she even eats like Liz Taylor did in *Virginia Woolf*, and Geraldine Page is like a grown-up Honey, chaos hanging onto a man for order.

Com: Yeah, well, agreed, it's not a European art film, it's an American art film with American rhythms, but there is also the less exalted influence of songwriter Paul Simon. "The Dangling Conversation." The whole movie is in that one song: So we sit and drink our coffee, couched in our indifference, like shells upon the shore, you can hear the ocean roar. Speaking of ocean: Don't you think it's a bit much that Maureen Stapleton, who breathes life into E. G.'s life, also literally breathes life into a drowned daughter?

Trag: A trifle excessive, but symbolically neat.

Com: What about the Jewish-Gentile issue?

Trag: Come again?

Com: This is a movie about Gentiles by a filmmaker whose humour has always involved his Jewishness and the one vital character, Stapleton, is a Jewish mother type. It's an anti-Gentile movie.

Trag: Get serious.

Com: Well, it's a movie about Gentiles by someone who doesn't know the score: does Woody Allen really think that Gentiles are so bloodlessly beige?

Trag: Some of them are. Been to the Granite Club lately?

Com: Been to El Mocambo lately?

Trag: *Interiors* does not claim to be representative. It is about a specific segment of upper middle-class life, in which the people have educated themselves into ennui. People like this do exist.

Com: Why should I care? Why should I settle for a dreary Diane Keaton?

Trag: She's very good at being dreary –

Com: – yes, she is, but why should I settle for Dreary Girl when I can have *Funny Girl*, and why should I settle for serious Woody Allen when I can have *Annie Hall*'s Woody Allen, the Woody Allen who makes serious points buoyantly?

Trag: Because you can't always have everything.

Com: Now you sound like the screenplay.

Trag: But you must admit that *Interiors* is made with care and conviction, and a lot of it works.

Com: Yes, it is. It does. But it's limiting. Would Callas want to confine herself to singing "Blue Suede Shoes"?

Trag: She never did.

Com: Exactly. And Woody Allen should never have made a serious film.

Trag: But if Callas had sung "Blue Suede Shoes," she probably would have done it well, at best, or interestingly, at least.

Com: I see your point. It's the old Dr. Johnson line: you're not so much pleased by the performance of a dog dancing on its hind legs as you are by the fact that it can dance on its hind legs at all.

Trag: Something like that.

September 30, 1978

❖

The Big Fix

Directed by Jeremy Paul Kagan
Written by Roger L. Simon
Starring Richard Dreyfuss

Moses S. Wine (Richard Dreyfuss) is an anachronism from the sixties. He drives a yellow 1969 convertible Volkswagen. When invited to a seduction, he says, OK, you make the hash brownies, I'll bring three bottles of tequila. When imagining the ideal *mise-en-scène* for a seduction, he says, We could pretend there's tear gas coming through the door and we could put on an old Buffalo Springfield album. When watching films of the good old student demonstration days, he weeps with nostalgia. When asked what happened to his cast-confined hand, he answers, "Bar fight with a Bircher." In fact, Moses S. Wine shattered his hand on his son's skateboard, trying to come to terms with the seventies.

The Big Fix, from a screenplay by Roger L. Simon, who wrote the first Moses Wine mystery in 1973 at the behest of *Rolling Stone* and Straight Arrow Books, follows the lead of Robert Altman's *The Long Goodbye* in de-glamorizing the private eye, but it goes much further and is much more poignant. Altman's Phillip Marlowe was a forties hero confined in the sixties; Moses Wine is a sixties anti-hero who's gone reluctantly straight in the seventies.

The situation is bristling with comic, satiric possibilities and, by the end of *The Big Fix*, most of the barbs have found their targets. Set in Los Angeles, the film has the slick, hip ambience of a *New West* magazine article, and because it deals with Moses' rejuvenation as a human being, it could have been called Shucking the Sixties: New Wine From Old Dregs.

Dreyfuss' acting style – all intense, earnest, scenery-chewing manic high spirits, the salesman as intellectual (would you buy a used world view from this man?) – is anachronistic in and of itself. The stars of the seventies (Travolta, Gere, Beatty and all the rest) are softly sensitive at the centre. Dreyfuss' Moses, posing at being burned out, is still smouldering – there is nothing soft about his centre, though we can see that he is sensitive, far more sensitive than his ex-wife (Bonnie Bedelia), who spends most of her time, and most of his money, on sensitivity-training seminars.

Moses doesn't want to care, but he can't help himself, and we can see why when we meet his Aunt Sonya (Rita Karin), an old socialist who offers to read Moses' kids a story about the Albanian Labour Party. To Moses, she says, "I remember when you used to believe in something."

Dreyfuss, doing his best work since Duddy Kravitz (this is a performance that approaches perfection), gives Moses Wine an astringent, acrid bouquet; it's difficult to conceive of a better role for him.

As a slice of sociologically accurate life, *The Big Fix* is resonant, compassionate, improbably funny; as a mystery, it's improbable and obtuse. One of the movie talents that was lost in the quick-cut sixties was the ability to solve a mystery with cinematic coherence, and the talent has yet to be regained. At the end, when things are supposed to come together, you may feel that you, like Moses Wine, have been playing the Parker Brothers' game of Clue solitaire.

Normally, a mystery with a mucked-up solution is something like an omelette without eggs, but with *The Big Fix*, the absence of a major ingredient is forgivable. Who can cavil loudly about a movie that gives us a former revolutionary, author of *Rip It Off*, hiding out as an adman because "I can write copy faster than any alcoholic on this floor"?

Surveying his Hollywood Hills pool, the underground hero concludes, "The reason there will never be a revolution in this country is because it's like being a spoilsport at an orgy. All those goodies . . . and you feel like a shit for saying no." You'd feel the same way for calling *The Big Fix* anything less than one of the best movies of the year.

October 10, 1978

❖

Midnight Express

Directed by Alan Parker
Written by Oliver Stone
Starring Brad Davis, Randy Quaid and John Hurt

Why has *Midnight Express* been causing a furor? Critics have been reacting to it as if it carried bubonic plague. Audiences have booed and walked out; have cheered and given it standing ovations. When it was screened last month in Toronto at the Festival of Festivals, Billy Hayes, the young American whose adventures in a Turkish prison are the foundation of the fictionalized film, was standing in the lobby of the Towne Cinema. A Columbia Pictures executive, noticing Hayes' nervousness, said, "Don't worry, Billy. It's a young crowd, very hip, very bluejean." When Hayes walked up the aisle at the conclusion of the movie, the crowd jumped to its work-booted feet. Adulation.

Obviously, *Midnight Express* must be more than just another prison-break movie: "The Great Hashish Escape." Mustn't it? Not really. *Midnight Express*, regardless of the reaction it has engendered, is just another prison-break movie, but with one significant, 1978 addition: there hasn't been a movie since *Straw Dogs* that has tried so consciously to make violence look good, look right, look natural. The penultimate violent scene, when Hayes bites a prison informer's tongue out of his mouth and spits the flesh in a graceful arch, is photographed from under Hayes' chin in slow-motion, and it's photographed with the sensually romanticized reverence hard-core pornographers reserve for the male climax. At that orgiastic moment, the lines are drawn in the audience; from then on, most people either hate *Midnight Express* or love it.

I liked it. And I think the other objections that have been raised – predominately that the Turks are presented as slobberingly inhuman – are misunderstandings of form masquerading as objections to content. *Midnight Express* is a melodrama (with documentary overtones) and it is easy to forget that the entire film is told from Billy Hayes' point of view. There is an esthetic rationale for the depiction of the guards as yowlingly sadistic and alien: they would appear that way to a white middle-class kid from the United States. Prejudice and an attraction to violence are on the screen because they are in the prisoner's mind, and the prisoner's mind is on the screen.

Alan Parker, the British filmmaker who gave us (thanks a heap) *Bugsy Malone*, has directed the film as if he were a sniper: you never know when you're going to get hit next, but from the first moments you know you're being aimed at. The opening, with Hayes taping hash to his chest only to be apprehended at the airport, must have looked like standard stuff in Oliver Stone's script, but on screen it's unadulterated adrenalin, filmed with fast cuts timed in counterpoint to the sound of Hayes' pounding heart. Inside the prison, there is no mercy – bullets keep whistling by your ears and when Hayes' appeal is denied, when he calls the Turks "Pigs!" in court, when he murders the informer, and when he's transferred to an asylum, you're pinged between the eyes. In the midst of the brutality (Dante could take lessons from *Midnight Express*) there is an aching tenderness in the performances of Randy Quaid, as a potentially psychotic inmate, and John Hurt, as a junkie Brit. There is a wounding poignancy when Hayes' girlfriend comes for a visit and at his request allows him to lick her breast, through glass, while he masturbates – I don't know if there has ever been a scene that dramatized so clearly and with such economy the denial of dignity that imprisonment entails. There is also an idyllic interlude between Hayes and a Swedish prisoner (male) which ends, coyly, when Hayes spurns the Swede's sexual advances (Doris Day in the inferno?).

That scene is one of several deviations from Hayes' book (he did have sex with the prisoner; he did not kill a guard; he did not call the Turks pigs in court) but it is the only one that feels false. Stone has compressed the experiences of many North American prisoners; if the fictionalizations didn't happen to Hayes, they did happen. Few of the departures bothered me because Parker is dealing with a compacted emotional reality, a concordance of prison experience, which is why the violence is glamorized: you'd probably want to kill, too. How do you make a film with this subject and ignore those impulses? Brad

Davis, the actor playing Hayes, doesn't ask for easy sympathy – he seems pretty dense, in fact – but his actions are explicable if not exculpable.

What did alienate me was the excessive prettiness of the cinematography (this movie was born to be black and white) and the casting of actors such as Quaid, Bo Hopkins and Mike Kellen (as Hayes' father) – able actors, but actors whose faces are familiar. They crack the documentary façade and you are aware, at times you shouldn't be, of watching a re-enactment. It also annoyed me, initially, that Parker left himself open to charges of ignoring the Turkish point of view by not subtitling the Turkish court sequences, in which a prosecutor speaking the native language (a friend who has lived in the Middle East for a decade translated) says that Turkey has a North American reputation of being a sleazy drug paradise, yet it is Americans like Billy Hayes who provide the money for the perpetuation of the drug trade, even as their government deplores the punishment. The prosecutor has a point, of course, but it is a point that would be lost on Hayes; Parker was right, esthetically, not to translate – we know only what Hayes knows. If we knew more, *Midnight Express* would no longer work as a melodrama of Middle East misadventure. On that level, it works like a hand grenade.

October 15, 1978

Comes a Horseman

Directed by Alan J. Pakula
Written by Dennis Lynton Clark
Starring Jane Fonda and James Caan

All of the actors in *Comes a Horseman* sound as if they were required to gargle with oatmeal just before moving in front of the cameras – the words bubble up from the depths, but only two-thirds of them make it to the surface. Were the microphones implanted in the performers' cowboy boots? The credits list eight people as sound technicians. What were they doing? Manning the mush pots? Fully one-third of the dialogue in this movie, directed by Alan J. Pakula and written by Dennis Lynton Clark, is indecipherable: lines I scribed phonetically in my notes include Hermalda's dea, Honeymaze these, Yes moam I did sat by one, and You ain't nothin' but a paperback couldn't lick his upper lip. Lewis Carroll is not credited.

The entire film is a technical travesty, with indications that at one time the writer (it's his first film) and the director (*All the President's Men, The Sterile Cuckoo, Klute*) knew what they were doing but utterly lost control. A scene that must have taken hours to get – of a rancher returning to the corral while lightning plays across the Colorado horizon – bumps against scene after scene fashioned from garbled dialogue and visual incongruity, reaching a climax when Jane Fonda, as Ella, a woman rancher fighting for her land, is locked in a burning, smoking attic. Her eyes don't water.

The story – Frank (James Caan), discharged by the Army during the Second World War, arrives to help Ella fight the erosion of her lifestyle by oil barons, represented by George Grizzard, and cattle barons, represented by Jason Robards – must have been conceived as a triple homage to John Ford, Howard Hawks and Edna Ferber, but the real deity receiving tribute is the Great God Boredom: the audience at the matinée I attended was grateful for the drama provided when children kept scooting past, banging on the outside exit doors, forcing an usher in platform booties to give wobbling chase.

Comes a Horseman has the look of a movie whose budget was slashed in the middle of production – at any rate, that's what one hopes occurred, because there are so many fine things in it one would hate to think the waste was the result of creative disregard or managerial incompetence. James Caan and Jane Fonda are among five or six movie actors who have the grit and guts (and in Fonda's case, the moral force) to play ranchers without looking like they're on their way to a Beverly Hills costume party with a Stetson theme. When they are on screen together, and when you can understand them, their chemistry is surprisingly complementary. In his first film role, Richard Farnsworth, playing a grizzled ranch hand with bones as brittle as a colt's temperament, brings an immeasurable dignity to the proceedings, the kind of dignity one expects of Jason Robards, who is here reduced to villainous malevolence – a butch Vincent Price with a baritone.

The film concludes with the burning attic sequence, as Fonda and Caan try to escape while Robards and two henchmen bear down on them in a scene that has classic written all over it; as it should, since it's lifted from any number of classic westerns. Every now and then, *Comes a Horseman* had seemed to be about individual dignity, resistance, the loss of autonomy. But you realize, in the end, that it is a movie that speaks mostly about other movies, mostly in borrowed tones enhanced by an original speech impediment. As the final scene galloped across the Panavision screen, the patrons in the theatre were hoping the kids would come back and bang on the door again. That message was at least comprehensible.

October 30, 1978

Superman

Directed by Richard Donner
Written by Mario Puzo, David Newman, Robert Benton and Leslie Newman
Starring Christopher Reeve and Margot Kidder

He has been, from the moment of his inception in the mind of a Canadian teen-ager in 1933, one of the strangest of the strangers in our strange land, one of the most potent pulp messiahs ever marketed.

This week, his powers reach their peak with the glorious film version of his incredible life and amazing times. He was and will be again the man who is more of a man than most men dare to be: the Superman. He was and will be again a symbol for the goodness inherent in his disciples. Although it may sound blasphemous, he was, for a large number of gentle readers at a certain stage in their development, more interesting and more relevant than their Sunday school messiahs. He may be again. Disapproving parents should know, if they have forgotten, that his story is the archetypal messiah fable, related in a lexicon children can appreciate and understand.

Director Richard Donner and his screenwriters, Mario Puzo, Robert Benton, and David and Leslie Newman, who have given us *Superman*, know and have not forgotten. This most expensive of all motion pictures begins in black and white, on a small screen, with tiny hands turning the pages of a comic book. We are then catapulted, as the mind of the child was, into space, to Krypton, Superman's home, where Superman's father Jor-El (Marlon Brando) is predicting the imminent destruction of the planet. The prediction is discounted, ignored. Jor-El places his only begotten son into a crystalline manger, a quartz womb that, when launched into the cosmos, bears the unmistakable outlines of the Christmas star. As the child travels to earth – the resemblance to the foetus at the end of *2001: A Space Odyssey* is not coincidental – he absorbs the knowledge of the eons.

The star lands in a Midwest wheatfield (which is really in Alberta) and is discovered by Ma and Pa Kent (Phyllis Thaxter and Glenn Ford), who rear the foundling as their own. Throughout this section of the film – an overture, really – the tone of Donner's direction is magisterial; the Superman tale is accorded the reverence any re-telling of any great religious myth receives in the chronicles of believers.

When Pa Kent dies of a heart attack in the yard of his home, the demise is treated as it would be in Sophocles. When Superman stands in a field and bids Ma Kent farewell, the leave-taking is mythologized: the camera moves back and up from the pair, taking in the field, the horizon, the world. John Williams' music rises to a crescendo. Until now, Superman has lived the life of any kid in any Smallville anywhere (except that when he jogs he paces himself with freight trains). The Mission is about to begin.

This build-up to the more familiar aspects of the Superman legend ends when the Man of Steel builds his Arctic fortress and his tape-recorded father gives him his final charge: "I have sent them you, my only son." Suddenly, Clark Kent-Superman (Christopher Reeve) is at the Daily Planet, working for Perry White (Jackie Cooper) and with/against girl reporter Lois Lane (Margot Kidder). Abruptly, astonishingly, effectively, we are wrenched from myth-making into the quasi-camp world of comic books. A James Bondian villain, Lex Luthor (Gene Hackman), is conniving under Park Avenue with a female assistant (Valerie Perrine) whose cups runneth over, and with a male sidekick (Ned Beatty) whose brain runneth dry.

Reeve's Clark Kent is a shy, sexless, innocent eunuch; his Superman is a shyly sexy, semi-innocent male, a mean man with a pun ("Bad vibrations?" he enquires solicitously when a hood conks him on the head with a crowbar that proceeds to shimmy like Kate's famous sister) and a good guy with no need of a gun – he's a green Cary Grant who's spent a couple of years in a gym. He's wonderful.

He's a romantic. Margot Kidder's cracklingly contemporary Lois Lane finds that she is, too – she eulogizes her conquest as he takes her for a convincing nighttime spin over Manhattan/Metropolis. (How can the image of one man flying – and the special effects in this area are marvellous – be more poetic than *Star Wars*' fleets?) Even Lex Luthor's grounded moll falls for him. Before removing deadly Kryptonite from his body, she kisses him, because, she explains plaintively, she wasn't sure he'd do it on his own. Why is it, she wonders, I can't get it on with the good guys?

The genius of *Superman* – and on a pop level, this is a work of genius – has been to eschew condescension while setting out to achieve both visual elegance – Geoffrey Unsworth's cinematography effortlessly slides from the blanched, gauzy antiseptic brightness of Krypton to the heavy, boiling, pestilence-laden skies of America – and nostalgia at its most honourable, nostalgia for a common past, for a childish past when heroics weren't corny and when death didn't sting.

For a lot of people, *Star Wars* functioned in the same manner, but *Star Wars* was a hollow technological victory, dazzling but calculatingly one-dimensional and manipulatively sentimental. *Close*

Encounters of the Third Kind wore out its welcome by dressing its comic strip effects in ratty metaphysical robes. *King Kong* camped itself into lugubrious cuteness: King Korn. *Superman* succeeds where those movies succeeded, but it goes beyond them to do what so many movies claim to do but so few (*The Wizard of Oz*, Cocteau's *Beauty and the Beast*) actually accomplish: *Superman* makes you feel like a child again.

Estimates of the movie's costs range between $35- and $70-million; whatever the price, it was not too much to pay. As gods go, Superman is one of the godliest; his movie is one of the best.

December 16, 1978

The Deer Hunter

Directed by Michael Cimino
Written by Deric Washburn
Starring Robert De Niro, Meryl Streep and Christopher Walken

Some years ago, Dick Cavett asked the poet James Dickey what his first novel, *Deliverance*, was about. Dickey smiled and in a low voice dripping with molasses replied, "It's about why decent men kill." *The Deer Hunter* is constructed symphonically, in three movements – it lasts three hours – with a recurring motif that never quite becomes a theme; but it, too, is about why decent men kill.

It is late in the day late in the decade – 1968 – in a steel mill town, Clairton, Pa. Three buddies, Michael (Robert De Niro), Steve (John Savage) and Nick (Christopher Walken), are preparing to ship out to Vietnam. Steve, the youngest, will marry before leaving. The extended, allusive first movement of *The Deer Hunter* takes us through the Russian Orthodox wedding, the reception, an early morning hunting trip organized by Michael, and the hunt's drunken aftermath.

33

The milieu is sub-culturally specific, but the emotional dynamics are not: director Michael Cimino, who once worked as a medic with a Green Beret training unit in Texas, draws the outlines of American machismo better than any other filmmaker in memory. He does not try to explain what he sees – I don't think he understands intellectually what he's doing – but he is able to make us feel the synergic relationship between patriotism and religion common in the white working class of the time. As a sign at the reception reads: Serving God and Country proudly.

We also feel the frustrations of the three bonded males. The night is one long beer bust. The three men and their two friends, Stan (the late John Cazale, who was dying of cancer when the movie was shot) and Axel (Chuck Aspergren) are constantly diddling danger and coming on to violence. Their high spirits are sexual and aggressive.

Linda (Meryl Streep), a woman attracted to both Michael and Nick, is beaten by her father. He drinks and stares out of his window. The buddies drink and career from macho cliché to cliché. Cimino shoots Michael's deer hunt mystically, with a Russian choir in the background. One feels that the boredom in Clairton is profound.

Vietnam explodes on the screen. In the first few seconds, heaving helicopters descend, a Viet Cong soldier throws a grenade into a bomb shelter full of women and children, Michael immolates the soldier with a flame-thrower, and pigs tear the corpses apart. Although Michael acts chivalrously, one easily imagines turned tables; My Lai hovers like a phantom helicopter over these scenes. The second movement ends when Michael goes home.

Earlier, the three buddies were reunited in a Viet Cong prison camp where they were forced to play Russian roulette – the recurring motif – in a sequence so well edited the technique is assaultive. Nick vanishes in Saigon and Michael finds Steve, crippled and withdrawn, in a Stateside hospital. Linda expends energy controlling her hysteria. "I get along," she says. Just. Michael is unable to comfort her: he is an ascetic enigma, to her and to himself. When his two friends recommence their good ol' boy byplay, he is enraged and forces one of them into Russian roulette.

The third movement takes Michael back to Vietnam in search of Nick, who is found in the pits of Saigon during the city's fall. He is on drugs and plays Russian roulette for money in a casino. The return to Pennsylvania is a coda; Michael and his friends sing "God Bless America" in a bar.

One of the catch phrases of the sixties was, If you're not part of the solution, you're part of the problem. Cimino's illuminating film is part of the problem. Other Vietnam movies have looked at the war from the outside in, from a pacifist perspective. *The Deer Hunter* is conceptually apolitical and emotionally conservative – it sees from the inside out.

Its lack of a coherent point of view, its romanticism, its indifference to the Vietnamese and its fumbling attempts to characterize women, are its great esthetic weaknesses – and its great sociological strengths. It's one-sided, but you get to know that one side as you never have.

The Russian roulette motif refers not only to the suicidal behaviour of the United States, but to the internalization of violence that ensued in many recruits and also to war's ability to provide what the existentialists call authenticity – an authenticity neither Michael nor Nick could locate in Clairton.

The writing has been criticized as superficial. And yet, most of the people I knew who went to Vietnam went without knowing why and came back without knowing how to articulate what they had been through or what it meant to them. The war may already have been explained (politically in *The Best and the Brightest*, psychologically in *A Rumor of War* and *Winners and Losers*) as completely as it can be. In comparison, *The Deer Hunter* is circumscribed, fabricated not by the Ivy League mentality that planned the war, nor by the movement that opposed it, but by the sensibility that executed it.

Cimino wants us to reconsider those people: look, he says, they were not monsters. They should be granted compassion for their situation and respect for their grief. Without detracting from the performances of De Niro and Walken, which are exceptional, Cimino could have saved himself a lot of grief if the actors playing Michael and

Nick had been draft age; their hell-raising would appear less indulgent, their shallowness more natural, and their ordeal even more harrowing.

To judge *The Deer Hunter* solely as a movie is to judge it an honourable failure with redemptive sequences of great power. But to judge it as part of a cultural process is quite another matter.

As I watched the "God Bless America" conclusion, feeling slightly sickened by Cimino's avoidance of a moral statement, I remembered a high school friend who left home the same time I did. I went to college. He went to Vietnam. We were friends, but we had argued – I enthusiastically, he reluctantly – about the war. I came home at Christmas in a jet. He came home in a shoe box. Hank was serious in his support of what we called the U.S. involvement. He has been dead for ten years. Now, a movie is weeping for him and for the thousands like him. It weeps in a way he, and they, would understand. One does not have to agree with *The Deer Hunter* to sympathize. One does not have to like it to recognize its value.

February 17, 1979

Norma Rae

Directed by Martin Ritt
Written by Irving Ravetch and Harriet Frank, Jr.
Starring Sally Field

Norma Rae Webster (Sally Field), tight body squeezed into tight jeans, loose morals squeezed into a tight town, has been to Henleyville, Ala., and on down the road to Piston. She's been married, been divorced, had one child by a Southern gentleman who begat the baby in the back of a car, had another child by her husband. Norma Rae works in the textile mills with her Daddy (Pat Hingle) and her Momma (Barbara

Baxley). One of her favourite songs is Dolly Parton's "It's All Wrong But It's All Right."

In Martin Ritt's film of Norma Rae, Sally Field gets so far into character you lose consciousness of her technique – there hasn't been a performance of this calibre by an American actress since Jane Fonda's in *Klute*. The screenwriters, Irving Ravetch and Harriet Frank Jr., have taken the real story of union organizer Crystal Lee and mixed it with incidents from the lives of several other militant Southern women.

The homogenization has resulted in a bona-fide folk heroine on par with Cicely Tyson in *Sounder* (also directed by Ritt) or *The Autobiography of Miss Jane Pittman*. It's a once-in-a-lifetime role, and Field squeezes it for every ounce of juice it harbours, without once appearing to apply pressure stronger than a lover's caress. Like Fred Astaire, she's in the business of making the impossible appear inevitable.

When Reuben (Ron Leibman), an advance man from the Textile Workers Union of America, arrives in Henleyville, Norma Rae's sour grapes are ripe for squeezing – she's broken up with a travelling salesman, the mill is making her mother deaf and living with her parents is driving her around a dead-end bend.

Just when you think this is going to be a predictable pairing of union man and maid, the movie throws a switch and Sonny (Beau Bridges), a crackling cracker, wins Norma Rae's heart – a good portion of which is located somewhere below her navel, as she lets Sonny know when he proposes. Kiss me, she orders, and if that's all right, everything else will be.

Ritt and his screenwriters carefully calibrate Norma Rae's odyssey to social consciousness. In a moving scene in a country-western hangout, Norma Rae talks about her past without a trace of self-pity. Sonny, sitting beside her, is asked by Reuben what he does when the fact that he's underpaid and overworked gets to him. "I just wash down the beer," he replies defensively.

Norma Rae, never one to settle for what is offered or expected, eventually devotes her considerable energies to Reuben's cause –

which she now understands as her own – and the film becomes a warm but realistic celebration of the working class's drive toward self-determination.

At a time when unions are unpopular, Ritt has taken a chance that viewers will respond to Norma Rae's plight. It was a chance that needed taking: there are unions and there are unions, and anyone who has spent time in the rural South will not quarrel with Ritt's even-handed contemporary depiction. (Two union bigwigs are image conscious; Reuben is irritatingly abrasive when dealing with management; Southern racism is shown as crossing class barriers.)

Their evident belief in this movie's message seems to have exerted a sobering effect on all the actors. Leibman does his finest, most understated work to date; Bridges holds his jejune charm in check, offering a dimensional performance that overcomes the significant obstacle of scanty screen time; and with practically no lines at all, Barbara Baxley captures the lights and shadows in Momma's life as vividly as in a Walker Evans photograph.

In the end, though, this is Sally Field's movie. Her performance – hyperbole completely aside – is peerless, one of the major achievements by an actress in the movies of any place and of any time. Reuben tells Norma Rae that when he wants a smart, loud, profane, sloppy, hardworking woman he'll call on her. From now on, when directors want legerdemain that becomes art, they're going to call on Sally Field. Reacting to a promise from a factory supervisor that "You're goin' up in the world, honey," Norma Rae retorts, "Yeah, how far for how much?" The film is carefully guarded about Norma Rae's prospects. But the answer, in Field's case, is obvious: way far, and for a whole lot.

March 10, 1979

❖

Apocalypse Now

Directed by Francis Ford Coppola
Written by John Milius and Francis Ford Coppola
Starring Martin Sheen, Robert Duvall and Marlon Brando

When it was all over, when the audience had applauded desultorily, too devastated and perhaps too heartbroken and certainly too depressed to summon the bravos that were demanded, Francis Ford Coppola's $30-million Vietnam War movie, *Apocalypse Now*, would dissolve in the mind into one long, fluid camera movement, a movie fabricated from a single operatic take to a single operatic purpose, a movie commencing with the mundane and ending with the monstrous, a movie made with the swiftness, the silence, the subtlety – and the savagery – of a spear thrown home to the centre of the heart.

Apocalypse Now is the Vietnam movie a lot of us were waiting for, but it turns out to be more than that: it turns out to be the *movie* a lot of us were waiting for. Movies have always been – at their most extravagantly appealing, sensually exciting and rationally disturbing – pieces of art with the power to bypass our defences. A few times in the history of movies, one caught glimpses of a power that could turn the screen experience into a hallucinatory celebration of irrationality, of pure feeling, and even, perhaps, of insanity. *Apocalypse Now* goes further in that direction more successfully than any movie ever has: like its main character, a special-forces assassin named Willard (Martin Sheen), like the nation whose Southeast Asia involvement it excoriates, and like the times it talks of, it is larger than life and every bit as crazy. Filming Vietnam as the product of a madman's hallucination was – it now seems so obvious – the only way to film it, the only way to separate it from good wars, and the only way to re-create the experience so completely that questions of *Apocalypse Now*'s flaws (and it has them) sound like questions posed by an academic teetering on the edge of an abyss.

The first shot is of palm trees undulating in tropic heat. Jim Morrison sings "This is the end, my friend" on the soundtrack, and the palm trees explode into flames. Immediately, we are yanked into a naturalistic Saigon. Willard, the assassin, is given a mission: to travel up a river into Cambodia and put an end to the reign of a madman, an American officer named Kurtz (Marlon Brando) who has set up a kingdom among the Montagnards. "He's out there operating without any decent restraint," Willard is told, and we see without further assistance that Kurtz is the United States in Vietnam. Later we see, with a great deal of assistance, that he is also the dark side of all of us, the side of our face that avoids the sun – he is Mr. Hyde to Willard's Dr. Jekyll.

The plot will sound familiar: it is taken from Joseph Conrad's *Heart of Darkness. Apocalypse Now* flies into that pulsating black hole on the wings of a hawk, with compassion carried symbolically on the wings of a dove. The rest of the movie charts Willard's journey, and it is nothing less than a history of the American presence in Vietnam. Americans – the fun-loving, aggressive Americans of *The Deer Hunter* – water-ski on the Nung River and overturn sampans. Robert Duvall, as a Commander in a black cowboy hat, leads his troops to the beach and allows them to surf under enemy fire. Coppola himself appears as a network television reporter, exhorting soldiers to stop looking at his cameras and start looking at the village they are in the process of incinerating. A helicopter attack that destroys a hamlet is filmed ecstatically to Wagner: this movie hates war but it is strong enough to show you, and to make you feel, the giddy excitement and almost sexual gratification of devastation and danger. Then Playboy Playmates of the Month are dropped into the jungle and undulate like the palm trees for the benefit of our boys.

The film is going crazy. The boys on the boat take drugs -- one of them drops acid at the Playboy concert. The atmosphere partakes of Carnival time – Tivoli Gardens at dusk or Disneyland at midnight. Willard's boat detains a vegetable-laden junk on the river – the soldiers are very young and very frightened and very nervous and for no reason at all massacre the Vietnamese going to market. They are just boys. Nice boys. A lot of people die.

Willard meets Kurtz. "Are my methods unsound?" the king with the glistening and hairless head asks. "I don't see any methods at all, sir," Willard responds. But he does. Kurtz is the United States in 1968 – someone says of him, "the man is clear in his mind but his soul is mad" – and the method of his madness is to appear utterly sane. *Apocalypse Now* ends the only way it can: there is a new order but nothing changes. Joseph Conrad will not soon go out of date.

The obvious comparison can be dispensed with summarily: esthetically, philosophically, historically and psychologically, *Apocalypse Now* is to *The Deer Hunter* what James Joyce is to Ernest Hemingway. Coppola focuses on his Americans – the only Vietnamese characters in *Apocalypse* are victims and murderers seen peripherally – as sharply as Michael Cimino did in *The Deer Hunter* – and he demonstrates their reasons for being in Vietnam even more succinctly than Cimino did. But *Apocalypse* is not filmed, as *The Deer Hunter* was, entirely from their point of view, and it is not, therefore, a work of nascent fascism. And on a purely technical level, it makes *The Deer Hunter* look like something shot within the confines of a movie studio outhouse: the scope of *Apocalypse* is Shakespearean, its incidents (unlike the notorious Russian-roulette business in *Deer Hunter*) historically accurate and its choreography magnificent.

Martin Sheen is on screen for the duration and gives a performance of amazing restraint. Brando does not appear until the end of the first two hours – he has little to do, but does it well. The film is narrated to words written by Michael Herr, author of *Dispatches*, and they are very good words, but I'm not sure they are necessary. Neither am I sure that Brando's jungle palace should resemble a pre-Columbian Tarzan temple – it's hallucinatory in the most banal fantasy-art way. But none of that is retained by the audience. What is retained is the fact that this film is a direct descendant of *The Birth of a Nation*, the fact that its importance would be difficult to overemphasize, the fact that it has made some sense of the senseless.

August 16, 1979   41

❖

Orchestra Rehearsal

Directed by Federico Fellini
Written by Federico Fellini and Brunello Rondi
Starring Balduin Baas

There is one sort of person to whom Federico Fellini's new film, *Orchestra Rehearsal*, will prove to be of value, and that is the sort of person who wants at all costs to keep up. If that sort of person has missed the extravagant outpourings of the master's later years – the *Satyricon*s, the *Casanova*s, the *Juliet*s *of the Spirit* – then that sort of person can catch up relatively painlessly by watching *Orchestra Rehearsal*. Everything Fellini has been up to in the past decade is in *Orchestra Rehearsal*, but this time he is up to everything for seventy minutes. Brevity is *Orchestra Rehearsal*'s greatest and only virtue.

An Italian orchestra is rehearsing in a hall that is also a tomb. (Could that be a metaphor for The World? Could it ever.) A TV crew is going to interview the musicians. Fellini, who has forever evinced a bottomless capacity for being surprised at the obvious, is surprised that beautiful music is made by unbeautiful people. (This is a Fellini film: you know what everyone looks like.) They listen to soccer matches (the boobs!) and squabble (the cretins!) and read *Playboy* (the degenerates!) and demand extra money for being interviewed (the mercenaries!). They rebel (silly children!) and bring down the end of the world – a wrecker's ball bashes in the side of the tomb, dust flies, the conductor reassembles the sorry lot and they make music. For a while.

There are two themes: art is made by dingdongs and unions are going to lead us all to wrack and ruin. (In the promo material, *Orchestra Rehearsal* is subtitled *The Decline of the West in C-Sharp Major*.) The first theme is sometimes true, sometimes not. The second is the gospel according to Margaret Thatcher, of course, but Fellini is not nearly as articulate as Mrs. Thatcher, and he hedges his politics – it is possible to interpret *Orchestra Rehearsal* as saying exactly the opposite of what I have said it says. In fact, it is possible to interpret it as saying any old thing you'd care to have it say.

There is no ambiguity about its subsidiary themes (call them themettes), however, because they are all too apparent from Fellini's other recent work, with the double exception of the splendid *Amarcord* and the whimsical *Clowns*:

Themette number one: Sex is revolting. The one sexual act in *Orchestra Rehearsal* takes place under a piano while the woman nonchalantly eats a sandwich. The one big joke concerns impotence, which has obsessed Fellini to a degree that goes beyond the esthetic and into the clinical.

Themette number two: People are revolting. No elaboration necessary; again, this is a Fellini film; you know what the people look (and act) like.

Themette number three: Directors are not revolting. The one character with any sense in *Orchestra Rehearsal* is – naturally – the conductor.

Themette number four: The work of Fellini is important. I counted five direct references to earlier Fellini films. The name *8½* is evoked in the first five minutes.

The Italians have a word for Fellini: *Basta*. It means Enough.

October 13, 1979

The Black Stallion

Directed by Carroll Ballard
Written by Melissa Mathison, Jeanne Rosenberg and William D. Witliff
Starring Kelly Reno, Mickey Rooney and Teri Garr

The Black Stallion is the most remarkable film debut since Marco Bellocchio's *Fists in the Pocket* thirteen years ago. Carroll Ballard, its neophyte director, was a contemporary of Francis Coppola at the UCLA Film School, from which he graduated in 1963; until 1967, he made movies for the United States Information Agency; prior to being assigned to *The Black Stallion* by his now-famous, now-wealthy, film-school buddy, he directed educational products. As you think about that résumé, as you think about it while *The Black Stallion* comes to a close, the prospect of the movies Ballard could have made in those years is enough to make you giddy; the fact that he didn't make them is enough to make you sick.

Based on a children's novel published in 1941 by nineteen-year-old Walter Farley (who went on to write sixteen sequels), the film's story is lean: Alec (Kelly Reno), a young boy travelling by ship with his father (Hoyt Axton), is attracted to a wild black stallion on board. The ship sinks and the horse saves the boy's life. On the island to which the two are consigned by fate, the boy returns the life-saving favour by slashing the ropes that have trapped the animal.

The relationship between man and beast develops slowly and mystically – the island interlude, utterly without dialogue, lasts fifty minutes, and is one of the most sustained, lyrical, rapturous sequences in the history of motion pictures, a visual symphony whose beauty cannot be oversold. (*The Black Stallion* is a children's movie, but it is a children's art movie and is in the esthetic company of *The Wizard of Oz* or Jean Cocteau's *Beauty and the Beast* rather than *Pippi Longstocking* or *The Absent-Minded Professor*.)

Once rescued, Alec returns to his mother (Teri Garr) and to his average American hometown (played nicely by Toronto). The horse eats fruit salad in the backyard but one day escapes to a farm run by an aged horse fancier, Henry Dailey (Mickey Rooney), who undertakes the double training of boy and horse. Henry wants to prove that he's not washed up and Alec wants to prove that his pet – named, tersely, The Black – is the fastest animal on four feet.

National Velvet has nothing to do with this. Ballard's visual scheme (he studied design at the Art Centre in Los Angeles) is so rich and sensuous the hackneyed story is nearly incidental. The island sequences, filmed in Sardinia, are right out of Ansel Adams, but there are also minimalist, abstract compositions (such as the first shot after the credits, an almost non-representational study of the side of the boat and the ocean). When framing a picture, Ballard never takes the expected angle. (The last movie I can remember in which every set-up was as carefully put together as a Van Eyck miniature was *The Chant of Jimmie Blacksmith*.)

Solely by manipulating static close-ups, he can create high drama and breathless momentum out of a visit by a cobra on the sand, and when the boy finally rides the horse, a startling aerial shot has the vertiginous – and ecstatically transcendent – quality of the sudden shifts of rhythm in Stravinsky.

Those are rarefied comparisons, but Ballard's ability demands them: if this is the only movie he ever directs, he is going to be remembered as a great filmmaker. *The Black Stallion* is virtually silent, but one never has the impression that dialogue is avoided – Ballard just doesn't need it. The interactions between Alec and Henry are marvels of mime and, in the climactic race sequence, all naturalistic sound is gradually leached out in favour of Carmine Coppola's music (exceptional throughout), which points up the non-competitive spiritual union between Alec and The Black.

The climax is thrilling, but it's thrilling in a much deeper, more satisfying way than the climax of something like *Rocky* or *Breaking Away* – it's thrilling because the romanticism is a matter of style, not sentimentality. Ballard is, in fact, an emotionally austere director (he reminds me a little of Werner Herzog) who prods responses from an audience with an asceticism especially welcome in these days of thundering soundtracks and soap-opera relationships. The terrifying shipwreck is terrifying largely because of the editing progression (it has already been compared to Eisenstein's *Potemkin*) and the plight of a boy abandoned on a desert island is never given special emphasis. Ballard is strangely matter-of-fact when filming the corners of the script upon which most directors would hinge their dramatizations.

45

Austere or not, he obviously gets along with actors: Rooney is worth the price of admission; the young Reno (who could ride but not act when signed for the movie) is a dignified, dimensional child-hero;

and as his parents, Hoyt Axton and Teri Garr, with almost no screen time and not a single scene together, give us all the material we need to piece together their relationship. Ballard's powers of suggestion are on par with his powers of depiction. In both cases, they are potentially peerless.

March 15, 1980

Urban Cowboy

Directed by James Bridges
Written by James Bridges and Aaron Latham
Starring John Travolta and Debra Winger

The *Urban Cowboy* blues: One night in Gilley's, a half-acre, country-western shoot-'em-up and knock-'em-down night club in the Houston suburb of Pasadena, the song being played is "Stand By Me," and a marriage is coming apart. Bud (John Travolta), who is married to Sissy (Debra Winger), is trying to make Sissy jealous, so he's dancing the two-step with Pam (Madolyn Smith), a society gal slumming at Gilley's, and Sissy, trying to keep up with Bud's meanness, is dancing with Wes (Scott Glenn), an ex-con who has muscles like sailors' knots.

Over the shoulders of their new partners, Sissy and Bud stare at each other, eyes full of hurt and hate and lust and love. Then Bud hugs his new honey closer, and Sissy, real near to crying, eases her hand on down past the place where Wes' back meets his belt, on down past the hand-tooled belt on Wes' jeans, on down past the tops of his pockets, on down to where the presence of her hand is making a statement. And the pain in Bud's eyes just about runs over, and he pulls his uptown honey even closer and rubs against her as if she were a warm blanket on a cold night. And the band plays "Stand By Me."

Good news and bad news: *Urban Cowboy*, from which that extraordinary scene of sexual stand-off is taken, is being promoted as a remake of *Saturday Night Fever*, with solely superficial (and largely sartorial) variations. We are given to believe that we will see the same dudes, but wearing duds from a funky closet: Tony Lama cowboy boots, $35 Stetsons, Larry Mahan pearl-snapped cowboy shirts. We will see the same star (Travolta), the same working-class cut-ups (transposed from the claustrophobic concrete of Brooklyn to the mesquite-studded, polluted vistas of the land of the yellow rose) and the same theme ("Hard hat days and honky tonk nights"). Instead of the Bee Gees – Jimmy Buffett. Instead of the hustle – the polka. The good news is that *Urban Cowboy* is not *Saturday Night Fever*. The bad news is that *Urban Cowboy* is not *Saturday Night Fever*.

John Badham's film of Nik Cohn's *New York* magazine article "Tribal Rites of the New Saturday Night" softened Cohn's justified pessimism, but James Bridges' film of Aaron Latham's *Esquire* cover story "The Urban Cowboy" does not stop with softening: real life is whipped into glistening fantasy peaks. The last half hour of this very long film (more than two hours) leaves Houston in the lurch and goes Hollywood with a puffy series of coincidences, melodramatic twists and sentimental resolutions that are not only forced from the unwilling material, but are antithetical to it. In the last half hour, Bridges (who co-wrote the script with Latham) seems to develop a fear of the truth he has so far recorded ("Damn, this is depressing!") and sets out to sabotage his achievement. He almost succeeds.

At no time is *Urban Cowboy* especially well-directed – Bridges, director of *The China Syndrome* and *The Paper Chase*, has yet to learn where to put a camera and when to move it. But the performances are so fresh, the dialogue so prickly and arid, and the milieu observed with such accuracy, that one's reservations regarding the cinematography, editing and a raft of other technical matters are held in check. The way people of any socio-economic class really live in the New South has been the subject of very few films (*Stay Hungry* and one or two others) and the way people live in the modern Texas sector of the Sunbelt has been left pretty much alone – except by TV's baroque "Dallas" – since *Giant*. Not all people in Texas are big, oily and rich: *Urban Cowboy* is about the ones who aren't (but might like to be).

It is also – who'd-a-thunk it? – a movie that looks at sexual jealousy with the steady, saddle-sore ache and sudden, blister-popped burn found in the slow rhythms and twanging guitars of hurtin' country songs. Bud arrives in Houston a bearded hick. (When he shaves, Bridges gives us a shot that crawls up Travolta's body, from high heels to hat brim, the same shot we got in *Moment by Moment* and *Saturday Night Fever* – does Travolta's contract demand that his body be caressed by the camera once in each movie?) He meets and marries Sissy in short order. They are both married to (and in) Gilley's, which Latham described in *Esquire* as "just a honky tonk, but it looks about as big as the MGM Grand Hotel or St. Patrick's Cathedral . . . When Willie Nelson played Gilley's, 4,500 people crowded inside." The Bud-Sissy romance starts there. The trouble starts there.

Sissy wants to ride the mechanical bucking bull. Bud doesn't want her to. One damned thing leads to another. Sissy moves out of her new mobile dream home and takes up with the ex-con. Bud takes up with the society woman (crudely drawn in the script, well played by Madolyn Smith). She says she patronizes cowboys because "I like men with simple values." Fool-headed woman: she doesn't know that Bud is no cowboy. As Latham wrote of him in *Esquire*, his cowboy hat "temporarily drives from his head the memory of his job at the refinery. When he pulls on his cowboy boots, he can temporarily forget that he is a member of Insulators' Union Local 22 which ties him to the city that he is always saying he is going to leave."

Most of *Urban Cowboy* is fascinating because that contrast is sharp; because Travolta – from the first time he opens his mouth and the soft tones of the Texas drawl descend like yellow rose petals – is quietly but utterly convincing; because his back-up crew is nothing short of terrific, with especially fine performances from Barry Corbin and Brooke Alderson as Uncle Bob and Aunt Corene; and because the chemistry between Travolta's Bud and Debra Winger's Sissy is hotly volatile – Winger, a squeezed-dry Sally Field, doesn't have a star's presence, but she is exactly right for the kinda-cute, kinda-sexy, independent Sissy. When the script's asinine plotting later requires her to put up with her ex-con's viciousness longer than she put up with Bud's chauvinism, Sissy's credibility as a character is destroyed, but not Winger's as an actress.

Urban Cowboy will be seen years from now as a classic example of commercial Hollywood compromise: a tight, hard-tack magazine article is loosened and leavened by the perceived demands of demographics. You're not going to have a hit, start a fashion trend and cover the country with soundtrack albums if the movie is a downer, if its whole point is that the things you want to market – the shirts, the boots, the tunes, the way of life – don't make the people in your movie happy, don't ease the sores or soothe the blisters. Writing of one Houston couple, Latham observed, "Eddie met Betty Jo Helmer at Gilley's. At the time, he was 19 and she was 18. It seemed like destiny. After all, their names rhymed the way the names of lovers in a good country song should. At the time, it didn't occur to them that all country songs have unhappy endings." It has occurred to the folks who made *Urban Cowboy*. And it has been dismissed by them. Cravenly.

June 7, 1980

The Shining

Directed by Stanley Kubrick
Written by Stanley Kubrick and Diane Johnson
Starring Jack Nicholson and Shelley Duvall

The theme of *The Shining*, Stanley Kubrick's three-years-in-the-making movie version of pulpmeister Stephen King's novel about a haunted Colorado hotel, is that evil is as omnipresent in human life as breathing – and perhaps as inescapable. It's the identical theme lurking behind the same director's *2001: A Space Odyssey* (until the foetal transfiguration) and *A Clockwork Orange*, but Kubrick has never expressed it so ponderously, with such literal ill-humour, and with such clinical contempt for the expectations of an audience. *The Shining* is not, the ads warn us, only a horror movie – it's an epic horror movie – but the real problem is that it's not even a horror movie. It's an American *Last Year at Marienbad*, a movie that sees the demands of the horror genre in opposition to the demands of Art, and a movie that opts for Art by trying to transform the genre into what can only be designated as – deep breath – a cinematic opera of the metaphysical.

It's bound to work for some people, especially for people who haven't read the King novel and don't know that Kubrick and Diane Johnson, his collaborator on the screenplay, have stuck closely to the basic plot – Mr. and Mrs. Jack Torrance and their small son arrive at the Overlook Hotel to look after it for the winter – while removing the explanations and mystifying what remains. When Jack (Jack Nicholson) brings his wife, Wendy (Shelley Duvall), to the Overlook, a gargantuan structure of Art Deco and American Indian yei motifs, we know that he has a drinking problem and that he once harmed his son, Danny (Danny Lloyd), a preternaturally mature child who physically resembles a miniature Georgie Jessel.

For two of this film's almost two and a half hours, we are led to believe that its haunts are in Jack's increasingly deranged mind, but then Wendy sees them, too, and Danny, blessed with second sight ("the shining"), has seen them all along (the presumption was that he had been peeping through a psychic porthole into his father's oily engine room). There is never a clarification of the confusion Kubrick and Johnson have created, unless you are prepared to believe that they have refused to tell the story coherently because doing so would not have suited their high-minded purposes.

What are those purposes? Assume that everything in *The Shining* is intentional, including its refusal to give the audience what it came for (a scare). Assume that Jack Nicholson's face-straining performance, which lets us know immediately that the man is a murderous lunatic, is by design (and not merely the result of immersion in Rod Steiger movies). Assume that the ever-changing temporal titles ("Tuesday," "Wednesday," "9 a.m.") are calculated to raise derisive laughter (which comes because they separate so many sequences in which nothing happens). Assume that a pair of murdered twins are supposed to be dressed in the style of the twenties, even though they were murdered in 1970.

Assume all that, and what have you got if you don't have a glacially beautiful but blatantly illogical and badly acted horror film? Perhaps you have a movie about the liquidity of time (Last Year at Overlook) and the immortality of evil (A Clockwork Hotel) and the vileness of the family (George Burns and Gracie Allen in Hell). You may have a movie in which nothing makes much sense because nothing in life makes sense; a movie in which everything is confused (insanity? possession? ghosts?) and questions are unanswered because – another deep breath – Life Is Like That. A movie in which things move backward and forward with great speed, but never get anywhere. (The most notable technical kink in *The Shining* is Kubrick's use of gliding tracking shots – I think he's seen Fassbinder's *Chinese Roulette*.) And you have a movie in which Jack Nicholson is allowed to stare and glare and drool because he's not giving anything so banal as a performance (he's acting an aria).

Kubrick certainly doesn't fail small. One could fast forget *The Shining* as an overreaching, multi-levelled botch – with moments – were it not for the use to which Jack Nicholson's uncanny audience rapport is put. Since the theme has to do with the devil in Mr. Everyman, Kubrick wants to make us accomplices to the horror, as he did in *A Clockwork Orange* when we were ordered to stop worrying and learn to love the psychopath. Nicholson, one of the few actors capable of getting the audience to love him no matter what he does, is an ideal vehicle for Kubrick – when Nicholson is trying to kill his ninny of a wife, Kubrick orchestrates the chase to get us intermittently on the murderer's side.

The vignette in which Nicholson crashes through the door with an axe and screams, "Wendy, I'm home!" and "Heeeere's Johnny!" has been cited as an example of Kubrick's satirical gift, but it's more likely that the humour is intended to cinch our queasy identification with Nicholson until the climax, which takes place in a topiary maze and is calibrated to bring us face to face with our own murderous impulses – we who are Kubrick's audience of evil Everymen.

We're supposed to realize that we're all brothers in brutishness under the hairless skin, killer cousins to the weapon-wielding apes from the beginning of *2001*, and that's why we have come to see *The Shining* – to get our sadistic jollies, to get high on horror. Kubrick sabotages his thesis in the most knuckle-headed way conceivable: we can't be charged as accomplices in horror when there is no horror.

June 14, 1980

Knife in the Head

Directed by Reinhard Hauff
Written by Peter Schneider
Starring Bruno Ganz

There is a sub-species of North American commercial art – epitomized by *Love Story* – that canonizes the suffering of unfortunates afflicted with various ailments (crippled appendages, malfunctioning organs, disordered brains) and uses that suffering as An Example to Us All in the task of persevering with grace and a sense of humour even though our left ear may be rotting. At one time, the sufferers in these upbeat object lessons usually survived and we were meant to be ennobled by their fortitude; now, movies having gone on a death-with-dignity kick, they often expire and we are meant to be ennobled by the honesty (and, sometimes, by the style) they bring to the bidding of their final adieus.

52 *Knife in the Head*, a German film directed by Reinhard Hauff and just now opening in Toronto although it was released in 1978, belongs to that sub-species only by virtue of its quickly summarizable plot: Bertolt Hoffman (Bruno Ganz), a biogeneticist, is shot in the head by the police one evening when trying to visit his estranged wife, Ann

(Angela Winkler), at a building under seige by police, a building sheltering a group of young, fearfully disorganized terrorists with whom Ann is in some way connected.

Hoffman had been thinking of committing suicide, a feasible explanation of his foolhardiness in pushing through police lines to attempt to rescue a woman he knows no longer loves him, but if he did have a death wish, the police bullet that lodges in his brain does not do the job: the bulk of *Knife in the Head* unsentimentally documents Hoffman's rehabilitation, from his first muttered syllables ("All . . . b . . . basta") to his carefully articulated statement of metaphysical condition ("I am nobody") to his bitter third-person characterization ("I don't have any consequences; Hoffman is inconsequential").

There are sub-plots and supporting textures: the desperate efforts of the police to acquit themselves, by lying and intimidation; the effect of Ann's love affair with a terrorist on her life, on the terrorist's, and on Hoffman's; and the arid, 1984-like state of the German nation in general, familiar to viewers of films by Herzog, Wenders and Fassbinder, directors whom Hauff resembles in his hatred of what has happened to Germany and in his willingness to allow an individual case to stand as a symbol of human nature (in many respects, *Knife in the Head* is Hauff's version of Herzog's *The Enigma of Kaspar Hauser*), but whom he resembles not at all in the lumpish straightforwardness of his work.

As Hoffman, Bruno Ganz holds the not always well-timed or well-edited episodes together in a fist as tightly coiled as the claw his character's right hand becomes after the shooting incident. The performance is masterly, and largely (and necessarily) mimed. Ganz individualizes Hoffman so much that while one wants badly for his recovery to be as complete as possible and for his vengeance to be as swift and thorough as is consonant with his own safety, one never wants to be him.

Those Example to Us All movies make suffering and even dying look awfully pleasurable: the pain is outweighed by the opportunity to trot one's virtue forth, as if it were fine china and the occasion festive. *Knife in the Head* shatters commercial crockery: it allows suffering its pain, and in its unsparing delineation of how randomly and totally human dignity can be threatened, it allows for realistic fear. Beyond freedom and dignity, the film finds both.

July 14, 1980

The Chant of Jimmie Blacksmith

Written and directed by Fred Schepisi
Starring Tommy Lewis

The first words spoken in Fred Schepisi's *The Chant of Jimmie Blacksmith* – one of the great films of the seventies, at long last opening in Toronto – are "Blast blacks." The blacks in question are Aborigines; the speaker is a white, turn-of-the-century Australian who, like the rest of the whites in Schepisi's monumental dissection of race relations, is convinced of his own rectitude and lack of bigotry. He is a monster, but he's not a bad man.

The picture bulges with that sort of paradox. Basically a record of the fitful and finally unsuccessful (or perhaps too successful) acculturation of a half-breed Aborigine, *The Chant of Jimmie Blacksmith* offers no sweeping generalizations and no surcease from the pain of prejudice; it charts the course of conflict between two cultures and shows how both are dehumanized, with an objectivity that is occasionally terrifying. Visually – the ultimate stylistic paradox – it is ravishing, formed from a pearly succession of images that recall Vermeer and David in tone, but that are of awesome antediluvian landscapes and primordial aboriginal camps, images unique to Australia.

54

Sadly, nothing else in the film is in any respect unique. The half-breed Jimmie (Tommy Lewis) is not at home in his own culture (when he makes love to an Aborigine woman he calls her a "black bitch") but he is accepted by whites solely when it suits their purposes; he proves a handy husband for a promiscuous and slightly retarded woman impregnated by a white man. Throughout the first part of the film, Jimmie goes from one situation to another in which he is treated poorly (and sometimes worse) by the dominant culture, but we are never sure exactly how he is reacting to his abasement – he plays Uncle Tom to the whites and to the camera – and we can see that the Australians who are humiliating him mean him no real harm. They simply cannot believe that he is fully human, and consequently treat him with the same mixture of contempt and affection experienced by unpredictable children. We can also see that his white ambitions (he is proud that his wife knows where to put the soup spoon when she sets the table, for example) are bewildering to his aboriginal brothers.

The preamble is necessary if the tragedy that follows is to make sense. When Jimmie rebels against his oppressors, he does so randomly and irrationally, explosively and self-destructively. He gets revenge, all right, but against the innocent as well as the guilty (Schepisi has made it clear that the concepts are meaningless: everyone contributes to Jimmie's desperation, but no one is responsible for it), and your feelings about him and about the film will probably be decided during the scene in which he takes the top of a small boy's head off with a hatchet.

That description is by way of a warning. When *The Chant of Jimmie Blacksmith*, based on actual incidents, was screened two years ago at the Festival of Festivals, there were many walkouts, a number of them from sympathetic liberals outraged that their sympathy had been defiled and their good intentions questioned. Schepisi, who both wrote and directed the movie, and who is now in Hollywood making a Western with Willie Nelson, is not interested in ideology: he is interested in showing what genocide does to both sides, and one of his conclusions is that revenge in the form of terrorism results in the total dehumanization of those once victimized. By the time he has become a fugitive, the half-breed is as racist as any of the whites for whom his existence, until he began his killing spree, was so trivial. *The Chant of*

Jimmie Blacksmith is a powerful, heartbreaking dirge for the casualties of colliding cultures. On some level, that includes all of us.

September 5, 1980

Bad Timing: A Sensual Obsession

Directed by Nicolas Roeg
Written by Yale Udoff
Starring Art Garfunkel and Theresa Russell

While Tom Waits growls "Invitation to the Blues," lovers Art Garfunkel and Theresa Russell contemplate the *fin de siècle* paintings of Gustav Klimt and his pupil Egon Schiele; in Klimt, the space surrounding the subjects has been shattered into glittering shards, and in Schiele, distorted men and women cling maniacally to each other, as though their lives will end if their pathological contact breaks. The gallery visited by the lovers is in Vienna, the city where – what with Freud and Wittgenstein and all the rest – it has been said the modern world began.

Bad Timing: A Sensual Obsession, directed by Nicolas Roeg, one of the world's great cinematic puzzle-makers, could have been entitled Anatomy of a Love Affair or Last Waltz in Vienna. Garfunkel is a gelid research psychoanalyst ("I prefer to label myself an observer") whose initially innocent flirtation with Russell, a wild and free-spirited or neurotically immature and irresponsible woman (the characterization depends on your prejudice), leads to an emotional Götterdämmerung. *Bad Timing* recalls Klimt in technique, Schiele in content and Dostoevski in attitude.

Like *Performance*, the Roeg film it most closely resembles, *Bad Timing* is open to infinite analysis and interpretation – it will probably become this year's most pummelled film-school film. But Roeg realizes that at heart his story is chillingly basic; the film's courage in paying tribute to the primitive is its salient achievement. What *All That Jazz* did for death, *Bad Timing* does for love: people who disliked the former will undoubtedly loathe the latter.

"I just wanted us to be nice together, that's all," Russell, whose performance is a protean revelation, tells Garfunkel. So easy, but so hard. "They're happy," she says, as they view a Schiele in which two lovers are emphatically unhappy. They are happy "because they don't know each other well enough yet," Garfunkel, who is no better at recognizing misery when he sees it, responds. In that one exchange, we have been given the algebra of *Bad Timing*: to love me is to know me is to hate me. And we have been given the seed of this couple's ruination: their ignorance of their atavistic impulses may destroy them. Love is a killer.

Impossible relationships have been popular in movies as long as there have been movies, but *Bad Timing* is something new, a popular movie that save for the picturesqueness of its locales makes few concessions to popular taste or accepted romantic myth. (It may be the strongest statement against romantic love since Bertolucci's *Last Tango in Paris* or Oshima's *In the Realm of the Senses*). While Garfunkel makes love to Russell, her groans of ecstasy are the bridge for a cut to her groans of anguish as her throat is being surgically slit. Her relationship has ended in a suicide attempt, and throughout the film the efforts of Viennese physicians to save her life – stomach pumps, a tracheotomy – are intercut with the sweetest and sexiest moments of her love affair.

The film earns Dr. Freud's Seal of Psychoanalytic Approval: the connections between sex and death, between love and hate, between pleasure and pain, have rarely been as graphically visualized. These are the sequences in *Bad Timing* that many people hate, just as they hated the open heart surgery and egotistic deathbed production number in *All That Jazz*. Some species of truth are too misshapen to fondle with equanimity.

Not everything works. There are cross-cuts that are facile (a stripper whirls; cut to a sheet of paper pulled from a spinning typewriter platen) and Harvey Keitel's Viennese detective is more interesting in theory than in fact. The detective protects himself against criminal "contamination" by incessantly confirming the worst of his fears about human nature – he's a homage to the Robert De Niro character in *Taxi Driver*. Roeg has explained that Keitel and Garfunkel are "both watchers and analysts – men who want everything to be tidy, obedient, pliant to their wills." That is apparent in the film, but at best it adds a footnote to the major thematic construct: that voyeurism is the seat of agony and ecstasy.

Roeg puts the theory together this way: Garfunkel is a professional observer. He watches. When he involves himself with Russell, every moment of her life comes under his scrutiny; in watching, he becomes jealous; in becoming jealous, he becomes murderous. At first, Russell does not watch – she reacts. But when she involves herself with Garfunkel, she too learns to watch; becomes uncertain; and in becoming uncertain, becomes suicidal (which is murder internalized). The camera watches everything; we watch through the camera. Roeg is arguing that by nature the human animal is a voyeur. By nature, and under certain circumstance, the human animal is a killer: he murders for love. Under what circumstances? Sometimes, all it takes is bad timing.

September 27, 1980

Ordinary People

Directed by Robert Redford
Written by Alvin Sargent
Starring Timothy Hutton, Mary Tyler Moore and Donald Sutherland

Judith Guest's 1976 novel *Ordinary People*, in which an affluent WASP high school student named Conrad Jarrett attempted to take his life (razors and wrists), was spare and lean and vigorously unsentimental. In the film adaptation, written by Alvin Sargent and directed by

Robert Redford, what was spare seems stingy, what was lean seems thin and what was unsentimental has franchised a Kleenex concession: *Ordinary People* has all the earmarks of an earnest hit, *Kramer vs. Kramer* division. The only thing that could keep it from box-office bingo is the fact that it is earnestly boring.

The setting is Lake Forest, Ill., Chicago's Rosedale, where the luggage is suede, the cars overpowered, the lipstick pale, the swimming pools aquamarine and the autumns auburn. These are not Ordinary People: they are Ordinary Rich People, and John Cheever, worst luck, is nowhere in view. Into their careful yet paradoxically carefree existence (wealthy WASPs in Hollywood movies have earned the right to be carefree because they have been careful) comes Conrad (Timothy Hutton) and his dripping wrists. They ooze all over monster mummy's carpets (Mummy is played, and played very well, by Mary Tyler Moore) and they burn like acid through plastic poppa's façade (Poppa is played, equally well, by Donald Sutherland).

Mum, a snooty soul with a large circle of golfing friends, discovers that she cannot forgive Conrad for having bled on her carpets and she's not too happy about his failing to save the life of her favourite son, either (a boating accident). Pop, on the other hand, wants to get to know his boy: he wants to be rid of masks, to be Real, to Understand.

Naturally, knowing how to be Real and how to Understand do not come easy in Lake Forest – which Redford records with the same libellously slick condescension Mike Nichols brought to the "plastics" party scene in *The Graduate* – and Pop sends Conrad to Dr. Berger, a godlike if not godfearing shrink (Judd Hirsch, in the Robert Redford role).

Dr. Berger is the one character in the film who really does have all the answers, including the big one: there ain't any. He is the one character who does not want to be in control of his surroundings ("I'm not big on control," he says). He is the one character who believes emotions should be expressed. He is the one character whose environment – his office – is a mess. He is the one character who is wise beyond his income and profound beyond his syntax. (He is the one character who sounds like Jack Webb on "Dragnet" – after est.) And he is the one character who is Jewish.

This final fact is absolutely essential to exposing the myths by which *Ordinary People* operates: its WASPS are as colourless as the WASPS in Woody Allen's *Interiors* (Moore's Mum is no more than a younger version of Geraldine Page) but its Jew is a brand new stereotype: to Dr. Berger goes the Sidney Poitier Pristine Pedestal Award.

In his debut as a director, Redford has treated his cast lovingly. Within the boundaries of their wizened roles, his actors perform competently, although Timothy Hutton's Conrad can be caught calculating his effects, and his big *Night Must Fall tour de force*, when he regresses psychologically to the scene of his suicide trauma, is a psychiatric and esthetic embarrassment. If the problem is neither in the acting nor in Redford's direction (workmanlike), where is it? The filmmakers have said repeatedly that they have been "true" to Guest's novel, which is not entirely accurate. Where, for instance, is the Epilogue, in which she graciously acknowledged the essential banality and ephemerality of her tale? But they have treated her words with more reverence than might have been necessary. Or wise.

That other manipulative domestic tearjerker, *Kramer vs. Kramer*, was also based on a novel of merit but, when the story reached the screen, it had shifted tone and altered allegiance; it had been reconceived for the movies. The problems of adapting *Ordinary People* are greater – its predominant virtue cannot be transferred to the screen. How do you pictorialize an author's analysis of the psychic states of people notable for refusing to articulate their thoughts, or even to feel their feelings? How do you communicate in images an omniscient psychological dissection? Redford and Sargent sidestep the conundrum and settle for blindly reproducing Guest's dialogue.

Unfortunately, out of Guest's precisely composed context, the words are archly literary: *Ordinary People*'s people are ordinary, ordinary TV people in an ordinary, overwritten, overprocessed TV drama. The most this sincere little movie expects of you is tears; it would be modestly pleased if its mirror reflects a little sliver of your life; it does not want to shock you, provoke you, frighten you, intellectually stimulate you, or even teach you anything you do not already know. If the hero of "Leave It to Beaver" had grown up, gone to high school and taken it into his head to off himself, the made-for-TV-movie that could have ensued – Leave It to Beaver Tries to Leave It – might have been a lot like *Ordinary People*.

September 27, 1980

Resurrection

Directed by Daniel Petrie
Written by Lewis John Carlino
Starring Ellen Burstyn and Sam Shepard

The Elephant Man

Directed by David Lynch
Written by Christopher de Vore, Eric Bergren and David Lynch
Starring Anthony Hopkins and John Hurt

Notes on two bad movies, about two memorable freaks, that share one admirable theme: that if humanity could learn to love what it loathes, to embrace what it fears, and to accept what it finds inexplicable, the world would be a better place.

In *Resurrection*, the character played by Ellen Burstyn dies (momentarily), is brought back to life and rehabilitates herself. Along the way, she discovers that she has been blessed with the gift of healing – just put her paws in the vicinity of a disease and those old hands heat right up and get to work, closing gaping wounds, straightening crooked limbs and in general lightening the loads of the heavy laden. (Originally, the script was about Jesus Christ coming back to earth as a female: cooler craniums prevailed.)

61

In *The Elephant Man*, the character played by John Hurt is John Merrick, a man whose early life was a kind of living death. Merrick, one of the most deformed beings ever to be documented ("From the brow there projected a huge bony mass like a loaf, while from the back of the head hung a bag of spongy fungus-looking skin, the surface of which was comparable to brown cauliflower," his physician wrote, in a description that went on for many more paragraphs), was brought to a Victorian hospital and placed under the care of Sir Frederick Treves (Anthony Hopkins); in a twist of fate worthy of Dickens, the outcast was fêted by London society and died, in 1890, at the age of twenty-seven, a celebrity.

It is often said the camera loves certain faces. It is less often said, but it is equally true, that it despises certain themes. On screen, the mystical almost always becomes ridiculous. Visions, for example, assume a psychedelic aura neither religious nor pharmaceutical; attempts to render the perceptually extraordinary invariably look like optical experiments (which of course they are). When Burstyn "dies" in *Resurrection*, director Daniel Petrie slavishly reproduces the cross-cultural descriptions of the process culled by respected researchers: there is a light at the end of a tunnel and as Burstyn moves toward it, she is greeted by departed friends urging her on. When one reads of this process, it seems as reasonable as anything unknowable can be, but when one sees it on screen, with divine illumination that is clearly a spotlight, and with actors and actresses waving their arms as if proffering martinis, the whole thing becomes hilarious. Death looks like a tour of a movie studio party.

John Merrick's make-up in *The Elephant Man* poses a similar problem. In the Broadway play (there is no connection, save subject, between film and play), Merrick is represented by an actor who simply alters his posture. In David Lynch's film, the Elephant Man has become a drooling Latex monster. There is nothing wrong with Hurt's performance – it is quite moving – but there is a great deal wrong with a movie that adds insult to injury by unconscionably holding back the revelation of the make-up. Lynch, who previously made the low-budget horror flick, *Eraserhead*, begins *The Elephant Man* with a surreal sequence in which Merrick's mother is raped (or trampled – with the surreal it's so hard to tell) by a herd of elephants. Then Treves finds the Elephant Man in a sideshow, strikes up a bargain with his "owner" and exhibits him to the College of Surgeons. The audience has yet to see the creation. Why? Because Lynch is making a horror film (in horror films, you make 'em wait) and because when we do see the make-up, the movie falls fatally apart. It is good make-up, but it is make-up.

Resurrection is sillier than *The Elephant Man*, but less offensive: in attempting less, its sins are smaller. Director Petrie, his screenwriter, Lewis John Carlino, and Burstyn, without whose interest and support the picture would not have been made, were out to film a study of healers that took the phenomenon seriously, as I've no doubt it should be taken. They have enlisted the aid of Sam Shepard, who is very good as Burstyn's boy friend, and as her grandmother they have unearthed the legendary Eva Le Gallienne.

They have chosen their Midwestern locations with an eye for the eye-filling; and they have scrupulously held to the known facts – Burstyn's character, for example, refuses to attribute her powers to any deity. What they have not managed to do is to make *Resurrection* believable for longer than a demi-second. But with lines such as "If life only gives you lemons, remember you can always make lemonade," belief is difficult to sandwich between groans and giggles.

The Elephant Man has chosen its locations with care, too, but they have been chosen for their horrific qualities: Victorian England is one endless, dimly lit corridor of squalor. For no reason, we are present while Treves performs grisly surgery (not on the Elephant Man); villains snarl slimily; and the gratuitous images of ugliness are jerkily held together by irritating fade-outs, the refuge of the unimaginative director.

The thrust of this appears to be that it is Victorian society that was deformed, not the Elephant Man. Lynch, who had a hand in the sodden screenplay, has retroactively applied the theories of R. D. Laing.

When Merrick recites the Twenty-third Psalm – the movie's most touching moment – we get a glimpse of the movie that might have been, if the make-up problem had been solved (I'm not sure it could have been). The movie that might have been was a quiet ode to a child-man fighting for a tiny corner of control in a world revolted by his physical presence. Little of that movie exists here, but *The Elephant Man* could become a hit anyway: the basic story, like Merrick's dignity, cannot be completely sabotaged, and Lynch's high-toned horror techniques make leering almost respectable.

October 4, 1980

The Stunt Man

Directed by Richard Rush
Written by Lawrence B. Marcus
Starring Peter O'Toole, Barbara Hershey and Steve Railsback

"My own tastes are for Proust and Batman." – *Richard Rush*

The Stunt Man, which is scary and sorrowful and stirring and sexy – in other words, everything a big Hollywood popcorn-cruncher of a movie should be – is the best movie about making a movie ever made. The achievement merely begins there: this is the Hollywood dream movie, the flick every producer thinks he wants to make, the perfect marriage between art and commerce, the picture that should pack 'em in for blistering action while critics are off in corners constructing spidery exegeses of debts to Luigi Pirandello and Jean-Luc Godard.

This is also the movie Hollywood wouldn't touch: not only did every studio reject the script (financing was raised privately, and the picture was shot in San Diego in 1978), but every studio rejected the film – Twentieth Century-Fox agreed to distribute it only after Richard Rush, the director, opened it in Seattle himself and demonstrated that it had an audience.

In superficial specifics, *The Stunt Man* is as simple as a silent movie: Eli Cross (Peter O'Toole), a director reminiscent of Patrick Dennis' outlandish Leander Starr in the novel *Genius*, is making an anti-war First World War movie with Nina Franklin (Barbara Hershey), a semi-competent actress and completely competent bitch, when his set is invaded by Cameron (Steve Railsback), an apparently paranoiac Vietnam veteran running from the police. Eli, a magisterial figure who plays God because that's the name of the directing game, decides to use Cameron as a replacement for a dead stunt man. Asked if he has stunt experience, the nutsy Cameron replies, "I got outta 'Nam in one piece; that's a helluva stunt." The rest of the movie is about the making of the rest of the movie.

How can a picture in which a stunt man falls in love with his leading lady and maintains an ambivalent relationship with his director operate on virtually every level open to a work of movie art? In that opening sequence, which is bound to become very famous, Cameron runs smack into a scene being played out on Eli's movie set. But we don't know that a movie is being made. When at long last we get our bearings, something else has thrown us off kilter, has put the sky where the sea should be. Nothing is what it seems. There are no red herrings, but we are constantly provided visual information from which we draw erroneous conclusions. *The Stunt Man*'s message is in its method.

I am being nebulous intentionally because I don't want to spoil the fun. For all its depth, or maybe because of its depth, *The Stunt Man* is as much fun as any great movie extant; imagine a comedy an eight-year-old and Wittgenstein could love with equal fervour. The entire picture is a shimmering mirage, as dizzyingly complex, unpredictable and original in tone as any American movie since *Bonnie and Clyde*, and as justifiably self-celebratory as Robert Altman's *Nashville*.

"It's life's illusions I recall." – *Joni Mitchell*

Like the anti-war movie Eli is directing (the film within the film), *The Stunt Man* is concerned with heroism and mortality. "We're afraid we're going to die of nothing more important than wrinkles," Eli observes. His stunt men risk death to prove they are alive; his audiences risk involvement with the characters portrayed by the stunt men for the same reason – movies let them hang from cliffs, face speeding locomotives and battle entire garrisons. By proxy.

"If God could do the tricks that we can do, He'd be a happy man," Eli smirks. Once upon a time, God could. But *The Stunt Man* argues that movie (or television) magic – media magic – has replaced the magic of yore, when little boxes holding bones of saints were worshipped and the appearance of the face of the Virgin on a dishcloth was a decade's marvel. "Everybody wants something to believe in – even policemen," Eli says. Without something to believe in, life is meaningless. So Eli plays God: he gives the masses movies. Stars. Stories. Something to care about. Something to make the pain go away.

There's a catch. Eli, who's seen life from both sides now, knows he's not God. (As played by O'Toole, in his finest performance since *The Ruling Class*, he is a variation on the half-mad Lawrence of Arabia. Except that this world-weary, effete figure in Dr. Zhivago shirts is Larry of Araby – a deity who shops on Rodeo Drive.) He knows the only time his stunt men feel alive, the only time their problems cease to be petty, is when they have faced and vanquished danger; that's the only time Eli feels alive. His movies, at their best, reproduce for the audience some of the excitement that went into making them. Eli is a purveyor of a very modern religion: Vicarious Living. But he is a leader with no place to take his followers, and he would like to make a movie about that, about the impotence of his art in the yawning maw of death; but to come right out and say that nothing makes sense, you would have to "sneak it in," he suspects. Toss it to the audience between the laughs, the tears and the sex-cum-violence turn-on. Eli is talking about *The Stunt Man*'s own *modus operandi*: the phenomeno-logical sophistication of this movie is extraordinary. The irony is that an incredibly self-conscious, analytical film can make you care deeply about its characters: when one of them is placed in great danger dur-ing the climax, you may find yourself clawing your arm rests.

"Truth and illusion, George. You don't know the difference." – *Martha, in* Who's Afraid of Virginia Woolf?

Side by side with the originality, any number of movie clichés are recycled, as they must be – one of the tasks *The Stunt Man* has set itself is to illustrate how the dynamics of the filmmaking process have been reflected, historically, in the movies themselves.

In the eyes of Eli and his leading lady, for example, the tattooed, blue-collar Cameron is an object of romanticized respect (because he has lived), fear (because he is volatile), condescension (because he has no social graces) and erotic attraction (for all those reasons). Roman-ticized respect, fear, condescension, erotic attraction: not a half-bad summation of Hollywood's dominant attitude toward working-class teen-agers – in the fifties, they became known as "anti-heroes" – all the way from the *Dead End* kids to Tony Manero in *Saturday Night Fever*, or to his Stetson clone in *Urban Cowboy*.

The Stunt Man examines an important symbiotic relationship: Hollywood movie rebels are nearly interchangeable because, in many cases, the filmmakers base them on the only working-class kids they know, the men in their movie crews; meanwhile, out in the real world, working-class kids pattern their behaviour after distorted reflections in the movies. (Cameron is the most obvious example but every character in *The Stunt Man* has been moulded by the movies. The actress comports herself as she thinks a hip leading lady should; her notions of how to orchestrate her love affair with Cameron are all movie-oriented.)

Truth and illusion collide in Cameron: part of *The Stunt Man*'s mystery involves the kind of person he really is, as opposed to the kind of person Eli and the actress (and a wonderful cast of supporting characters) think he is. On this level, too, we are toyed with: personality is just one more special effect. Cameron is convinced that Eli is out to get him, that the actress may not love him, that nobody is what he seems. Is Cameron paranoid – or aware? Crazy or sane? Do people care or could they care less? Cameron can be seen as Everyman on the lam: his message is that we are all stunt men. We are all forced to find authenticity by threatening life itself (in big ways or small), to support values that the next move of the camera may reveal to be false fronts. What knowledge of the nature of life is possible, finally? *The Stunt Man*'s answer comes from Cameron, in a description of a Vietnam booby trap. If a man stepped on this trap, nothing happened; if he removed his foot, it exploded. "So all he could do was just stand there."

October 11, 1980

Steve McQueen (1930-1980), An Appreciation

In *Tom Horn*, one of the two movies Steve McQueen came out of a four-year hiatus to make last year, there is a scene in which he is introduced as "a vestige of that heroic era just past." McQueen plays a hired gun at loose ends: the twentieth century has dawned, the West has been settled, killing has been outlawed, outlaws have been domesticated. The First World War is around the corner. McQueen goes grimly to work for a group of modern cattle barons – already cognizant of corporate image, they need someone to do their dirty work. Work, dirty or otherwise, was something a Steve McQueen character seldom turned down.

In his most successful movies (and there were many; at the time of his death, he could command a $3-million fee for a film), McQueen frequently could be found laundering someone else's soiled linen. John Wayne, the actor to whom he was often and inaptly compared, did his own dirty work (in Wayne's movies, killing was rarely perceived as "dirty") for his own self-aggrandizement: he was an independent operator in a country that worshipped independent operators.

McQueen played men who thought they were independent. They were often proved wrong. *Tom Horn*, which may be viewed as a kind of summing up – it is to McQueen's career what *The Shootist* was to Wayne's – closes with the actor on the gallows, a fall-guy for corporate intrigue. Tom McGuane's script tells us that if Horn would give in and play the game, his life would be saved. McQueen's portrayal tells us Horn would rather die by his own rules than live by the opposition's. Consistently the laconic rebel, McQueen's jousts with authority were two things: admirable and doomed.

He was a logical extension of the James Dean era, but he was cooler – a bona-fide minimalist, and much more passive than either Dean or Brando; he could make Paul Newman seem hysterical. As writer Roger Angell has pointed out, his characters were invariably at home with the mechanical or inanimate: the ship in *The Sand Pebbles*; the motorcycles in *The Great Escape*; the yellow Winton Flyer in one of his best films, *The Reivers*; the cars in *Bullitt*, *Le Mans* and *The Getaway*; the nags in *Junior Bonner*; the blob in *The Blob*; Natalie Wood in *Love With the Proper Stranger*.

Human society was his albatross. It is no accident that the one project for which he campaigned tirelessly was his film version of Ibsen's *An Enemy of the People*. It was the intellectualized, "high art" analogue of what he had become in the popular mind, a man who could be trusted to do the right thing if he were left alone. He was the apotheosis of the whiz-kid garage mechanic who can lubricate a chassis with élan but who is never promoted and is always exploited by those richer – but not necessarily cleverer – than he.

Considering his effortless sex appeal, his remarkable relationship with the camera and his limited but authentic acting skills, it was perhaps inevitable that he would became one of Hollywood's most popular and durable stars in an era (the sixties and seventies) when stars were said to be dead and durability confined to German and Japanese automobiles. In the sixties, he communicated with hard-hat and hippie alike. In the seventies, his sense of isolation and his brave but ultimately impotent disdain for propriety found a knowing response in the middle and lower classes – especially in the young of those classes.

(He was never an upper-class icon. Although incredibly rich, and highly visible as a jet-set race car driver, he nonetheless managed to retain a volatile grittiness that warned his fingernails might be black-rimmed if they were to shake a white-gloved hand.)

The conclusion of his life yesterday in a Juarez clinic, where he had gone for Laetrile and other conventionally castigated treatments, was an ending as fitting as any ending can be. Once again, he had refused to listen to the modulated tones of official wisdom; he had refused to give up. For more than thirty years, he had played men who had defied the authorities and had tried to live by their own, difficult-to-define codes. Steve McQueen was not about to die following orders.

November 8, 1980

Raging Bull

Directed by Martin Scorsese
Written by Paul Schrader and Mardik Martin
Starring Robert De Niro

As Jake La Motta, a world champion welterweight prizefighter whose career collapsed in the mid-fifties, Robert De Niro brings to Martin

Scorsese's new film *Raging Bull* one of the most astonishing metamorphoses in the history of movies: he ages by more than twenty years and balloons by more than forty pounds – real pounds – in the space of two harrowing hours.

When we first see La Motta under the credits (*Raging Bull* is in glorious black and white, save for a few home-movie sequences in faded colour), he is warming up in the ring in 1941 and De Niro is clearly in the best shape he has been in his life. A title (New York City, 1964) appears and Scorsese cuts to a dressing room in an unidentified theatre where a paunchy, gross-featured figure with a battered puss that has the texture of potato skin is reciting doggerel in front of a mirror: "So give a stage/Where this bull here can rage." As the camera glides toward the face, recognition comes slowly: poked into the almost monstrous flab are two porcine eyes that could belong to Brando, or James Caan. De Niro flashes his goofy, moronic grin and one accepts the incredible.

The story of Jake La Motta, rags to riches to rags, is an actor's dream, but both De Niro and Scorsese have been careful not to make their palooka into a conventional (or even an unconventional) hero. Violent, vindictive, volatile, childish and psychotically jealous of his beautiful second wife, a succulent blonde named Vickie (Cathy Moriarity), La Motta is portrayed in a melodramatic format – a homage to Warner Brothers of the thirties – that deliberately suggests tabloid newspapers and newsreels.

Scorsese achieves his remarkable effects through surprisingly modest means. Period music ("Big Noise" from Winnetka, Monroe singing "Bye Bye Baby") is used sparingly; the original score is MGM pastoral (the lyric theme recalls "Over the Rainbow" in both melody and orchestration). There are simple but stunning visual contrasts between De Niro's *café au lait* skin tones and the creamy vanilla of Moriarity's cheeks. La Motta's slippery grasp of reality is signalled by photographing scenes of Vickie through La Motta's eyes, in slow motion – very fast slow motion, a nearly imperceptible shift of speed. Where *Rocky* and *Rocky II* saw boxing as a groaning waltz of dinosaurs

(Rocky Balboa was a heavyweight), the battles in *Raging Bull* are jitter-bugs of death danced by stinging insects – quick, vicious, blistering exchanges of venom.

Over all, *Raging Bull* is so tough (it is, however, restrained in comparison to Scorsese's most expressionist exercises, *Taxi Driver* and *Mean Streets*) and so intransigently anti-romantic that some viewers are certain to wonder why it was made at all. Where's the moral? Twice married, La Motta beats both wives and throttles Joey (Joe Pesci), his long-suffering brother, when he paranoiacally decides Joey has been fornicating with Vickie. La Motta is not a nice guy; *Raging Bull* is not, and does not want to be, a nice movie – Scorsese is after verisimilitude, not myth.

(Sexual possessiveness and its inevitable vitriol, the strong subtext of *Raging Bull*, has always been a major motif in Scorsese's work. The most illuminating example is perhaps *Taxi Driver*, where Scorsese himself plays one of Robert De Niro's fares. He orders De Niro to park outside a high-rise, points to two figures silhouetted in a window and calmly informs De Niro the figures belong to his wife and her black lover. He is going to kill both of them, he says. Jake's attitude toward Vickie in *Raging Bull* is neither as concentrated nor quite as pathological; in all other respects, it is identical, and it, more than the boxing, gives *Raging Bull* its edge.)

Miraculously, La Motta's relationship with his wife survives the beatings – for the time being – though the relationship with his brother does not. Retirement provides a nightclub in Miami (called Jake La Motta's, of course) and it seems likely the old pro will settle into a reasonably profitable and pleasantly easy dotage. Except that the old pro, who has turned his free-floating hostility toward his patrons and does a stand-up comedy routine – he's an unfunny Don Rickles precursor – is allergic to the profitable, the pleasant, the easy and the reasonable. The boxer who gratuitously smeared an opponent's nose "from one side of his face to another" because Vickie found the opponent "good-looking" is not about to stay out of trouble.

In the scene that climaxes De Niro's performance, La Motta has been thrown into the Dade County Jail. For the first time, the fighter sees the brick wall – the prison of his own personality – he has been shadow-boxing all his life, and he bangs his head and his hands into the concrete blocks lining his cell over and over again, screaming, "Why?! Why?!" The intensity of the film verges on the intolerable.

Hemingway would hate *Raging Bull* – it's about the life of boxing, not the art – and many of the men in yesterday's audience who had come for a true-life Rocky and who had originally egged La Motta on regardless of his activities (a tantrummy up-ending of the dinner table set by the first wife was greeted with cheers and applause) were finally bludgeoned into silence by Scorsese when their hero had become aged and corpulent and unmistakably cruel. La Motta lost them, but De Niro didn't; one may lose empathy for the bruiser, but one never loses sympathy for the human being. "I wanted this film to be real," Scorsese has said, and in his smoky primal world, heroes are something taking up space on TV sets in the background. When La Motta, in the neatest, sickest joke of the movie, appears at a benefit and reads the "I coulda been a contender" speech from *On the Waterfront, Raging Bull* comes full circle: Jake La Motta was champion of the world, but he's one of the world's champion losers. And he's still raging.

November 15, 1980

Tess

Directed by Roman Polanski
Written by Roman Polanski, Gerard Brach, John Brownjohn
Starring Nastassja Kinski, Leigh Lawson and Peter Firth

The supranaturally beautiful, three-hour Roman Polanski adaptation of Thomas Hardy's 1891 novel *Tess of the d'Urbervilles* has been hailed by many observers, and indeed by Polanski himself, as a departure for the incisive director of *Chinatown, Repulsion, The Tenant* and *Rosemary's Baby.* It is a relief to be able to report that *Tess* is a continuation and elaboration of the themes that have always attracted Polanski, and that it represents a maturation of those themes, rather than a departure. What Polanski has been exploring all these years is far too valuable to leave behind.

What has been bypassed, naturally, is a certain explicitness in the presentation of the products of passion: violence and eroticism. The story of Tess (Nastassja Kinski) is melodramatic tragedy, formed from undesired seduction, unwanted pregnancy and unpremeditated murder. But in Hardy the hint is stronger than the howl and Polanski, who in his 1971 visualization of *Macbeth* proved a master of Shakespearean sound and fury, is here equally proficient at the whisper and the whimper. It may be impossible for a filmic compression of a great novel to be considered definitive, but this treatment should render future attempts superfluous, in the way that David Lean's *Great Expectations*, John Ford's *Grapes of Wrath*, Ken Russell's *Women in Love* and (on a different level) Victor Fleming's *Gone With the Wind*, have stymied in the daydream stage directors who would better the originals. (*Gone With the Wind*'s producer, David O. Selznick, dreamed of making *Tess* with Jennifer Jones, but the only previous version is a 1924 silent with Blanche Sweet.)

The screenplay, by Polanski, Gerard Brach and John Brownjohn, lifts huge chunks of dialogue from Hardy's pages, and gets away with it. "Tess, I'm dying for you" and "I want to take you away from this wretched place" – even those lines play well. The scrupulously pellucid pacing, the sophistication of the screenplay's frieze-like structure, the fluidity of the camerawork and the compositional colouration (*Tess* has the look of a *Barry Lyndon* that is about something) coalesce to tell Hardy's tale of a woman victimized by Victorian society – and unable to learn from her victimization – with sensual lucidity.

Kinski was seventeen when shooting began on *Tess*; a year earlier, she spoke no English, but she mastered with putative ease a functional if inexpressive facsimile of a Dorset accent. As an actress, she is something of a post, albeit a splendiferously bedecked post – less a physical reminder of the young Ingrid Bergman than an eerie reincarnation. Polanski's careful control of her every nuance is reminiscent of the hushed camera with which he caressed Catherine Deneuve when he handed her, in *Repulsion*, the performance of her career, a performance that in common with Kinski's was most effective in repose. (When Kinski reclines, she suggests volumes; when she talks, she speaks captions.) Adequate though the Kinski Tess is, it appears to have been edited rather than acted. What this willowy, doe-like ingenue may be able to accomplish in the future is at present a matter for palmistry.

The cast with which she has been surrounded, including Leigh Lawson as her first seducer and Peter Firth as her husband, is first-rate. The extras are among the most convincing ever photographed for a period film and Lawson recently explained, with thudding demystification, the reason: "National Health hasn't come to Northern France, so the peasant faces are still peasant faces; they haven't been equipped with dentures."

Polanski may see Tess as a victim of society, but she is by no means a sacrificial victim and the film by no means an implicit feminist tract, although its supporters and detractors have agreed on that reductive reading. If they are correct, then why does Tess eventually, maddeningly, abet her persecutors, first through shame, then stubbornness? She is more woman than symbol, and more a creature of the psychological interaction between novelist and director than an exponent of any political position. In this heroine's understandable but nonetheless maladaptive aversion to men there are overtones of the Deneuve character in *Repulsion*, and in the fetid incestuous claustrophobia of her relationships there are dank reminders of Faye Dunaway in *Chinatown*.

The extraordinary empathy this director has for women in peril, the generative force behind *Rosemary's Baby* (where Mia Farrow gave the performance of her career), helps to explain why he was drawn to the novel and why the voice in which the film speaks is so well-modulated: Polanski has been working through his feelings toward women for a long time. The fact that *Tess* is dedicated to the late Sharon Tate indicates that, through Hardy, much of the work has been accomplished and a resolution achieved. The detached tone of

Tess – contemplative and fatalistic, resigned and melancholy – may be non-romantic and in the end not entirely true to Hardy, but it is full of love and compassion for those who seek both in a world where there is so little of either.

February 14, 1981

❖

Melvin and Howard

Directed by Jonathan Demme
Written by Bo Goldman
Starring Paul Le Mat, Jason Robards and Mary Steenburgen

Out on the Nevada desert near Tonopah, a land where even the lizards are dried and salted like beef jerky, a lone figure – an old, old man – is racing a motorcycle. All grey hair and gristle, he bends jubilantly over the handlebars, a wino Ichabod Crane cackling in delight at his daredevilry. When he wipes out and is picked up at the side of the road by a pudgy, slow-talkin', slow-thinkin' local boy in a western shirt and pickup, he begins berating his benefactor in a mellifluous, educated, intelligent voice. "I am Howard Hughes," the wino says. And the pudgy local, whose name is Melvin Dummar, squints into the desert night and replies, "I believe people have the right to call themselves anything they want to."

The meeting is the stuff of legend, and the real Melvin Dummar, who appears briefly in *Melvin and Howard* as a hash-house waiter in Reno, claims to have met Hughes on just such a night, and further claims that Hughes, grateful for Melvin's courtesy, left a hand-written will in which he, Melvin Dummar, was named recipient of $156-million of Howard Hughes' money, one-sixteenth of the aggregate fortune. Scriptwriter Bo Goldman and director Jonathan Demme (*The Last Embrace, Handle With Care*) have accepted Dummar's story as blue-collar gospel and have used the alleged 1967 act of good

Samaritanism as the pivot for what is easily the best and funniest American film of the new year, a picture that views the desiccated psychic flatlands of game-show America with the precision, humour and sympathy of the early sequences of *Breaking Away*, and with a stylistic fluidity that recalls *Alice Doesn't Live Here Anymore*. *Melvin and Howard* is a screwball farce that reads like reportage – a docu-comedy.

"I've had a lot of jobs, but I can't seem to get the right one," Melvin (Paul Le Mat) tells Howard (Jason Robards), before bullying Howard into accompanying him on the chorus of an original song, "Santa's Souped-Up Sleigh." So Howard Hughes, who had a lot of jobs and couldn't get the right one, either (until Occupation: Hermit, happened along), realizes he has something in common with this sun-belt cracker, and grudgingly agrees to sing a solo to pass the time. Hughes' rendition of "Bye Bye Blackbird" has already become, justifiably, the movie's most famous sequence.

But when Hughes leaves the film, the good spirits hold up. Melvin is a professional victim with more dreams than brains and with a lack of opportunism that amounts to a crippling mutation. When he was a milkman, he reminisces, he would see wives home alone while their husbands worked the graveyard shift. Did that give Melvin ideas? Yep: "I thought maybe I should be doin' that – workin' the graveyard shift." His wife Lynda (Mary Steenburgen), a luscious cupcake with a brainpan approximately the size of a Twinkie, does nonetheless possess enough smarts to see that Melvin possesses none and takes off to Vegas to be a hootchie-kootchie dancer; what she actually becomes is a stripper, but Steenburgen gives her character such a radiant, unaffected ingenuousness that the term stripper sticks in the throat. Melvin, appalled, tracks her down and enters her bar. "Let's go!" he orders, grabbing what little clothing she has left while Mick Jagger sings of Satisfaction. "I caaaaan't!" Lynda wails. Melvin, puzzled: "Why not?" Lynda, matter-of-fact: "I love to dance."

Thanks to Easy Street, a game show that combines "Let's Make a Deal" (magic doors) with "The Gong Show" (performing bores), their fortunes soar and then settle, like restless sparrows heralding the onset of a thunderstorm. A fed-up Lynda makes room for Bonnie

(Pamela Reed), who inveigles Melvin into sharing her get-rich-quick scheme, running a gas station in Willard, Utah, where the presence of snow-capped peaks dwarfs their aspirations – until the so-called "Mormon Will" left by Hughes comes to light and Melvin comes to celebrity.

Both Mary Steenburgen and Jason Robards have been deservedly nominated for Academy Awards, but it is on Paul Le Mat's puffy shoulders that the movie rides piggyback. His Melvin, the kind of gregarious jerk men count as a friend (he is no competition) and women count as a pet (sweet to scratch under the chin, simple to toss in the backyard) is dangerously close to sentimentalization in the script, but Le Mat pulls Melvin back from a plush-lined pigeonhole with distinct individuality: something that is not nice beats its wings at the corner of Melvin Dummar's eyes when he is pushed too far. While one cannot imagine him intentionally harming anyone, it is remarkably easy to envision the damage he might cause unintentionally if cornered.

He is cornered toward the end of *Melvin and Howard*, when the Mormon Will is investigated in open court and his claim is jeered at, but Melvin reveals – with the blend of humour, irony and dignity that makes the film such a warmly memorable experience – that he never expected to see the Hughes bequest. Demme means us to see that Melvin has developed a new realism; he understands why the money is denied to him, but he is not about to let the experience poison him with bitterness. Demme also means us to see (and we do, without a trace of condescension or embarrassment) that Melvin Dummar and his people, inhabitants of a cultural and economic wasteland, of an isolated desert hollow barred by impassable peaks from the American dream, are the salt of their unenviable earth.

February 23, 1981

❖

In a Year With 13 Moons

Written and directed by Rainer Werner Fassbinder
Starring Volker Spengler

"Much of modern art," Susan Sontag wrote in *On Photography*, "is devoted to lowering the threshold of what is terrible. By getting us used to what, formerly, we could not bear to see or hear, because it was too shocking, painful or embarrassing, art changes morals – that body of psychic custom and public sanctions that draws a vague boundary between what is emotionally and spontaneously tolerable and what is not." A paragraph earlier, writing of the photographer Diane Arbus, Sontag observes that her pictures "are typical of the kind of art popular among sophisticated urban people right now: art that is a test of hardness."

Rainer Werner Fassbinder's *In a Year With 13 Moons* was undertaken in 1978 – *The Marriage of Maria Braun* and *The Third Generation* were products of the same year – in reaction to the suicide of Fassbinder's lover, Armin. For Fassbinder, the film is an act of penance, a leap of empathetic imagination and a way of providing a personal memorial. Functioning, as usual, as writer and director, he also served as executive producer, cinematographer, art director and editor; only the score was entrusted to an associate, Fassbinder's brilliant collaborator Peer Raben.

But the movie begins with the music of Mahler, in a Frankfurt park in the early hours of the morning in – as a title tells us – 1978, a year of thirteen new moons and a year therefore in which "many lives are in danger." (Attributing the events of the film to celestial bodies is a typical Fassbinder joke – as well as his deadly serious method of calling into question pat, systemic explanations of behaviour.)

Elvira (Volker Spengler), a transsexual, is beaten by a homosexual pickup for having posed as a man. Already, in the first few seconds, Elvira is the quintessential Fassbinder victim/hero – an outcast rejected by outcasts. The film proceeds to follow Elvira's slow slide into suicide and, like Arbus' photographs of freaks, it can be seen as a test of hardness, as a work "devoted to lowering the threshold of what is terrible." But unlike Arbus' photographs where, as Sontag says, "the point is not to be upset," the point of *In a Year With 13 Moons* is precisely the opposite: the movie is a relentlessly uncompromising, keening *cri de coeur*, a movie that has turned a wake into a work of art.

Related in the form of long monologues of clotted, operatic prose, Elvira's life leads with a terrible, tranquil inevitability to its tragic conclusion. Fassbinder sees the seeds of Elvira's destruction everywhere, but most obviously in society at large, which has no place for individuals who believe, as Elvira fervently does, in "love." The nun (Lilo Penpeit, Fassbinder's own mother) who reared Elvira theorizes that "the order human beings have made ruins them."

For Elvira, the ruin began when he was deserted in a convent by his parents, but was solidified when, as a man, he fell in love with another man – Anton Saitz (Gottfried John), Elvira's partner in a meat-packing business. Saitz, who was not homosexual, made an off-hand comment about Elvira (called Erwin in those days) having a sex change operation; before long, Elvira was off to Casablanca for the surgery, only to be rejected on his return by Saitz (who patterned his efficient capitalist management techniques, we are told, after what he saw as a child in Nazi concentration camps). Elvira's best friend in the last five days of his life is a prostitute, Zora (Ingrid Caven), but even she unwittingly betrays Elvira.

Never before has the intense, depressive, claustrophobic interior world of the potential suicide been brought to the screen with such force. But *In a Year With 13 Moons* is of more than clinical value. One of the minor characters tells of walking through a graveyard in a dream, a graveyard in which, according to the headstones, no life had lasted longer than three years and in which several had lasted no longer than a moment. He realized that the dream was not about life – the dates on the tombstones were the dates "when the people had been really happy."

At screenings of *13 Moons*, the dream's denouement generally calls forth gasps and nervous laughter. Sontag warned that a "pseudo-familiarity with the horrible reinforces alienation." In the work of

Arbus, for example, there was "no intention of entering into the horror experienced" by her subjects: "Her view was always from the outside." Fassbinder's view is, on the contrary, from the inside. Nervous laughter is the laughter of recognition.

March 9, 1981

The Postman Always Rings Twice

Directed by Bob Rafelson
Written by David Mamet
Starring Jack Nicholson, Jessica Lange and John Colicos

"Then I saw her. She had been out back, in the kitchen, but she came in to gather up my dishes. Except for the shape, she really wasn't any raving beauty, but she had a sulky look to her, and her lips stuck out in a way that made me want to mash them in for her."

Thus is Cora Papadakis, the wife of a Greek gas station owner, described by Frank Chambers, the narrator of James M. Cain's tight, tough, sexy 1934 novel *The Postman Always Rings Twice*. (The book is said to have been banned in Canada and Boston. It was filmed by Visconti in 1942 as *Ossessione*, filmed in 1946 with John Garfield and Lana Turner, and said by Camus to be his inspiration for *The Stranger*.) Frank has arrived at the Papadakis place during the Depression. He stays because he has no reason to go. He stays because "from the filling station I could just get a good view of the kitchen."

From the first scene of playwright David Mamet's screen adaptation for director Bob Rafelson, the tone is set – existential foreboding. More frightening than most horror movies, more erotic than most pornography, *The Postman Always Rings Twice* is a sour slice of bonafide Americana, a relentlessly pessimistic melodrama that conjures memories of *They Shoot Horses, Don't They?*, *Bonnie and Clyde*, *The Godfather* and *Chinatown*. It is not conceived in homage to *film noir*: it is *film noir*, but in colour, in an Edward Hopper palette that Ingmar Bergman's cinematographer Sven Nykvist correctly considers the finest work of his distinguished career.

Noted for elliptical, unstructured films – *Stay Hungry, Five Easy Pieces* – Rafelson is not always interested in reproducing the simplicity and clarity of the novel's plot: what builds in the book to a climax drifts along in the movie from catastrophe to catastrophe. The sexual, violent and sado-masochistic interludes are brutally, brilliantly paced and edited – they become arias of hysteria – but the film feels as if it could end several times before it does, and several plot points are fuzzy. In addition, because the novel's ending has been altered, the metaphoric title has lost its resonance. (Postman is slang for the hanging judge: in the book, Frank ends his days on death row, paying for a crime he did not commit – ironic retribution for having earlier got away with a crime he did commit.)

Oddly, none of this detracts significantly from Rafelson's achievement, which is immense. The episodic nature of the film may even be its own reward – the novel has been inadvertently modernized. As Frank Chambers, Jack Nicholson gives his most dimensional and controlled performance since *One Flew Over the Cuckoo's Nest*, and I think it is possible that he has never been better than he is here, scanning the world through suspicious (but not suspicious enough) eyes, controlling his impulses toward destruction (but not controlling them enough) and sizing up the limited possibilities available to him (but not sizing them up cleverly enough).

Jessica Lange, best known for the black I. Magnin dress she was barely wearing when she was discovered in the remake of *King Kong*, holds her sultry, aggressive own against Nicholson. Her Cora is a hot, lewd, snarling tramp trapped by the era's prejudice against women and by the era's economics, which have forced her to live with an aged Greek husband (Canada's John Colicos, in a portrayal so natural it seems a found object) who might as well be her old-country grandfather, so little can she relate to him. When she cries, "I can't have his baby," you can feel her skin crawl. When she says, "I'm tired of what's right and wrong, Frank," you can feel your skin crawl.

Cora's relationship with Frank is volatile – tempestuous in its tenderness, sizzling in its sensuality, terrifying in the ease with which it moves from the erotically consuming to the maliciously devouring. If it seems remarkable and strange, it is only because it is contained in a commercial American film, and because the lovers' lack of intelligence allows them to be viewed as practically pure id – a primal Adam and Eve re-enacting the acquisition of Original Sin. The movie's argument, dramatized forthrightly, is that sexual excitement is allergic to the settled – when Cora and Frank murder the Greek, their first act is to make love, but when they have lived comfortably together for months, they grow restive. To sustain their attraction, they whirl, biting and scratching and spitting, on each other.

In the end, the villain (no wonder Camus was fascinated by Cain) is the randomness and the absurdity of existence, an existence in which insurance companies can decree that murderers will go free and in which an accident can rule that a loved one will die. God Himself is a hanging judge, and He determines the identity of the dead by shooting craps. "She wanted something, and she tried to get it," Frank said of Cora in the novel. "She tried all the wrong ways, but she tried." Like the book, the movie admires effort: in their shared universe, effort is all there is.

March 21, 1981

This Is Elvis

Directed by Andrew Solt and Malcolm Leo

Ol' swivel hips is back and in one of *This Is Elvis*'s many magic moments, in a segment from a 1960 television special celebrating Presley's liberation from the U.S. Army, he sings a duet with Ol' Blue Eyes. There they are, the two sex kings of contiguous musical kingdoms, doing each other. Frank Sinatra croons "Love Me Tender" and tries to get Elvis down and can't, and Presley – one of the most versatile rock singers of all time – sings "Witchcraft" and impersonates Sinatra perfectly, satirically.

"There is nothing original about Elvis Presley's music," pop music historian Tony Palmer wrote in what has remained the best one-sentence summary of the Presley career, "except Elvis Presley, and that is enough."

Carrying the blessings of the Memphis Mafia – the technical adviser is Presley's Svengali, Col. Tom Parker, who once said it was his "patriotic duty" to keep Elvis in the 90 per cent tax bracket – *This Is Elvis* is three movies in one. The first is an invaluable collection of documentary footage, much of it previously unseen. The second is an embarrassing series of "dramatic re-enactments" – three actors play Elvis at different stages in his life – swimming in syrupy narration from real people in Elvis' life (and from actors posing as real people in Elvis' life). The third is a combination of the first two, a movie that goes beyond anything the directors, Andrew Solt and Malcolm Leo, may have envisioned, a fascinating artifact in which the very vulgarity of the re-enactments works to explain the Presley milieu in a way that a tempered, objective approach could not.

He was a good boy who loved God, but his temper was legendary. He became a favourite of the intelligentsia, but his Graceland mansion was a tacky, plush, red-velvet fantasy, ante-bellum whorehouse chic. He loved his mother, but the teen-aged girl he would marry, Priscilla, was tarted up to look like a streetwalking Liz Taylor. Although he made his reputation with sartorial and musical simplicity (blues-based rock, leather jackets and jeans), in his later years he adopted a bejewelled style of attire best described as chorus girl caca, while his entrances were preceded by a famous-to-a-fault Richard Strauss fanfare also used in that period for heralding salad dressings on TV commercials.

He personified the contradictions and paradoxes, the achievements and shortcomings, of American pop culture, the most influential culture in the world. He was the embodiment of animalistic, anti-puritanical sexuality (listen to the flagrantly perverse "Jailhouse Rock," with its lines, "Number 47 said to Number 3, you're the cutest jailbird I ever did see"), but also of Southern piety (wearing a powder-blue cape, he invoked American martial religiosity with "Battle Hymn of the Republic").

Those who banned and burned his records came around, and by the time he died, he had become a god to many Americans – his likeness would be embroidered on samplers next to the faces of Jack Kennedy and Martin Luther King. He made thirty-three movies, sold half a billion records, never played to an unsold seat, and conquered television over and over again. He was careerism and consumerism incarnate.

Early in *This Is Elvis*, there is a performance of "Hound Dog" from a Milton Berle television show. Already, the charisma, the self-mocking sexuality and the ironic distancing – almost a satire of James Dean, whom Presley adored – are in place. Already, with his superficially contemptuous but unmistakably sweet sneer, he is an unforgettable icon.

Ed Sullivan, who promised his audience that Presley would never appear on his show and then signed him several months later for a record $50,000, tells the world, his arm around Elvis, that "this is a real decent, fine boy." Elvis's smouldering, heavy-lidded and slightly feminine dark eyes glare blackly into the wings; it was the beginning of the taming process – the outcast was on his way in.

Once caged, Presley escaped only once, for a 1968 TV special given lamentably short shrift in *This Is Elvis*. The promising *King Creole* and the impudent *Jailhouse Rock* aside, his movies were benign, inter-changeable integers: their mediocrity is excellently communicated by clips counterpointed to Presley's rendition of Chuck Berry's "Too Much Monkey Business."

After the TV special, he went to Vegas and the decline began in earnest. The movie ends with the bloated potentate of kitsch, in a white jump suit emblazoned with a gold Aztec calendar plate, singing "My Way" six weeks before he died. One watches, transfixed, as a montage of the lithe, youthful Elvis is expertly, ghoulishly, tragically intercut.

Throughout the picture, the narration tells us one thing ("We always had so much fun at Christmas!" Priscilla gushes) while the images tell us another (Priscilla and Presley always seem strangers). "It's very hard to have to live up to an image," Presley said at a New York press conference before returning to Las Vegas. This is a movie about just how hellishly hard that can be: even though the man is dead, the image-mongers are still polishing and protecting their product. That they have not been successful is what gives the movie its unique – culturally sobering and musically invigorating – charge. *This Is Elvis* could have been called This Is America: it's a portrait of a face full of wounds, warts and wonders.

May 9, 1981

Lili Marleen

Directed by Rainer Werner Fassbinder
Written by Manfred Purzer, Joshua Sinclair and Rainer Werner Fassbinder
Starring Hanna Schygulla

Lili Marleen, German director Rainer Werner Fassbinder's first big-budget film – a hilarious, hateful fictionalization of the life of singer Lale Andersen, who made famous the song from which the film takes its name – is as close to camp as an artist can get and still be conscious of his intentions. This sumptuous, excessive "biopic" is *Mary Hartman, Mary Hartman* crossed with *A Star Is Born* and filmed on the scale of *Apocalypse Now*.

Famed for an impressive body of stylistically extravagant and intellectually invigorating work, the unpredictable Fassbinder was offered $5-million by a German producer to come forth with a commercial breakthrough, a musical that would star Hanna Schygulla (of

The Marriage of Maria Braun) as Andersen and would feature Giancarlo Giannini as a blond Swiss Jew (!) and Mel Ferrer as his father (!!).

Politically an anarchist and temperamentally a satirist of sadistic thoroughness, Fassbinder has endeavoured to Brechtianize Hollywood melodrama of the Imitation of Life era: *Lili Marleen* is nothing less than a fascinating – albeit, failed – attempt to radicalize kitsch, to use camp to corrosive political purposes.

Renamed Wilkie Bunterberg, the singer – a singer of scant talent – becomes famous through a fluke when she records in 1938 a sentimental anthem dating from the First World War. Interested equally in smuggling Jews out of Nazi Germany and in the hue of her eye shadow, Wilkie is always hitching a ride on the main chance and when invited by Hitler to an exclusive audience is only too ready to comply. (Her visit best exemplifies the style of *Lili Marleen*: doors the dimension of Bernini's slowly open, and from heaven's gate shoots a shaft of divine white light while, as Wilkie enters the presence of his satanic majesty at his request, soundtrack music swells to a Wagnerian crescendo.)

This Teutonic Lana Turner (Wilkie's wardrobe is even patterned after the designs of Edith Head) is a self-proclaimed "survivor" who emigrated to Zurich not because she opposed the Nazis but because "I thought Switzerland would be a good place to start singing; after all, it's international." Of her pedigree, there is no doubt. "I'm German," she proudly announces when it is to her advantage to do so. "Aryan. Back to the Stone Age."

Not since the Jack Clayton remake of *The Great Gatsby* has a film been so full of glitz – mirrors reflecting mirrors, gowns gossamer as angel wings, eyes twinkling like Christmas stars, teeth with the sheen of fine porcelain – and never before has the director of *The Third Generation* and *In a Year With 13 Moons* so indulged his ambivalence toward mainstream Hollywood filmmaking.

87

Invariably, just at the point at which the audience begins to believe Fassbinder's interior decoration send-up of the Third Reich – a send-up of the fantasy style of UFA, the official German film studio – and to care about his characters, he dumps on the emotions engendered with line readings or camera angles that emphasize the artificiality of the film and the venality of the people within it. *Lili Marleen* is beautiful, but poisonous; it is funny, but malicious.

Fassbinder himself appears as a "secret Resistance fighter" and were that not enough of an in-joke, his real-life mother pushes her way through a crowd gathered around Wilkie and says, "My son asked me, can he have your autograph?" The performances, with the exception of Hark Bohm as Wilkie's musical muse, are universally and intentionally terrible. Filmed in English, dubbed into German and overlaid with English subtitles, there is an eerie, disembodied, alienating ghostliness to the voices that Fassbinder no doubt finds to his liking.

The less said of Giannini the better, but even the protean Hanna Schygulla is an object of beefy ridicule, a lumpen Garbo, a deglamorized Marlene – she's the fishwife one felt might be hiding under the Dietrich fishnet. ("Hanna," Fassbinder actress Ingrid Caven said after seeing *Lili Marleen*, "has always had a cow-like quality, but Rainer didn't have to do this to her.")

Fassbinder is a genius – the most wildly talented, prolific filmmaker of his generation – but *Lili Marleen* is far from his best work, and not so far from his worst. Still, it is worth seeing for its audacious ambition: from the garbage of schlock Nazi culture, Fassbinder has sought to alchemize art. There are a few authentic nuggets (especially the scenes intercutting the gushing syrup of the song with the gushing blood of the battlefield) but much of the product is iron pyrite – fool's gold.

Lili Marleen bears the same problematic relation to Fassbinder's career that Martin Scorsese's *New York, New York* bears to his: both are stylized attempts to use style against itself. Dismissal would be dangerous: as the years go by, *New York, New York* looks better and better. The same fate may be in store for *Lili Marleen* and Nazi Disneyland.

July 24, 1981

❖

Chakra

Written and directed by Rabindra Dharmaraj

In Bijapur, a small town in India, a beautiful young wife gives birth to a baby. All is well. A civil servant, aged and jaded, happens by and, seeing the mother unguarded, attempts a rape. The woman's husband happens by and, hearing his wife's screams, commits a murder. The family, knowing there will be no mercy from the authorities, flees to a shack city on the outskirts of Bombay. Only then do the credits for *Chakra* (Vicious Circle), a remarkable, courageous Indian movie, appear on the screen.

Showcased in competition at the Montreal Film Festival, *Chakra*, a first film written and directed by Rabindra Dharmaraj, who died earlier this year at the age of thirty-four, is unlike any film ever to have come out of India, a country with censorship laws worthy of Darius' Persia. Reports of Indian poverty, like nuclear survival scenarios or pictures of Auschwitz, have become part of the informational content of our lives – insane aspects of contemporary existence we accept with equanimity to remain sane.

Chakra humanizes those reports by giving the statistics flesh; humanizes woebegone photographs of starving Indian children by giving them personalities; and humanizes a culture we may have thought is more alien than it actually is by illustrating that hope, love, pain and grief are identical, regardless of region or religion.

It does this with a sense of humour that is nothing short of astounding – *Chakra* is a movie about the slums of Bombay that is also, for long periods of time, a satiric comedy dealing with rebellious and lazy teen-agers (adolescent angst and arrogance are no strangers to this strangest of all subcontinents) and with their rebellious and lazy elders.

When the heroine's husband is killed, she takes up with two men, a cocky pimp and an emotionally remote truck driver. The pimp is idolized by the heroine's son (the baby from the beginning has grown into a troublesome teen, decked out in a spiky Rod Stewart hairdo) and flowers under the rays of that adulation. Convinced fate is on his side, he discharges his days in petty scams in order to support the heroine, in order to get drunk on cheap hooch or high on cocaine-laced betelnut, and in order to instill in his adopted son his ideas of the way life should be: "To hell with marriage. I want to live free and go where I please."

But he also instills in his young charge an even stronger sense of the way life is: "Earn, eat and die," he says, "that's our life. No bastard will give you your rights, you've got to snatch your rights." Halfway through the picture, the pimp contracts gonorrhea, is unable to obtain the money needed to obtain the drugs to obtain a cure, and rots away – while making jokes about it – in front of our eyes. Like everything that happens in *Chakra* (a baby is found dead in the garbage, an old man trying to steal wheat from a truck is beaten to death by the police), his fate is presented unblinkingly, without a single sentimental tear. Dharmaraj – who was educated in England and worked as a correspondent in Vietnam for *Time* and *Ramparts*, in addition to Indian publications – is at heart a journalist, and has no interest in putting his people through the romantic *Grapes of Wrath* mill.

Those who see the poor as inherently noble will find *Chakra* tough going: Dharmaraj insists that the single thing that separates his subjects from the rest of humanity is the fact that their living conditions are inhuman. In all other ways, the people caught in this vicious circle are not inherently anything. Benwa, the teen-ager, picks his nose and gives his mother fits, for example, but is also capable of working hard as a shoeshine boy, his method of paying for his keep. There is a sense of community among the poor here, but it is as fragile as their lives. In one memorable scene, a wake for the old man killed by the police, we are shown how the villagers exorcise their rage: around a campfire late at night they pass a bottle, drenching their sorrow in a mass drunk that is for some cathartic and for others a prelude to pointless internecine squabbling.

How did this film get made and released? One possible answer is the caste system – because the subjects do not comport themselves as good Hindus, because they are utter outcasts, the authorities may have decided that *Chakra* was an exposé; they may have considered it an object lesson in what can happen to the undisciplined. It is nothing of the kind. It is a document of what can and does happen to the unlucky, to those unlucky enough to be born in a certain place at a certain time, and there is an unmistakable call at the conclusion of the picture for an overthrow of the system that created Bombay's slum shanty towns.

The director said before he died (the film came to Montreal without a representative – all efforts to discover the cause of Dharmaraj's death were fruitless) that *Chakra* was "a small attempt to explore the path from where Third World cinema can emerge and develop." It is much larger than small; and the fates that decreed the director would be unable to further explore that path were harsh indeed. The death of a talent of this magnitude after a film of this power, scope and clarity is a tragedy.

August 27, 1981

❖

Prince of the City

Directed by Sidney Lumet
Written by Sidney Lumet and Jay Presson Allen
Starring Treat Williams

Up front: a warning. Detective Danny Ciello (Treat Williams) is in bed with his wife. He wakes up in a cold sweat. She tells him there is nothing to be afraid of. She is lying. He knows it. In the opening scene of *Prince of the City*, director Sidney Lumet indicates to the audience that, during the next two hours and forty-eight minutes, it is going to learn why Det. Ciello is afraid. And is going to learn to share his fear.

Already the most controversial picture of the year, *Prince of the City* is an upper division survey of the inequities of the system in general and of the system of justice in particular. If it were a university course, it would be called Decline of Western Civilization 401. The prerequisites would be Lumet's earlier New York films, *Serpico* and *Dog Day Afternoon*. But next to the banquet of corruption afforded by the final chapter of the trilogy, the first two are canapés.

Divided into five parts, the film is the most ambitious, realistic, thorough and scrupulous feature yet released by a major studio on the subject of cops and corruption. It is neither liberal nor conservative; its political views are subordinate to, and must be inferred from, the facts. It is unabashedly subjective, however: Lumet and co-screenwriter Jay Presson Allen openly sympathize with Det. Ciello, an undercover narcotics cop who becomes a stoolie so he can get back to being "a good guy." Their prince is trying to regain his crown in a kingdom that has no place for honest rulers.

If Lumet sympathizes with Ciello, he does not romanticize him. Ciello's real-life model, Bob Leuci, sent more than fifty detectives (many of them friends) to court; two of his close associates committed suicide and a third went mad as the result of his activities. In the beginning, Ciello insists he will not wear "a wire" (a bugging device) and will not rat on his partners. He thinks (so did Oedipus) that he can control circumstance.

As portrayed electrifyingly – sometimes a little too electrifyingly – by Williams, Ciello's reasons for becoming a stoolie are as complex as his reasons for becoming a cop. They are bound up with being a good guy, yes, but they also have to do with his Italian background – a relative calls him "the black sheep" of the family because he has become a cop – and his cocky macho hubris.

He is a great deal like the people one dips into in daily life: under the surface, a mixture of cross-currents and depths difficult to fathom. Ciello's good intentions are twisted by a federal justice department that is itself corrupt, by laws that don't work, by courts that don't enforce them, by cops who don't care about them and by crooks ready to exploit them. Still, Ciello unwittingly co-operates: what the outside doesn't damage, the pride and prevarication inside sully.

Psychological motivation aside, we are asked to agree when he says, "You guys [the establishment] are gonna win in the end anyway.

We're out there selling ourselves and our families until these people [criminals, junkies, etc.] own us. We're the only thing standing between you and the jungle."

The script does not rationalize police corruption, but it does try to understand it, a decision that will be considered heinous by doctrinaire liberals. At the same time, it does not support the system that alternately feeds on and condemns corruption, a decision that will be considered blasphemous by conservatives.

Prince of the City, like Francis Coppola's screenplay for *Patton*, is a have-it-both-ways movie, a movie that can, if read through ideological glasses, be seen as opportunistically offering support to any number of positions. It can also be seen – this is closer to the truth – as a movie with the intelligence to allow the audience to form its own conclusions.

Cinematically, it is a triumph of casting and craftsmanship. There are a few familiar faces (Broadway's Jerry Orbach is one of Ciello's partners) but most of the performers are relatively unknown and each is exceptional. In the early sequences, there is a fair amount of fast cutting, but as the movie goes on, Lumet depends on increasingly lengthy takes. The excitement is in the script, in the actors' faces and voices, and in the declamatory speechifying, not in the camera's movements.

(The quintessential scene involves Ciello and one of his partners: they stand on opposite street corners and have a conversation by yelling across the chasm.) As in Lumet's other New York movies, the dialogue is fast, loud, loose and profane.

But the other New York movies came to recognizable, if not entirely satisfying, conclusions. There is no conclusion in *Prince of the City*. While we know that the real-life Ciello retired some months ago after having continued to serve the force peripherally, Lumet chooses to end with Ciello instructing a class at police academy. Ciello's wife has said, "Everybody's guilty," and we have seen that she is correct, and Ciello has said, "I don't know what the truth is any more," and neither do we.

Prince of the City plunges the viewer into a *Rashomon*-like maelstrom: pet theories regarding crime, law enforcement and informers are swiftly swept from sight while the audience is placed on a raft riding a whirlpool, the raft the justice system has been clinging to a long time. The movie bears a warning: sink or swim. Or, more precisely, think or swim.

August 29, 1981

Soldier Girls

Written and directed by Nicholas Broomfield and Joan Churchill

"I don't care how much of a man you are . . ." – *a drill sergeant addresses a platoon of women in* Soldier Girls

Soldier Girls, an utterly remarkable Nicholas Broomfield and Joan Churchill documentary, follows four female recruits through boot camp at an American army installation in Georgia. The four, two black privates and two white, had been prepared for the army by movies and television shows and by pitches from their home-town recruiters. Nothing could have prepared them for the spectacle of a drill sergeant biting the head off a chicken as an illustration of how to get along in the jungle. Nothing could have prepared the film's audience for the fantastic reality of women preparing for war.

Shot in 1980, in the midst of the Iran crisis and in the long shadow of Vietnam, *Soldier Girls* presents an army desperately in search of validity. On their morning marches, the women are confidently instructed to chant, "IIIIIIRAN! I WANT TO KILL AN IRANIAN!" and – a more traditional, ecumenical cheer – "BLOOD! GUTS! KILL!" (The sound of those words trilled in cheerful chorus by soprano voices is indescribable.) But at pep talks, the primary drill instructor, platoon Sgt. Abing, an ex-Marine from Washington, feels compelled to defend the honour of the military. "We didn't lose that sucker," he says of

Vietnam. "Politicians may have lost it. We didn't." He confronts the paradox of a peace-time army directly: quoting Patton, he says, "In peace we should train for war. Everything else is bull—. I believe that."

Sgt. Abing, the Great Santini come to good-looking white-trash life, is driven to the edge of madness by one of the black recruits, Joann Johnson, an eighteen-year-old rebel from Oxford, Miss. When Abing – macho artillery blazing – dresses down Johnson for making her bed improperly, the object of his scorn is unable to control her giggling. (The audience shares her glee: the first half hour of *Soldier Girls* is the real *Private Benjamin*, and much funnier because it is real.) As the weeks wear on, the problem gets worse, until Abing concludes that Johnson's very existence is an affront to decent people.

But the giggle-box infraction is shared by several other recruits; time after time when platoon sergeants (Sgt. Abing has two assistants, one male, one female) drape themselves importantly in the mantle of militaristic authority, the women they are supposed to be impressing and/or intimidating find it all but impossible to control their mirth. The difference in dynamic between a male platoon and this one is profound – purely by accident, the movie is excellent p.r. for being a woman.

Like its male counterpart, the distaff army in *Soldier Girls* is composed of women who had run out of alternatives: they are poor, mostly, and mostly uneducated. Some take eventually to the training (Jackie Hall, from New Rochelle, N.Y., becomes a squad leader and says, "We'll be better people when we come out, we'll be able to hold our heads up high back on the block") and others never do (Johnson is drummed out and so is Clara Alves, a woman who suffers gruesome abuse). In the end, the film ceases to be p.r. for being a woman. In the end, for the women who stay, the fact that the girls are soldiers is more important than the fact that they are girls. The army has done its work. Well.

But we are not left with a testament to the army's effectiveness. The directors ask where this effectiveness leads – it assuredly leads to good soldiers and to disciplined troops, but where else? We return to

Sgt. Abing, to the drill sergeant we have loved to hate, and in an incredible interview conducted by Pvt. Hall we learn on a personal basis what Vietnam meant and, more chillingly, what the army means. "A part of your humanity, a large part of it, your soul or whatever the hell you want to call it – it's never going to be there again," Sgt. Abing sighs with slight but sincere distaste, as if reciting the ingredients on a can of Spam. "It's gone. And you don't know it, you don't notice it, until after it's over. And then, long afterwards, as you grow older, you start missing it. This [the army] is all I've got. I can't give nothin' to anybody else any more. There's so much missing."

There is nothing missing from *Soldier Girls*. The audience is left speechless. A movie that began as a riff on *Private Benjamin* has ended in high tragedy. The dehumanization documented here is an intentional, well-designed dehumanization, a rigorous dehumanization deemed necessary by society; it is the method used to create guardians that theoretically protect the humanity of everyone else. The men and women in *Soldier Girls* are Aztec sacrifices: their hearts have been torn out so that others might sleep in peace.

September 15, 1981

Mommie Dearest

Directed by Frank Perry
Written by Frank Yablans, Frank Perry, Tracy Hotchner and Robert Getchell
Starring Faye Dunaway

"Joan Crawford from beyond the grave to Bette Davis: 'Don't die: people'll dish ya.'" – *Craig Russell*

On paper, *Mommie Dearest*, Christina Crawford's gloves-off memoir of life with monster mum, the redoubtable Joan Crawford, was a pathetic tale told by a badly bruised child who had grown into a wounded and understandably vengeful adult. On screen, with Faye Dunaway giving the performance of several lifetimes as the broad-shouldered, self-styled Queen of Hollywood, *Mommie Dearest* is the story of a madcap mother who beats her adopted daughter who in turn grows up and finds the happy ending by selling the glass slipper. It's the first full-scale comedy about child abuse: Auntie Maim.

That couldn't have been what director Frank Perry and three other scriptwriters had in mind, or could it? *Mommie Dearest* is such a mess it's difficult to be sure. What appears to be one of the worst movies this year – it was hissed at an invitational screening this week – might be a consciously subversive satire of hype, the American dream, the nuclear family, gossip-mongering and the movies themselves (no one ever goes out a door without pausing at the threshold to make a curtain speech), all filmed in the style of a Joan Crawford vehicle. Then again, it might be a hoot 'n' holler stinker, more dirty fun than mud wrestling.

Whatever it is – the truth lies somewhere in between – it's a terrific movie for audience back-talk. When the aged Joan Crawford moaned, "I'm scared, Christina, what will I do?" someone hollered, "Go to work." Laughter during Joan's beatings of her children was constant, capped by applause when the tiny blonde "Tina," having lived through another onslaught of mummerly love, rolled her eyes and said, "Jesus Christ."

The opening image is the best: an Art Deco alarm clock rings and a gloved hand emerges from satin sheets to silence it. Perry keeps the camera away from The Face throughout the credits; when we do finally see the bushy eyebrows and the red lips, the incarnation is eerie, as advertised. The Face is her face, the mannerisms are her manner-isms and Dunaway manages magnificently to depict a woman whose acting off-screen is no better than her acting on. But Joan Crawford was never particularly sympathetic and the movie – what with Mom-mie Dearest covered in cold cream and rolling her eyes like a demented Kabuki creature while demanding that little Christina scour the bathroom floor and submit to coat-hanger beatings at 4 a.m. – makes her less so. Dunaway has been quoted as saying she feels for Joan. Feels what?

Perry and his writers obviously do not believe Christina's account of life with Auntie Fame and they have therefore turned the volume into one long, lushly appointed joke. (This movie is physically and maybe philosophically what Fassbinder was after in *Lili Marleen*.) We are given a Joan out of *Whatever Happened to Baby Jane?* maniacally pruning rose bushes in the middle of the night with garden shears (a great line here: "Tina, bring me the axe!") and in Tina we are given a child victim whose poise and calculation are authentically creepy. So many alternate titles suggest themselves that it's hard to choose, but one has to be Christina, The Omen IV. The movie implies that Christina made mummy do it. Auntie Blame.

There's nothing to sympathize with but the sets, which get far too many drinks spilled on them. Well, not quite: there is a good supporting performance from the costumes, which also get too many drinks spilled on them. Both sets and costumes are sadly required to witness entirely too much empty hysteria from their unappreciative owners.

Because Perry, *et al.*, have taken Christina's account with a salt lick, they have eschewed excesses that would have been wonderful in the movie's trash-forties context. Christina reports that her mother died in the presence of a Christian Science practitioner: "The woman, realizing there was nothing more she could do, began praying . . . My mother raised her head. The last coherent words from her mouth were, 'Damn it . . . don't you dare ask God to help me!' " Why is that scene missing? And why aren't we told of the birthday and graduation present Joan sent her daughter – two boxes, a single earring in one box for graduation, its mate in the other box for birthday?

Dunaway's fear that Joan Crawford would be turned into a scapegoat may be the answer to the film's bizarre even-handedness. So instead of telling God to get along without her, Joan tells the board of directors at Pepsi-Cola they can't get along without her, in a scene clearly designed to correspond to revisionist feminist readings of

Crawford's career. Dunaway's fears that Joan would come across as a monster have, nonetheless, been fulfilled. But democratically: both Crawfords, victim and victimizer, have been trashed in *Mommie Dearest*. This is theoretically a modern horror movie about mother love but it is actually one of the funniest movies about how not to make a movie ever made.

September 25, 1981

❖

Pixote

Directed by Hector Babenco
Written by Hector Babenco and Jorge Duran
Starring Fernando Ramos da Silva

They call him Pixote, which is pronounced "Pee-shot" and which means "Peewee," but the ten-year-old boy to whom the name has been applied makes up in experience what he lacks in size; by the time Brazilian writer-director Hector Babenco's grim but galvanizing film of the same name is over, Pixote has absorbed the sorrows of the ages. J. Hoberman has described Pixote as "Dondi in Hell." He is also Christ reborn as a gamin: a tiny sacrifice for the enormous sins of his society.

Babenco, who appears in a prologue to explain that three million Brazilian children share a similar plight, is not interested in political pamphleteering, however; any political extrapolations to be had from *Pixote* are the responsibility of the viewer. And so are any solutions – solutions to a problem that appears all but insoluble. This hallucinatory tour through Brazil's urchin underside is overwhelming and unforgettable, and Babenco has mercifully allowed it to speak for itself. It speaks merciless volumes.

Abandoned to an institution for the children of parents too poor to take care of them, one of Pixote's first "adventures" (the film is structured like a grotesque parody of Tom Sawyer) is the witnessing of the nocturnal gang rape of a room-mate. When Pixote (Fernando Ramos da Silva) leaves the institution, in the wake of beatings and the cover-up of a murder, he sets out with three friends – a seventeen-year-old drag queen, Lilica (Jorge Juliao); Lilica's macho lover, Dito (Gilberto Moura); the camp-follower Diego (Jose Nilson dos Santos) – to find the Brazilian dream. What he finds is a cocaine scam and an aged hooker, Sueli (Marilia Pera), whom he attempts tragically to make his mother.

Although fearless when it comes to staging pyrotechnical, theatrical climaxes – as when Lilica keens over the body of a former lover – Babenco is equally alive to the power of understatement. One of the film's most moving moments records the singing performance of an institutionalized teen-ager, a crippled and unattractive but not untalented boy who dreams of an impossible stardom. And there is throughout the picture a blackly astute comic sensibility that finds ephemeral humour in continual horror.

The performances are marvels. Jorge Juliao's Lilica is the most human, least sentimentalized gay teen-ager imaginable; Marilia Pera's old whore is equally tough, but with an absolutely magical interlude when she dances, hair thrown back and skirts hiked, in front of the headlights of a car; and Fernando Ramos da Silva's Pixote is nearly beyond praise. The young-old face, with its hugely uncomprehending and sadly unquestioning eyes, is an icon in a cathedral of the needlessly damned. But you do not pray to this image; you pray for it.

October 9, 1981

❖

Circle of Deceit

Directed by Volker Schlöndorff
Written by Volker Schlöndorff, Jean Claude Carrière,
    Margarethe von Trotta and Kai Herman
Starring Bruno Ganz and Hanna Schygulla

Volker Schlöndorff, whose cinematic adaptation of *The Tin Drum* shared the grand prize with Francis Coppola's *Apocalypse Now* several years ago at the Cannes Film Festival, has come forth with his own answer to Coppola's odyssey: *Circle of Deceit* was filmed on location in Beirut and though it purports to examine the civil war in Lebanon, it does so through the guilt, angst and ennui of modern Germany. Coppola used Vietnam to make a metaphorical film about what was wrong with America; Schlöndorff has used the Middle East to take the pulse of the heart of German darkness.

Of the group of West German directors who came to prominence in the early seventies – the group that includes Werner Herzog, Wim Wenders and Rainer Werner Fassbinder – Schlöndorff is the least innovative, the least interesting and yet the most reliable; he's the plodding heavy hitter of the new wave, and *Circle of Deceit* is a plodding, heavy-hitting film of great power, no small part of which is owed to the fact that it is a war film that takes place in an actual war zone.

When journalist Georg Laschen (Bruno Ganz) arrives in Beirut with his photographer Hoffman (Jerzy Skolimowski), he leaves behind in Germany a romance that, like Laschen's love of life, has all but died. "I am not afraid to live or die," he tells us. "I'm only afraid that I'll stop noticing." This fear of a "meaningless metabolism," of a sleepwalking existence, is reflected in a question he asks but does not answer until the end of the film: "Is peace at home so unbearable because it's peace?"

Laschen's odyssey to his answer is horrifyingly staged by Schlöndorff on locations that are not stages, on locations where horror is as common as the sunset that serves to lift the curtain on the war. The journalists with whom Laschen associates are housed in a hotel in the centre of the city, in the centre of city blocks claimed in common by warring factions (for simplicity's sake, those factions have been reduced in the picture to Arab and Christian). The press pool is a continual cocktail party in no-man's land, a chatty, hedonistic fête attended by entrepreneurs who sell atrocity photographs to the highest bidder – "People need that, to appreciate their own lives," the salesman says, as he points to eight-by-tens of raped women, orphaned children and charred corpses – and call girls who dispense frantic, fulfilling sex.

Outside, Catholic orphanages sell Arab children inexpensively but will not part with Christian children if they are destined for a mixed marriage. Laschen surveys Beirut, an outpost of anarchy, a rehearsal hall for the end of the world, with growing disgust and begins to loath everything, including his occupation. "I stick to the facts," he says, "but it's still mere entertainment." His initial sympathy for the Palestinians – "because they are weaker" – cools when he discovers that both sides, in attempting to "purge their God of all competing gods," travel the circumference of the same circle of deceit.

And yet, Beirut has overcome his ennui; disgust is not boredom. For a journalist, stasis is death. Warned that "snipers go for sitting targets – never stand still in Beirut," Laschen is appalled – and excited. In addition to the fear and disgust that have jolted him free of his boredom, his odd rejuvenation is aided by a romance with Arianne Nassar (Hanna Schygulla), the German widow of a wealthy Arab. Arianne is "gradually forgetting about Germany" and enjoys the contradictions of Lebanese living, where shopkeepers are gunned down next to stacks of Marlboro, where sheiks watch an Ann-Margret TV special with fascination, where a Christian guerrilla who studied music at Karlsruhe obligingly places his machine-gun on a gleaming grand piano before launching into an *étude*, and where a Christian despot who prefers to speak French because he considers himself Phoenician rather than Arab announces: "I have to force myself to be violent." Danger troubles Arianne not at all: "I've never thought less about death. I'm never even sick," she informs Laschen. Schlöndorff's suggestion is that Arianne may not be forgetting Germany after all. She may be finding it.

But it is not Germany that gives *Circle of Deceit* its value, nor is it Schlöndorff's attempt to find within Laschen's personal relationships an image of political realities – Fassbinder can meld the personal and political effortlessly and evocatively, but Schlöndorff labours studiously and tediously at parallels already apparent. What does give the film its value is Lebanon, the Lebanon found by Schlöndorff's crew during several dangerous months of shooting in 1980 when – as the press material drily puts it – "for some of the more epic scenes of destruction, heavy munitions, such as dynamite, were obtained from the Lebanese government [and] the problem was to find blanks, since prop ammunition is little used in Lebanon." Like Costa-Gavras' *Missing*, *Circle of Deceit* is an adjunct to "objective" journalism. It fills in emotional gaps: it gives death back the pain that passionless reporting has killed.

April 22, 1982

❖

Les Fleurs sauvages (Wild Flowers)

Written and directed by Jean-Pierre Lefebvre
Starring Marthe Nadeau

"When the ship is sinking, one must learn how to swim." – *Jean-Pierre Lefebvre*

"Two years ago, I was dead. I thought I would never again make a film." Jean-Pierre Lefebvre, Canada's most accomplished and prolific director (seventeen features since 1965), poured a *café au lait*. It was early. The night before, just down the Rue d'Antibes from the Hotel Century, Lefebvre's modest residence in Cannes, his latest film, *Les Fleurs sauvages* (*Wild Flowers*), had been screened for the first time. He had been up until 5:30 a.m. drinking champagne with Jacqueline Brodie, who has promoted Lefebvre's work at the Cannes Film Festival for many years. But he was not tired. "As you can see," he grinned, "I am no longer dead. Now I have ideas for five films. I am thinking of them all the time."

Wild Flowers, the only Canadian feature invited officially to Cannes, was shot in fifteen days at a cost of $350,000. It is two hours and forty minutes long, and covers a week in a Quebec summer when three generations – Simone, who is seventy, her daughter Michèle and Michèle's husband Pierre, and two children, Claudia and Eric – get to know one another a bit better.

"It was a short, simple week in our lives," one of the characters reminisces. *Wild Flowers* is a long, complex film, "difficult because it is so simple," as Lefebvre says.

It is probably a masterpiece. Its budget was the smallest of any film made last year in Quebec. And it represents the resurrection of Jean-Pierre Lefebvre, who is famous in France, who is well known in Quebec, but who has not once in the seventeen years he has been making movies seen a picture open commercially in English Canada. Lefebvre's films are not easy. But they aren't that difficult.

Lefebvre attributes his despair of two years ago to several factors. Although well received at Cannes, his elegant, formalistic essay on teen-age rebellion, *Avoir seize ans* (*To Be Sixteen*), was greeted with critical hostility in Quebec. Meanwhile, he saw the camaraderie for which his industry was famous, dissolve in a flood of tax shelter productions. "It was worse than in English Canada, when those rotten films were being made. I always said the minimum for films was imagination and solidarity. We had neither.

"I chose to make *Wild Flowers* as a way of getting that back. I thought of it as a film for children, and it was written for the actors and actresses. That's why it is so long. It was meant to be two hours, but the actors brought so much to it that to cut it would not have been to respect them. I felt I had no right to cut it."

Wild Flowers was pieced together from seven times the footage in the finished product. The editor and the producer was, as always, Lefebvre's wife, Marguerite Duparc, whose contributions to his *oeuvre* cannot be overestimated. It was her last film for him: she died of cancer in March, not long after completing the editing, and that may be an additional reason Lefebvre has chosen to leave the length at more than two hours. The movie is dedicated to her.

This is the first film Lefebvre has made in years that is a "mosaic," which is to say it is his first film in years to make use of fast cuts: Lefebvre's movies have long been notable for their extended shots. Those certainly exist in *Wild Flowers* – one especially memorable four-and-a-half-minute example takes place – but the rhythm of the picture is more conventional than is customary in Lefebvre.

"Compared to the others, *Wild Flowers* is composed of fragments," Lefebvre says. "That was the result of the actors. Marthe Nadeau, who plays Simone, told me: 'Jean, I am much older than I was when we made *The Last Betrothal* [a small classic dealing with the death of an elderly couple] and I don't have the energy for those long takes. I tire easily. My memory is not so good.'"

Nadeau gives a magnificent performance, a performance that seems unlikely to be surpassed this year, and a performance that may pass unnoticed by the Academy of Canadian Cinema, which can honour Micheline Lanctot for her contributions to Canadian cinema after she has directed one film, but which has not seen fit to acknowledge the existence of Jean-Pierre Lefebvre. Nadeau's Simone, like the other characters in *Wild Flowers*, is trapped by the era of her upbringing, and understands keenly the truth of her daughter's accusation: "I feel that I know my friends better than I know you."

But Simone is philosophical. She reads *People* magazine, she has a regular Saturday card game, she misses her late husband once a week at mass, and she mutters to herself: "Like it or not, things never change. Everyone has his own little routine." There is some of Lefebvre in that philosophy – "I don't believe in artificial transformations," he says – but the film is more hopeful than a synopsis would indicate.

"I admire *Mon Oncle d'Amerique*, the Alain Resnais film about the biologist Henri Laborit, who tells us how little real freedom we have," Lefebvre announces with a cheeriness that belies the subject. "But if it is impossible to transform some things, such as the gap between generations, it is possible to transform our way of looking at it.

premise for the movie was: for those who cannot talk to each other, a movie about what they might have said."

Lefebvre brings the point home unforgettably when Simone and her daughter are walking down a country lane. Communication has broken down. The mother testily informs the daughter it is time to go home. They turn and walk away from us. Cut. The colour of the film vanishes into black and white. The same scene is re-played, but this time the daughter embraces the mother as they turn. Cut. Another replay, and this time Lefebvre breaks the sequence into still photographs, allowing us – as Godard did in *Sauve Qui Peut (La Vie)* – to examine each second of behaviour. The scene ends with a still photograph of the mother and daughter entwined, heads affectionately together, in a reunion that might have been.

"My only angle, as you say in English, was to love everybody and to make no judgements," Lefebvre explained. "Years ago, when my mother was dying, she asked me to take her to see *South Pacific*. This was the kind of film I already hated. But I took her, of course. I realized then – that was before my first film – that the only way to answer her, if she wondered why I did not like it, would be with my own films, and with this one especially. I wanted it to be simple. I wanted everything in it to be true."

May 22, 1982

Wasn't That a Time

Directed by Jim Brown

There was a time, a time in the early fifties, when everyone knew who The Weavers were – they were the most popular singing group in North America, responsible for making famous "Goodnight Irene," "On Top of Old Smokey," "Tzena Tzena," "Kisses Sweeter Than Wine" and their own "Hammer Song" (If I Had a Hammer). Even Carl Sandburg was a fan: "The Weavers are out of the grass roots of America," the prairie poet wrote. "I salute them. When I hear America singing, The Weavers are there."

During the sixties, when Peter, Paul and Mary turned "The Hammer Song" into a hit, older eyes would mist over and older voices would sigh, "You should have heard The Weavers sing that song." Younger shoulders would shrug. There were but three things most casual fans of popular music were apt to know about The Weavers: (1) they were thought to be influential – all neophyte folk musicians paid homage to them; (2) they had retired via a farewell concert at Carnegie Hall in 1963, a concert that music critics used as a benchmark for all other folk performances; (3) Pete Seeger had been a Weaver and wouldn't shut up about it.

Wasn't That a Time, an extravagantly joyous documentary in the *From Mao to Mozart* mode (*Mao to Mozart* is in contrast emotionally miserly), fills out the list and in so doing resurrects a meaningful chapter in musical history. But the importance of Jim Brown's loving documentary extends beyond the musical, beyond the historical.

Wasn't That a Time celebrates survival, and not in the Steely Seventies, Me Generation, survive-at-any-cost sense. The survival it celebrates is communal survival, in the best sense. Less than a year ago, the sentiments expressed in *Wasn't That a Time* might have seemed hopelessly recherché. Today, with one million people marching in New York City on behalf of global peace, with Joan Baez and Bob Dylan singing together again, with "ban the bomb" – that almost forgotten phrase of the fifties – on magazine covers once more, *Wasn't That a Time* should find a large audience. The movie is about two sides of the same political-cum-showbiz coin: Ronald Reagan and The Weavers grew up together.

The picture opens with testaments to the four singers. Studs Terkel tells us the group was the first to bring authentic folk songs into the mass marketplace. Mary Travers tells us "Peter, Paul and Mary were very much The Weavers' children." Harry Reasoner tells us the singers were "a unifying factor between the rebellious American of the thirties and the rebellious American of the forties." Don McLean tells us he wants to be The Weavers when he grows up. And then we meet Lee Hays, the sixty-ish Weaver who will narrate the film.

Hays is a diabetic. As a result of the disease, he is a double amputee confined to a wheelchair. He knows he does not have long to live. He is spirited, but not sentimental, realistic but not resigned. He looks at the compost heap in his backyard, remarks that he will soon be part of it and quotes Walt Whitman on the glories that can arise from waste. "I'm Lee Hays," he growls. "More or less."

We learn that when Hays, Pete Seeger, Fred Hellerman (now a record producer) and Ronnie Gilbert (an actress) formed The Weavers in the late forties, it was their intention to sing to labour unions. A fluke booking at the Village Vanguard extended to six months and the group's name was made: record contracts, tours, radio and television followed in the acceptable order. Gordon Jenkins, whose lush orchestral sound was synonymous with fifties middle-of-the-road music, was hired to "sweeten" The Weavers' first album with strings, making the sound more palatable (or so it was thought) to midwestern tastes. The Weavers, three guys and a gal, had nowhere to go but up.

(A TV clip of the period, with the group purveying an enthusiasm that is slightly off-putting – that is slightly Up With People, to be frank – is included. The contemporary Lee Hays watches the clip along with us. "Would you look at that?" he snarls. "Barbie Doll and the three stuffed dummies. If I'd known how foolish we looked, I swear on Pete's chin whiskers that I'd have given this up for something socially useful, like plucking chickens.")

Enter Joe McCarthy. A bizarre, tragic syllogism of the era was set in motion: The Weavers sing to unions. Unions are Communist. Therefore, The Weavers are Communist. Protests to the contrary were of no avail and The Weavers were blacklisted in 1952.

This forced sabbatical, Hays says, "stretched into a Sundical, a Mondical and a Tuesdical." Three years later, fed up and hurting, they persuaded Carnegie Hall to open its august doors to them and they came back. The 1955 concert, attended either in person or through records by Judy Collins, The Kingston Trio, Peter, Paul and Mary, The Limelighters and many others who would carry the group's style and substance forward, guaranteed The Weavers a significant historical niche.

Wasn't That a Time wisely spends little time on this period: its main focus is on the present, on The Weavers' Carnegie Hall reunion less than two years ago. The film may be suffused with nostalgia, but it is not itself nostalgic, and it does not depend in any way upon familiarity with the group's past. The reunion – it would be held, finally, at Carnegie on November 28-29, 1980 – was the product of a picnic held in May, 1980, at Hays' farmhouse; the group sat down to sing together and found the harmonies to be so beautiful even Gilbert, the most reluctant of the quartet, was convinced one last comeback-farewell might work. She worries about "four decrepit folk singers staggering out on stage" and Seeger worries that it might be "like the basketball team thirty years later trying to run through their old plays," but there is no denying the strength of their sound. "That day was so full of euphoria," Hays exults, "that I had to take a laxative that night."

Hays, for whom the concert will be a physical ordeal, spends hours singing with old Weavers records as his form of warming up for the rematch. Gilbert, determined to show her fans she has not stood still, lobbies for the inclusion of a Holly Near song about Chile and then rehearses it in a gorgeous duet with Near herself. Director Brown builds anticipation, but not mechanically, and, once the concert has begun (with a wonderful, wordless rendition of "Wimoweh, The Lion Sleeps Tonight"), he cuts away from the stage to provide further insight into his remarkable foursome. (If the movie has a flaw, it is that it is too skimpy with the music.)

Earlier, Hays offered his homey advice to the politically pessimistic – "Be of good cheer; this too shall pass. I've had kidney stones – I know" – and Gilbert discussed feminism. Brown stresses throughout the film that, although these four happen to be famous (or once-famous) singers and although it is their talent that has made the movie

possible, his interest in them is based on their basic human friend-
ships, foibles and fears; he is interested in them because they are great
old folks, in addition to being great old folkies. *Wasn't That a Time* is a
testament to growing up, and growing old, with grace.

June 25, 1982

❖

Lola

Directed by Rainer Werner Fassbinder
Written by Rainer Werner Fassbinder, Peter Marthesheimer and Pea Frolich
Starring Barbara Sukowa and Armin Mueller-Stahl

Lola is the first film to be released since the death of the thirty-six-
year-old West German filmmaker Rainer Werner Fassbinder – two
more completed Fassbinders, *Querelle* and *The Passion of Veronika
Voss*, are in the offing – and while it is a pleasure to report that the
movie makes a good tribute to a great director, one's enthusiasm is-
inevitably blended with a sense of loss. For *Lola*, Fassbinder's funniest
film and one of his most tender, is not the work of a man past, or even
approaching, his prime: this is the work of a genius still palpably in
love with his medium. The title Myra Friedman chose for her
biography of Janis Joplin applies – *Lola* indicates Fassbinder was buried alive.

Although the movie is the second part of Fassbinder's satiric,
postwar history of Germany (*Veronika Voss* concludes the trilogy),
knowledge of its predecessor, *The Marriage of Maria Braun*, is not
essential. The pastel pink, green and blue titles alert the audience to
the film's seductive, innovative visual scheme, which positions characters under pink or blue lights, depending on their mood, and which
comments brazenly and intrusively on the action. Fassbinder uses
lighting in *Lola* as he employs the music of Peer Raben, to spark emotion and, more important, to douse it. The lighting additionally serves

to give a hilariously apt, *Life* magazine-styled Scandinavian Modern ambience to the picture, set in a nameless German town in 1957.

Maria Braun, the chronicle of an independent woman's rise in postwar Germany, ended in 1954 on the day Germany won the world soccer championship (on the day, in other words, that postwar Germans felt for the first time they could cheer something German publicly). It ended with Maria Braun's demise and with, by implication, the demise of all women like her, women who took advantage of the absence of men to at least partially liberate themselves.

When *Lola* opens, the conventional sexual-sexist balance has been restored – the heroine (the miraculous Barbara Sukowa) is a singing whore working in a tony brothel frequented by the town's ruling class. We meet the élite, a cross between the creatures that slither through Sinclair Lewis novels and the monsters that move through Fassbinder's earlier films and plays, in the bathroom, where they spend a lot of time washing their hands.

But the early Fassbinder raised melodrama to high art; the tone of *Lola* is essentially comic. The shenanigans of the businessmen are a burlesque (the script, by Fassbinder, Peter Marthesheimer and Pea Frolich, follows the inception and realization of a corrupt construction scheme) and the consistently outrageous references to everything from *Imitation of Life* to *Don Quixote* and to everyone from Monroe to Bakunin are tossed about with an exultant sense of the absurd. If *Lola* is in some fashion a remake of *The Blue Angel*, it is also in a stronger fashion a high-fashion refashioning of Cervantes, with Lola as Dulcinea and with a building commissioner named Von Bohm (East German actor Armin Mueller-Stahl) as her Quixote.

The townsfolk fear that Von Bohm's putative integrity – he assumes his duties as the movie opens – will threaten their plans, summed up by the slogan, "We shall do our best to make sure progress can progress." In what at first appears to be a tangential plot development, Von Bohm meets and gets to know Lola – in a church, no less – without knowing that her claim to be a singer of the classics is ever so slightly exaggerated. The instantaneous love he feels for this deceitful woman could prove (as it did for the professor who fell for the dance-hall girl in *The Blue Angel*) his undoing. And then again, it might not. *Lola*'s debt to *The Blue Angel* is obvious, but Fassbinder has other folks to fry.

The director's attitudes toward the leading characters vacillate, much as one's attitudes toward the people one knows in real life reflect a combination of evolution, mutation and contradiction. (A technical motif present throughout *Lola* emphasizes the sticky, cotton-candy lack of certainty: the bridges between scenes are accomplished with what might be called "fuzz outs.")

Von Bohm is a good man but he is also a fool (Quixote); the singer is a pathetically exploited figure – "I'd like to know why the whole world thinks I've got leprosy!" she snarls – but she is also an opportunistic slut (Dulcinea). Von Bohm's employee and good friend Esslin (Matthias Fuchs) is a humanist who does not believe in revolution; in the film's terms, that makes him an impotent unit. The town's real power, the contractor Schuckert (Mario Adorf), is a pig – Lola tells him he can sell his haunch for pork roast – but he is a charismatic, energetic, attractive pig.

Everyone wears a mask with at least two faces. "People here have an inner life and an outer life and the two have nothing to do with each other," Lola warns Von Bohm, who seems at first to have but one face and one mask. That he does not gives Fassbinder the opportunity to stage one of his few "happy" endings – a "happy" ending that nonetheless groans with irony.

Still, *Lola* is less ironic than usual. There are exchanges between the whore and the commissioner that contain a gentleness rare in Fassbinder since *Ali – Fear Eats the Soul* nearly a decade ago, and there is a lacerating sequence in which the protean Lola rips herself to shreds while singing (the movie's most obvious nod to *Gilda*) after she and Von Bohm have discovered simultaneously that their visions of each other were illusory. In Fassbinder, that is the tragic flaw: to believe that virtue is incorruptible is to invite disaster.

Both Sukowa, who can appear as pretty and slack-jawed as Sandra Dee or as mysterious and conniving as Dietrich, and Armin Mueller-Stahl, who manages the difficult task of engendering sympathy for a man with a bit of the wimp about him, are perfection. The supporting cast, comprised of Fassbinder regulars, is equally exemplary.

In the end, the picture leaves one with a complex, frustrating political message. "The building commissioner condemns the basic principle of capitalism from a moral point of view but realizes that, without that principle, the country can't be rebuilt," Fassbinder said. "He has a liberal/social democratic attitude, which assumes that this sort of politics can somehow be contained. In the end he realizes it cannot be stopped. This is exactly what happened. Portraying this has nothing to do with resignation. As long as I still find it important and fun to tell such a story, I haven't resigned yet."

Those two words summarize this extraordinary movie, which might have been awarded an alternate title: Lola, or The Way Things Work. With its cautionary theme – never believe in inhuman virtue – and its bitingly witty analysis of the way human society goes about meeting its needs, *Lola* is a rarity, a work of art important and fun in equal portions.

August 13, 1982

❖

48 Hours

Directed by Walter Hill
Written by Roger Spottiswoode, Walter Hill, Larry Gross and Steven E. de Souza
Starring Nick Nolte and Eddie Murphy

Nick Nolte, blond and boxy in blue jeans, his voice vibrating with the ebony rumble of a cave-in at the bottom of a coal-mine, makes a great straight man for "Saturday Night Live"'s svelte and swaggering Eddie Murphy in *48 Hours*. A surreal sweep through San Francisco's tenderloin, a quick and clever thriller as nasty as a piece of shrapnel snapping the sound barrier, *48 Hours* is as violent as it is funny. It is very funny.

Nolte is Detective Jack Cates, owner of a sky-blue Cadillac convertible that saw better days a decade ago, right about the time Cates may have been in his prime. ("I'm a rag-top man," he growls in a bass-baritone that makes Kris Kristofferson sound like a tinkling Richard Simmons.) In order to crack a case, a case that is no more than a pretext for launching this little missile of a movie, Cates springs convict Reggie Hammond (Murphy) from the slammer for forty-eight hours. Hammond was a member of the gang that is giving Cates and the San Francisco Police Department fits for reasons that need not concern the viewer because they don't particularly concern Walter Hill, the director.

The pairing is blatant contrivance, an opportunity to film the antics of one of the oddest couples to reach the screen since Mae West took a shine to Ringo Starr in *Sextette.*

Hill, director of *The Long Riders, The Warriors, Hard Times* and *Southern Comfort,* has become the Hemingway of the modern movie house, a terse stylist with unapologetically macho attitudes: the only major female character in *48 Hours,* the gifted and criminally under-utilized Annette O'Toole, spends her time on the phone haranguing the hero; the other women are either whores or sluts; of the terms employed to characterize females, "chick" is the least offensive.

But Hill has a similarly primitive attitude toward males: he's an equal-opportunity chauvinist. The men in *48 Hours,* the bad guys, are scuzz-balls so alien to human feeling you expect them to leave snail-trails behind them. The good guys are not much better; what they've got that sets them apart from the bad guys is a sense of humour, and Detective Cates, the nominal hero, has something more, an attachment to a vestigial moral code. That attachment is romantic and perhaps idiotic in the lurid face of the glistening, pastel neon garden of urban blight Hill and cinematographer Ric Waite have nurtured.

114

For all its resolute roughness, *48 Hours* is a sleek entertainment machine, far more tolerable than Clint Eastwood's *Magnum Force* or Burt Reynolds' *Sharkey's Machine,* to name two other cop flicks that staked out similar terrain, because this time Hill is clearly at work in the cartoon mode. The movie, intentionally apolitical and nearly amoral, is an American *Diva* by way of Dick Tracy and Sam Peckinpah. If you can imagine one of Sidney Lumet's profane, hyperized New York cop pictures (*Dog Day Afternoon, Prince of the City, Serpico*) speeded up, with the social conscience Lumet brings to those movies tossed out in favour of a shamelessly opportunistic, devil-made-me-do-it comic spirit, then you have approximated the idiosyncratic tenor of *48 Hours*, which is probably going to be a big, big hit.

The camaraderie between the detective and the convict, supercharged and ambivalent, veers instantly from co-operation to hostility, and contains within its comic exaggerations more truth about American race relations than a dozen respectable movies.

Nolte occasionally relies on schtick – he flexes his forehead muscles, à la Walter Matthau, a few times too many – but his floppy, puppy-dawg charm is a nifty contrast to Eddie Murphy's well-tailored, wiry finesse. Murphy is wonderful in this movie, but who knows if he can act? The role of the convict dude, who dons a Giorgio Armani suit the second he is free of the pen, is so beautifully written in garrulous, razor's-edge ghetto-speak, it could have been played to acclaim by a well-oiled robot.

Hill's films, fabulously crafted fables vacant as a vacuum, are often irritating because they pretend not to be empty – *The Warriors* fooled Pauline Kael into thinking it had something to do with Xenophon, *The Long Riders* was supposed to be about the death of the West, and *Southern Comfort* called upon Vietnam for resonance. This time, Hill has had the grace to admit that his movie is empty; the movie is better for it. *48 Hours* has the wit, speed and technocratically veiled brutality of the new video games. You can argue with the concept, but it's hell arguing with the execution: attempting to rebut excitement is a thankless and wizened task, a puritan's miserly errand.

December 3, 1982

❖

Come Back to the Five and Dime, Jimmy Dean, Jimmy Dean

Directed by Robert Altman
Written by Ed Graczyk
Starring Sandy Dennis, Karen Black and Cher

Knowing exactly how to recommend Robert Altman's fabulously adept adaptation of Ed Graczyk's incredibly inept Broadway play, *Come Back to the Five and Dime, Jimmy Dean, Jimmy Dean*, is a problem: although the film is more fun than it has any right to be, customary critical kudos doesn't apply.

The play flouted any standard of excellence applicable – it's trashy, psychologically overscaled, pretentious, predictable and tasteless – but the movie is not only funny, it's moving, and it contains the greatest acting by women on view anywhere this year.

Shot for $800,000 on a single set, *Jimmy Dean* begins with a premise as hoary as a Christmas carol: this is a Dark Night of the Soul Movie, in the tradition of *Long Day's Journey Into Night*, *The Iceman Cometh*, *Who's Afraid of Virginia Woolf?*, *The Boys in the Band* and *The Championship Season*.

In the Dark Night of the Soul Movie, folks who knew each other years ago get together to strip the sleaze from each other's souls and find that all that surface sleaze was hiding deeper sleaze. Everyone laughs, cries and gets bitchy, and Truth is served straight-up.

In *Jimmy Dean*'s case, the folks are members of a fan club, the Disciples of Jimmy Dean, attending a twentieth anniversary reunion; the action alternates between 1975, the year of the reunion, and 1955, the year Dean, Elizabeth Taylor and Rock Hudson came to Texas to film *Giant*, and changed the lives of their fans.

Graczyk has combined the Dark Night of the Soul Movie with the My Grapes Are Sour and My Prose Is Purple Movie, Dixie Division – *Jimmy Dean* is misty with the steamy Southern sensuality of Tennessee

Williams and William Inge (Pierre Mignot's peach-coloured cinematography gives the dust of drought-ridden Texas the appearance of shimmering orange smoke) and it's bathed in the excesses of those writers, too. Baroque is too mild a word for the bizarre nature of the secrets eventually uncovered.

There are six women and one man in the cast. Of the women, three are important: Mona (Sandy Dennis), impregnated twenty years earlier, according to her, by Dean himself; Sissy (Cher), a good-time girl with an indigenously poetic method of expressing herself (Sissy to Mona: "You look like you been rode hard and put away wet"); and Joanne (Karen Black), who arrives at the party belatedly and who is a packhorse of irony. The women are to a man exceptional.

Sandy Dennis, high-strung and erratic, is better than she has been in years, and she makes use of the most eloquent pointing finger since E.T.'s digit glowed with palliative powers. When Sissy makes fun of Mona – of Mona's twitches, tosses of the head and holier-than-y'all attitudes – it seems for a second that Altman may be scoring a cheap laugh from Dennis' idiosyncracies as an actress, but the fear is groundless. Sissy gets her laugh, and Altman cuts to a close-up of Mona's face, rigid with pain; the sight is enough to force the most vociferous opponent of Dennis' adenoidal art to cry Uncle.

Cher is a personification of Altman's easy, rhythmic directorial style. Although Sissy is the tart of the piece, Cher gives her a gentle dignity untainted by pathos – it's a sex symbol performance, but the breezy, small-town good cheer is unique (Sissy could not become, like a Monroe character, a symbol for feminists: she is too individual to be anything but a symbol of herself) and her big monologue, shot in three-quarter profile with her face away from the camera, is a masterpiece of emotional economy.

Karen Black, as Joanne, offers the most spectacular performance of her career, in a role so spectacular the fact that it works at all – let alone wonderfully well – is something of a miracle. Stiff-limbed and romantically wasted, Joanne pulls herself up to her full height when she is about to deliver a zinger, raises her eyebrows, and then points her pupils at the floor, as if addressing a cockroach. Black hasn't been as weirdly likeable since the last time she worked for Altman, as Connie the country singer in *Nashville.*

The legerdemain Altman accomplishes here nearly ranks with his magic act in *Nashville,* his finest film. *Nashville's* style was equalled by its script, however, and the script for *Jimmy Dean,* at its very best, is never more than an entertaining groaner, despite Altman's exhilarating dexterity. Juanita (Sudie Bond), the fundamentalist proprietor of the Five and Dime, observes at one point, vis-à-vis the girls' "belief" in Jimmy Dean: "Believin' is so funny, when what you believe in don't even know you exist." Believin' in *Come Back to the Five and Dime, Jimmy Dean, Jimmy Dean,* is a little like that – but you're not sure it exists. "It's deceivin' to the eye," Mona says of the movies. Amen. And sometimes, if the director is good enough, it's deceivin' to the mind as well.

December 22, 1982

The Night of the Shooting Stars

Written and directed by Paolo and Vittorio Taviani
Starring Omero Antonutti and Margarita Lozano

Early evening, the night of August 10. A bedroom window. A woman's voice, hushed by the telling of a tale. Tonight, the woman says, is the night of San Lorenzo. Tonight is a night of special, magic meaning. Tonight is the night of the shooting stars – wishes are granted, dreams come true. Tonight the woman's thoughts turn to perhaps the most important night of her life, to the night of San Lorenzo in the troubled year of 1944, when she was six and her country was at war.

So begins, in the form of a prologue, Vittorio and Paolo Taviani's *The Night of the Shooting Stars,* one of the gentlest and yet most powerful anti-war films since Jean Renoir's *The Grand Illusion*. As the unseen narrator prepares the audience for her reminiscences – reminiscences transformed, as the directors have commented, "by forty years of story-telling, with all the exaggerations and gaps in memory, with all the artlessness and epic and fantastic leaps with which the collective imagination manages to heighten meaning" – the camera remains perched in front of the bedroom window. The bedroom is realistic (there is a TV set with a red plastic cabinet on a bureau), but the landscape beyond is fabulist, stylized, unreal, a landscape that could offer hospitality to Peter Pan.

The contrast between the mundane and the magical is the *raison d'être* of *The Night of the Shooting Stars*, which takes place in and near the tiny Tuscan town of San Martino. Italy has been at war for what must seem like centuries. Families are divided by fascism – a boy is a black-shirted follower of Mussolini, his brother a member of the resistance. The Americans are coming. The peasants of San Martino ache for liberation. One night a group led by a village elder, Galvano (Omero Antonutti), sets out in search of the Yankees; another group stays behind, hidden in the village cathedral. There is no other plot: The movie is an adventure in which the old become young, the young become old, and life is lived at the extremes.

Everything happens, but nothing follows logically from anything else – the movie has the exhilarating, disorienting, maddening and saddening unpredictability of life itself. A priest tells his parishioners it is their responsibility to survive, and then is a horrified witness to unspeakable carnage; young boys masturbate communally, watching a young woman urinate; an old man and an old woman bathe, fully clothed, in a stream, and give new dimension to the concept of the erotic; a battle in a wheatfield veers from the slapstick to the tragic – an old woman who croaks, "Who's winning?" is shot at point-blank range.

119

The Taviani brothers, winners in 1977 of a Golden Palm at the Cannes Film Festival for *Padre Padrone*, are not overly concerned with differentiating between the people to whom these events occur; as in a folk tale, it is the tale that takes precedence.

Still, the personalities of the exceptional actors chosen by the directors manifest themselves, and the burgeoning relationship between the old man Galvano and his "superior," the regal widow Concetta (Margarita Lozano, who has appeared in movies for Bunuel, Sergio Leone and Pasolini), is at the heart of the film's affirmative, spiritual sensibility. The Tavianis may not set out to persuade the audience to care for their characters by drawing psychological profiles or proffering "revealing" traits – their method of characterization is almost Chaucerian in its flat, ribald simplicity – but, by the end of this unexpectedly moving film, the people in it are engraved as deeply on the memory, and their adventures have become as elusively evocative as any of the people in any of the yarns spun by any of those travellers on their way to Canterbury five hundred years ago.

For the Taviani brothers, the war years "were of course atrocious, but they were also years when men were forced to show everything of which they were capable, both for good and evil . . . We think ourselves lucky to have lived so intensively a collective adventure while the world was turning upside down before our eyes." The Tavianis have approached their boyhood memories with all the wonder implied in that statement, and with a warm, unquenchable sensuality that may be as quintessentially Italian as the gelid, analytical intelligence Volker Schlöndorff brought to his film of Günter Grass's *The Tin Drum* is quintessentially German.

The Tin Drum really is the German version of *The Night of the Shooting Stars*, and like *The Tin Drum*, the Taviani film is a self-reflective work that lays bare the process by which the material of memory becomes myth and the chaos of life becomes art. But if that gives the impression that *The Night of the Shooting Stars* is dry or abstract, it is neither. It may be esthetically sophisticated, technically distinguished (there are sequences of bravura filmmaking) and politically astute, but it is also a work of popular art in the best sense: It launches a tall tale that rides high and dives deep.

February 4, 1983

The Stationmaster's Wife

Directed by Rainer Werner Fassbinder
Starring Kurt Raab and Elisabeth Trissenaar

The late Rainer Werner Fassbinder's *The Stationmaster's Wife*, based on Oskar Maria Graf's 1931 novel, *Bolweiser* (the title is the surname of the protagonist, a petty bourgeois stationmaster), was shot for Bavarian television in 1977, but there is nothing in it, in style or in substance, to indicate its modest origins. By any standard, this is a work of major movie art, one of the most corrosive and yet compassionate studies of hypocrisy ever unfolded on the screen.

Working close-up and indoors (when the camera strays outside, it comes as a pleasant shock), Fassbinder claustrophobically evokes the stultifying existence of the German lower-middle class in the twenties. His vehicle is the melodramatic, adulterous story of the diffident, unimaginative Bolweiser (Kurt Raab) and his restive, beautiful wife, Hanni (Elisabeth Trissenaar), a woman in the literary and psychological tradition of Madame Bovary.

The movie opens at their home, on their wedding day. All is well: passion is paramount. In the marriage bed, their hands, ringed in wedding bands, intertwine. "I belong to you, only to you," Bolweiser whispers. Peer Raben's music swells. And then, in a series of surgically sharp scenes – blackouts, really – the melodrama rapidly establishes a progression. As the novelty of the marriage erodes, desire and affection dribble away. The boring Bolweiser does not notice (or, more to the point, chooses not to notice) when Hanni takes up with a handsome, beefy butcher, Merkl (Bernard Helfrich), as a way of assuaging her ennui.

Another affair follows, accusations are flung with the abandon of water on wash day, and the passive Bolweiser – on one level, a symbol for the subservient, pre-Hitler German masses – allows himself to be manipulated into a court case from which he can expect nothing but grief. Perversely, his distrust of his wife reignites his passion; now, however, the lovemaking is bitter, savage, desperate, without release. When asked by Hanni to hurry, he snarls, "You're . . . my . . . property. I can do what I like with you."

Fassbinder assesses no blame, passes no judgement. His fluid, probing camera and Raben's emphatic music serve as emotional intensifiers of an exceptionally complex and analytic screenplay. The characters in *The Stationmaster's Wife* act with the near-randomness of people in life; the explanations they offer for their actions may or may not have much to do with reality. In common with Fassbinder's other first-rate films (*The Marriage of Maria Braun, In a Year With 13 Moons*), *The Stationmaster's Wife* stymies filmgoers accustomed to assigning emotional allegiance to sentimentalized characters, and it similarly frustrates those who would impose a clarifying ideology on chaotic events.

Hanni and Bolweiser are, in varying degrees, admirable and disgusting: they are partly good, partly bad and wholly human. Their universality is accentuated by the technical device of constantly photographing them in mirrors (or mirrored surfaces – an Art Deco coffee pot, for example). Fassbinder made use of mirrors more often and with greater dexterity than any other filmmaker, but the eloquence of their employment here is unmatched. They are an analogue for the camera itself, a self-conscious reflection on the process of moviemaking. Just as Hanni and Bolweiser peer into mirrors for some hint of their true identities, the audience in the theatre stares into the screen for a reflection of itself, and that, Fassbinder argues implicitly, may be exactly what the audience is getting, like it or not: the truth.

Fassbinder's "truth" is, of course, debatable. But, if his view of romantic relationships is despairing (exploitation is inevitable; morality is both expendable and expedient), it is not, for all its pessimism, a philosophy of melancholy: there is no self-pity and precious little sadness in *The Stationmaster's Wife*. The method is exacting, as if an important autopsy is under way, but rarely grim, as if the doctor conducting the autopsy has become so intent on his analysis he has ceased to notice that the thing he is cutting up is a corpse. The movie gives up on exorcism: it advises coming to guarded terms with the demons in the human heart.

February 11, 1983

The Grey Fox

Directed by Phillip Borsos
Written by John Hunter
Starring Richard Farnsworth and Jackie Burroughs

The aged outlaw, Bill Miner (Richard Farnsworth), is waltzing with his girl friend, a middle-aged, politically progressive photographer named Kate Flynn (Jackie Burroughs). They are dancing at dusk, under the roof of a Kamloops, B.C., gazebo, and their environment is immeasurably beautiful: in the background, jagged peaks dusted with pink-sugar snow are outlined against an indigo sky.

The Grey Fox, winner of the Academy of Canadian Cinema's best picture award, is about two kinds of beauty, the obvious and easily photographed beauty of British Columbia, and the less obvious and not so easily photographed beauty of human beings no longer young.

After serving thirty-three years in prison for an eighteen-year spree of robbery that began with the 1863 holdup of the Arizona Pony Express when he was a tender and sweet sixteen, Bill Miner is released from prison on June 17, 1901. He is released "into the twentieth century," as a title at the beginning of *The Grey Fox* puts it, but he is a nineteenth-century figure, a courtly coot nicknamed by the Pinkerton people "the gentleman bandit." Stagecoaches were Miner's speciality – his credo was, "A professional always specializes" – but stagecoaches no longer exist. It's a different world, and the old fox must find a way of moving in it.

The means to that end present themselves one night at the moving picture show. The feature is Edwin S. Porter's *The Great Train Robbery* and, as the jerky black and white drama unfolds on the rickety screen, Miner is entranced – his eyes widen, his cheeks redden, his breath shortens. "To a man my age, the future don't mean too much, unless you're thinking, maybe, about next week," he earlier told a salesman who tried to interest him in the glories of the twentieth century (Miner gave in and purchased one of the glories, a mechanical apple peeler). But his exposure to *The Great Train Robbery* transforms resignation into inspiration. Here is a new world for the old criminal to conquer.

Not much need be said about the remaining plot of *The Grey Fox* because not much plot remains. The film finds its compelling emotional centre when Miner meets Kate Flynn, a nascent feminist in a pillowy red Gibson, a woman of the kind once known as "eccentric" (that meant unmarried) and a woman who finds, to her shock, that she is capable of a great love. When Miner and Kate Flynn are together, *The Grey Fox* is a magnificent romance, and viewers may well wish history would stay out of the way to allow the film to follow the logic of the love affair. Even the B.C. landscapes photographed so sumptuously by Frank Tidy – the pristine images are dramatic and classic, as if Ansel Adams had decided to make a movie – cannot compete with the glory of a minor moment when Kate runs her hands flittingly across Miner's chest and asks him to tell her the stories trapped in his tattoos.

Jackie Burroughs gives Richard Farnsworth an invaluable gift, a gift that throws the film's title into two levels, and a gift without which the movie might be no more than a splendidly constructed but alienatingly austere elegiac western: she gives him sex appeal. Farnsworth, a former stunt man, has always been an attractively homespun and persuasively "real" screen presence; he's a less charismatic variation on the honest-as-the-day-is-long Willie Nelson theme. But Burroughs singlehandedly turns him into a romantic lead, and she arrives on screen to accomplish her alchemy exactly when the picture is in danger of becoming a series of pretty but empty pictures.

Her method is disarmingly simple: in her scenes with the townsfolk of Kamloops, Kate is brusque and efficient and tinged subliminally with hysteria. (This woman, an "old maid" with socialist opinions, is both a pioneer – an oddball, in other words – and an odd-ball among oddballs. Burroughs clues the audience into the difficulty of maintaining dignity under those circumstances.) But in her scenes with Miner, the normally businesslike and even arid Kate vibrates with ecstasy. During Kate's post-coital inventory of her lover's scratches and scrapes, she asks Miner about a bluebird tattoo and finds she is so charged by his touch she cannot keep his hand in hers.

The Grey Fox is being "presented" by Francis Coppola's Zoetrope Studios. The reason for Coppola's approval of the picture is apparent. Miner's aborted rustling of a gang of wild horses is shot with the grandeur of The Black Stallion, which Coppola produced, and the over-all look of the film has the slightly fantastic, hard-edged colour associated with Zoetrope (except that the fantasy colours Coppola laboured to produce in One From the Heart exist naturally in British Columbia).

Like much of Zoetrope's recent output, the emphasis in The Grey Fox is on the feat of filmmaking; Phillip Borsos, the gifted director, is fortunate to have found in Farnsworth and Burroughs performers who can hold their own against the pyrotechnics, and he is additionally fortunate to have found in John Hunter's script a charming, chivalrous argot – full of "please" and "thank-you" and "yes sir" as people are being ripped off – that cleverly differentiates the Canadian west from the macho American myth.

Westerns and science fiction, although placed in the past and future, are invariably about the aspirations of present, and The Grey Fox is no exception. This is a Western set in a mythic, nostalgic Canada where manners receive respect, where order is preferable to law and where fair play is more important than self-promotion. It's not what we are – it's what we like to think we are – but it's part of the truth, just as the American opposite number, which accords respect to bluster, preference to lawlessness and infinite importance to individualism, is not what they are, either, though it's part of their truth.

What's more, The Grey Fox provides that truth with an artistry that transcends nationality. Like Australians, Canadians have at long last found the quiet confidence to assume that the rest of the world may be interested in knowing about Canadians. That kind of confidence may not be an especially Canadian trait, but it's a damned healthy one.

April 8, 1983

❖

Lone Wolf McQuade

Directed by Steve Carter
Written by B. J. Nelson
Starring Chuck Norris

"My kind of trouble doesn't take vacations," Texas Ranger J. J. McQuade (Chuck Norris) says in *Lone Wolf McQuade*. Boy howdy, is he tellin' the Good Book truth! J. J. is called Lone Wolf cuz of his habit of workin' the El Paso badlands without a buddy, and in his new movie he's got more trouble than Ma's got grief.

F'r instance: his girl friend (Barbara Carrera), who looks like Raquel Welch, but meaner, is workin' for Rawley Wilkes (David Carradine), as bad a man ever crawled out from under a rock. Ol' Rawley sells machine guns to "all terrorists and subversives" and is known for martial arts lore but not for book learnin' – the licence plate on his car says CARATE. He meets up with Lone Wolf, who's hip to martial arts lore, too, only Lone Wolf doesn't feel the need to advertise it. Ol' Rawley, who wears gold chains and cashmere sweaters without a shirt on underneath, sissy style, says to Lone Wolf, who wears jean jackets with the sleeves torn out and combat pants, he-man style, "I understand you're very good with your hands and feet." Damned if Lone Wolf don't danged near blush!

Now Lone Wolf, who's watched a heap of Burt Reynolds, Chuck Bronson, Sly Stallone and Clint Eastwood flicks, is bein' pushed 'tween a rock and a hard place. His supervisor, Captain Tee Tyler

(R. G. Armstrong), wants him to take a partner, Chicano kid by the name of Kayo (Robert Beltran, same guy that got ate in *Eating Raoul* — as an actor, he makes a durned good sandwich), and then he wants him to settle down. "Your lone wolf attitude is gonna change," Capt. Tee says. "You're gonna start co-operatin' with state and federal authorities, understand?"

Not 'til the Rio Grande freezes over. Lone Wolf heads back on home, takes his shirt off: he's hairier 'n an Irish setter. He rolls around on the desert sand barechested, shootin' off guns bigger 'n oak trees. The man is tough, tougher 'n a scorpion in jackboots. How tough is that? He goes to a barbecue, Lone Wolf does, and asks the barkeep, "You got Pearl beer?" They got Dos Equis, Heineken and Michelob, barkeep says. "Forget it," Lone Wolf says. Now that's tough.

Afore you know it, Lone Wolf's best friend (L. Q. Jones, in white hair and goatee, lookin' like a hard-case Colonel Sanders) gets done in. He gets done in just about the worst way a man can go: somebody steps on his throat. That's bad enough, but the dude doin' the deed is wearin' a white shoe! A loafer! Lone Wolf gets mad as a bee-stung boxer dog. How mad is that? This here's the *Lone Wolf McQuade* body count:

Killed by guns: 35.
Killed by explosions: 9.
Killed by arrows: 3.
Hit by car: 1.
In car goin' over cliff: 1.
Killed by white shoe: 1.
And dog killed: 1.

It's Lone Wolf's dog. After the poor critter's been buried, Lone Wolf looks at his little ol' bitty water dish with a little ol' bitty tear in his foxy eye. It's enough to make the heart of a stone statue crack right in two.

April 18, 1983

❖

The Terry Fox Story

Directed by Ralph L. Thomas
Written by Edward Hume
Starring Eric Fryer and Robert Duvall

"I'm not the Bionic Man." – *Terry Fox*

But he was treated that way, during his one-legged run across Canada, and he became that rarest of all things Canadian, a hero. With his athlete's muscles and his cupid's curls, he was a natural, a shoo-in for page one, and if he was good in print, he was even better on the tube, ungainly but oddly graceful, his Marathon of Hope drama staged poignantly against landscapes that changed as fast as movie sets. By the time he hit Toronto, he was a star. *The Terry Fox Story* was a foregone conclusion.

What no one could have foreseen was that the movie would be good. Sure, Bill Conti's music is deafeningly dreadful, and there are problems here and there with performances and camera angles and even with wigs and make-up (the film was made mostly with television in mind), but all that is secondary to the achievement, which has been to humanize a kid who had been made larger – and paradoxically smaller – than life. In trying to explain Terry Fox, the media, the Great Explainers, had rendered him inexplicable: they transformed an alternately tranquil and angry, frightened and sanguine, self-centred and compassionate, manipulative and ingenuous kid – a dying boy – into a living doll.

Edward Hume's wonderful script restores the reality: when this Terry Fox (Eric Fryer) begins running, it is to convince himself that he is not going to die. "If you want to do something to fight cancer," his judgemental and seductive mother Betty (Elva Mai Hoover) tells him, "you just stop pretending to forget your X-ray appointments." Terry's girl friend Rika (a radiant Rosalind Chao), commenting on his extraordinary self-involvement, wonders, "When are you going to grow up? You've got to start giving a little." She does not mean to the

Canadian Cancer Society. "The reason I'm running is to raise money for cancer research," Terry says, but in the beginning that is a lie – and if it is not, it contains so little of the truth it might as well be.

Doug (Michael Zelniker), the long-suffering companion who drives the van for Terry's marathon (the tempestuous relationship is closer to a love affair than a friendship), initially sees the run as "one big ego trip." He has no other option. When Terry's arrival goes ungreeted in a small Newfoundland town, he is livid, and complains caustically to Doug, "That's your job, ——."

None too soon, Terry meets Bill Vigars (Robert Duvall), a representative of the Cancer Society, and his dreams of publicity come true with a vengeance. "By the time you cross the Ottawa River, you could be front page news," Vigars promises. Until then, the run has attracted so little attention, Terry asks querulously, "Don't people get cancer in Quebec?" (Even here: the two solitudes.) By the time Terry has left Toronto, Vigars is telling him they have to "make that reception in Barrie." "What do they want of me, blood?" Terry demands. "If you don't show," Vigars warns, "it's my ass. I could be back selling encyclopedias."

None of this is depicted by director Ralph Thomas (*Ticket to Heaven*) in a miserly, debunking spirit: the strategy is to trust the audience to admire Terry despite and because of his failings.

Fryer, the Ontario athlete who makes his debut as Fox, is remarkable at delineating Terry's growth; without him, the picture, which is otherwise a competent but pedestrian treatment of a first-rate script, would be unimaginable.

The hard, cold examination of the Terry Fox celebrity phenomenon and of Terry's contribution to it has the chilling overtones of Martin Scorsese's *The King of Comedy* – even a battle with cancer, the film suggests, is fodder for media sentimentality, a way to sell just one more paper and one more lie – but the difference is that at the centre of *The King of Comedy* was a vacuum gussied up as a man. At the centre of *The Terry Fox Story* is a painfully real boy, a boy learning to appreciate life and coming to terms with death. Hospitalized for the last time, Terry is visited by his father, who sobs out his anger at the "unfairness" of the situation. "It's not unfair; it happens to a lot of people," Terry responds. For those few seconds, he snatches an equanimity few ever find in the face of extinction. That's enough to ask of any hero.

Recovering from his own leg amputation, Eric Fryer learned to hate Terry Fox, director Ralph Thomas said several days ago: "Terry was always being held up to Eric as an example." How Fryer came to play the role has become a tale almost as legendary as the Terry Fox story itself – *People* magazine breathlessly tells its readers Fryer finally capitulated to an audition when his mother said he would be able to buy a Corvette – but there was a time when a "name" actor was considered. "Ralph had a long conversation with Matt Dillon," producer Robert Cooper recalls. "In an era of *Star Wars* special effects, they thought we should be able to do one leg."

But Cooper persisted in his resolve that an amputee play the role, if the right actor could be found. Cooper was able to push the point because he was producing for Home Box Office where, he says fondly, "the freedom they gave Ralph and me was in excess of what is given by the networks or the studios." *The Terry Fox Story* was HBO's first foray into film production, and the American reaction to its quality threatens to revolutionize the film business.

Cooper met Terry Fox in Vancouver toward the end of his life and found him to be as complex – at once charming and manipulative – as he is depicted in the film. "He was in good shape the first time I saw him. The day before he went out to a kung fu movie. When I walked in, he laughed and told me I looked like Peter Sellers, so I did my Peter Sellers imitation." Fox was firm in his desire that his run be neither glamorized nor sentimentalized. "He kept coming back to that," Cooper said, "in a droning way, over and over. He had a real scepticism and cynicism about what might happen."

The grittiness of the script, commissioned from American writer Edward Hume, who spent a good deal of time with the Fox family, did not offend Thomas. (Mrs. Fox herself inserted a line when Terry's plans are revealed to her husband: "Sit down, shut up and don't yell when I tell you.") On the contrary: Thomas was relieved by what he saw as the honesty of the script. "When I first met with Robert Cooper, I started by saying, 'Let me tell you what I won't do. I'm not interested in doing a story about a saint.' Listening to what Terry didn't want from the film, I felt we had a mandate."

Fryer meanwhile altered his opinion of Fox. He confided to Thomas that chemotherapy was as close to hell as he ever wanted to get and said, "Terry's real heroism was not running across Canada, it was going back to take chemotherapy the second time." During shooting, as Fryer learned to trust Thomas, Cooper and – most of all – co-star Robert Duvall, whom Thomas credits with teaching Fryer to relax as an actor, he was by turns as angry, frightened, socially uncomfortable and "short of fuse" – Cooper's phrase – as the character he was impersonating. "He also became," Thomas says softly, with pride, "technically better than any actor I ever worked with. I kept seeing what the film was about. I saw it in his eyes."

May 27, 1983

The Survivors

Directed by Michael Ritchie
Written by Michael Leeson
Starring Walter Matthau, Robin Williams and Jerry Reed

Letter from Des Moines:

Listen up, peckerwoods! There's a threat to all decent, clean-livin', Commie-hatin' Americans, and this here thing's a threat to all decent, clean-livin', Commie-hatin' Canadians, too! If there are any. We know y'all are decent – you got censor boards – and you're so goldurned clean you're downright sissified, but do y'all hate the Commies wors'n ya hate anything, except maybe hot beer and cold women? Some of you funny-talkin' Canuckian sissies must stand for the American way. Hell's bells, even the broad that runs Britain knows what the Russkies and other suchlike are tryin' to do to the precious bodily fluids of Yankee Doodle's dandies.

So listen up, mud-for-brains! This here threat's in the form of a movie, *The Survivors* by name. It's festerin' in lotsa theatres. Some are right near what they call the downtown core. Good place for this thing. Downtown core is rotten to the seeds already, bein' filled up with Commie lovers and wine drinkers. They're gonna dig this movie about Robin Williams goin' bananas and buyin' guns and takin' survival trainin' to defend himself.

What's wrong with doin' all that? Not a goldurned thing, but this here movie comes along, slick as you please, and makes fun of it, as if armin' yourself so you can blow people away is somethin' crazy! Director of this here movie, Michael Ritchie, has been makin' fun of America a long time. *The Candidate* made fun of our sacred political process. *Smile* made fun of beauty pageants. Beauty pageants, I'm tellin' ya. He even – Scout's honour – he even made fun of the Little League, f'r God's sake, in *The Bad News Bears*! A man that'll make fun of the Little League is lower than the low. That must be what they teach nowadays at Harvard. That's where this Ritchie went to school. Figures. They must give degrees in Low. Maybe he's got a Masters in Low.

Now what happens in this here movie is that Robin Williams wants to off a guy played by Jerry Reed. Sounds good to me. The Jerry Reed guy tried to rob Williams and Walter Matthau. So Williams goes after him. Sounds good to me. But the guy played by Matthau doesn't want Williams to do it. This Matthau guy gets real uptight when Williams goes on TV. Williams goes on TV because a TV editorial said Williams and Matthau were "hotshots" for fightin' back when they was attacked. Williams says, "I don't think we're hotshots. I just think we're non-victims." Sounds good to me. Then Williams wants to know, "Why is there crime? I think the root cause is criminals." Sounds good to me. But this here audience – the downtown core – laughed! They laughed at him, like what he said was stupid. Come to think of it, they laughed all the way through.

Now this is weird. Ya see, they laughed at everything. This movie's a wily one. Things have gone wrong with the good ol' U.S. of A., I'd be the first to admit it, and this movie shows it. It hooks the true blues along with the Commie lovers.

Matthau has a daughter played by Kristen Vigard – she's cute as a bug's ear – and all the poor thing knows is TV and partyin'. She says, "If you get killed, you can't party or anything, what a drag." The Jerry Reed guy claims he killed Jimmy Hoffa. Jerry Reed's killer shows what happens to morals when they're screwed around by the godless media and other wine drinkers. Reed plays a hired killer, Have Gun, Will Travel. He says, "I was raised a Southern Baptist and I place a high value on human life. $20,000 minimum." That's wrong, I'd be the first to admit it. And I admit there's something wrong when somebody asks Matthau's daughter what has got better in America in the past ten years and she says, "Video games." I couldn't think of anything else either.

So stuff is wrong with America. But then, this movie takes all the things wrong and shows how they could be set right – by guys really livin' the American way, at a survival camp in the hills, where they learn to kill creeps living the un-American way, and most of those creeps are not of the white persuasion, believe you me. And then it laughs at the idea of settin' things right with guns. Williams's girl friend won't take a gun, and he asks, "Suppose someone breaks in here? What are you gonna do? Stun 'em with your good taste?" That's pretty funny. But what's her answer to that, I'd like to know?

Williams is right wonderful in this thing, especially when he gets to do stand-up comic-type stuff, and Matthau is right funny, and Reed is right convincin' (Williams says Reed has "a face like someone in the road company of *Deliverance*," whatever that means – to me, he looks like Jerry Reed, only older) and everybody else is right friendly and downhomelike.

They got everything goin' for 'em, and then they turn around and make people laugh at how the country's collapsin' and blame it on folks that just want to be left alone and are ready to knock heads to do it. That's not funny, and any sucker says any different don't deserve to live in a God-blessed land where Popsicles and video games are open to anybody with enough goldurned gumption to get out and work for 'em.

June 27, 1983

❖

Risky Business

Written and directed by Paul Brickman
Starring Tom Cruise and Rebecca De Mornay

What if Benjamin Braddock, the hero of *The Graduate*, were to get out of high school this year? Fifteen years ago, young Ben had the luxury of eschewing luxury: he was above the tawdry, materialistic push and pull represented by the guy who accosted him poolside and whispered into his distinctly unreceptive ear the single word, "Plastics!"

Paul Brickman, the phenomenally talented writer and director of *Risky Business*, thinks today's Ben, seventeen years old and facing a perilous economic future, would drag the plastics guy into the house to take a meeting. "Today," Brickman says, "kids are praying for someone to walk up to them and say 'plastics' – or 'computers' or 'marketing.'"

The generalization may or may not hold, but Brickman's marvellously supple and theoretically absurd demonstration of it stands an excellent chance of turning out to be the finest and funniest comedy of the summer (if, that is, you don't consider Woody Allen's *Zelig* strictly a comedy, which it strictly isn't.) Already this season we have had John Sayles' wonderful but essentially serious examination of growing up, *Baby It's You. Risky Business* is *Baby*'s comic cousin, an adolescent-oriented farce so finely tuned it projects beyond its narrow intended audience – it's not only for adolescents, it's for anyone who remembers what adolescence was like.

Brickman, who wrote *Citizens Band* for director Jonathan Demme in 1977 and is author of the forthcoming William Friedkin film *Deal of the Century* (*Risky Business* is his first directorial effort), keys the picture around an archetypal situation: mom and dad go away on holiday, leaving sonny in charge of the house. Everything about the milieu, set in a Chicago suburb, is specific. Mom and dad are rich, the kid wants to get into Princeton and the house is full of valuable *chachkas*: there's a big crystal egg on the mantel, there's a Persian goodie on the floor and there's a purring Porsche in the garage. All three items figure in the plot.

The kid, Joel (Tom Cruise), is a member of the Future Enterprisers Club. He's ambitious and he's cute in a pink-gummed, Ivy-League way (he probably was born with an alligator stitched to his chest), but he's a little shy. His articulate friends – unlike the morons in *Porky's*, these kids construct complex sentences and, every now and then, have a thought that rises above their belt buckles – are always after him to loosen up. Freed from parental constraint, he follows their advice with a vengeance.

Because much of the pleasure of *Risky Business* depends on Brickman's delight in presenting the audience with ever more improbable coincidences and reversals (this is a picture in which a supporting character is given the line, "I've got a 'trig' mid-term tomorrow and I'm being chased by Guido, killer pimp!" and he does and he is), it would be unfair to reveal much more, except to report that not all the coincidences and reversals work equally well. When they do work, they are gleeful in their effrontery; when they don't, they are reminiscent of hearing a gifted, amateur singer slide off key – the failure belongs to the moment and is not especially distressing.

In the demanding role of Joel, Cruise gives a thorough, impeccable performance lacking only the *frisson* that brings stardom. Early on, in another of the archetypal situations Brickman is so good at unearthing, Joel, in his underwear and alone in the house, mimes to a rock recording. The sequence is a replay of Nastassja Kinski's narcissistic number in *Exposed*: Brickman has handed his lead a vehicle that could be exploited to the max. Instead, Cruise, who doesn't appear to have a vulgar bone in his body, refuses to go with it and stays resolutely in character. Rather than flatten the audience with an animal magnetism that would be uncharacteristic for his Chicago teenager, Cruise plays the sequence for reality. Imagine Barbra Streisand deciding to sound like the real Fanny Brice in *Funny Girl.*

Cruise and *Bad Boys* star Sean Penn are determined to become movie stars the hard way, on the basis of their acting, not their personalities. That's admirable and it can happen (it's the Paul Newman, Robert De Niro model) but both men may learn that in comedies or musicals an actor's purity is occasionally secondary to pumping as much life as possible into the material. (The Streisand model is an example of what happens when someone goes too far, and pumps so much "life" into the material that it's obliterated.)

Opposite Cruise, newcomer Rebecca De Mornay, as a whore with a heart of iron pyrite, handles the film's least convincing role with a pro's aplomb. The character is introduced during one of Brickman's more extravagant, fantastical and successful sequences. She strides into the house, asks Joel, "Are you ready for me?" and, as he demonstrates that he is by undressing her, is framed in nude silhouette against double doors that fly open to admit more blowing-leaf action than there's been in a movie since Bernardo Bertolucci buried his camera in autumn in *The Conformist.*

Elsewhere, Brickman pushes too hard for similar sumptuous effects, but even when he does, he never threatens the audience's goodwill: a talent too big for its breeches is a talent easy to forgive.

August 5, 1983

❖

Staying Alive

Directed by Sylvester Stallone
Written by Sylvester Stallone and Norman Wexler
Starring John Travolta

Flashdance

Directed by Adrian Lyne
Written by Tom Hedley and Joe Eszterhas
Starring Jennifer Beals

She looked like Lee Grant in *Shampoo*, only older: she was pushing sixty like Madame Rose pushed Gypsy, and she was wall-to-wall beige – beige hair bleached to the texture of mattress ticking, beige skin tanned to the texture of greased leather, beige face facelifted to the taut grimace of a Haida mask. But there was nothing beige about her apparel. Designer knapsack bulging with Beverly Hills bucks in the heart of Hollywood, at a store called Fred Segal's, in a joint for those who think – and sometimes are – young, she fit in, all the way. Standing in front of a dressing room, she was fit to kill in a torn T-shirt, pleated gold mini-skirt and green plastic pumps, and she was moving her tight, ropy Jane Fonda Workout muscles provocatively to the beat of Irene Cara belting the theme from *Flashdance*, "What a Feeling."

At her feet were two piles of belts, one containing three relatively tasteful leather accessories, the other formed from a knee-high mountain of plastic, chain and leatherette accoutrements. "That pile," a salesgirl whispered, pointing to the three forlorn belts, "is the rejects. The other pile, she's taking. She comes in about once a month, loads up her Rolls. She's on a roll now 'cause she just saw *Flashdance*." The salesgirl paused, surveyed the litter with the smugness of an eighteen-year-old who needs Jane Fonda like true love needs pain, and smiled. "*Flashdance* has been good to us."

And they said the musical was dead. *Staying Alive* and *Flashdance*, two of the hottest tickets of a red-hot summer, esthetic offspring of *Fame* and *Rocky* – *Flashdance* is *Rocky* with a sex change, *Staying Alive* is *Flashdance* in a jockstrap, and both are post-graduate *Fame*s – have given the lie to the eulogies. Whatever else *Staying Alive* and *Flashdance* may be, they are musicals, but of a new breed: they are workout musicals, soft-pornie health-club musicals, musicals that instead of making the difficult look easy make the easy look grotesque. They are musicals with ersatz dancing and no dancers. They are musicals with soundtracks, not songs. They are musicals that celebrate the body, not what the body can do. They are about sweat, not grace.

They are equal-opportunity musicals. They refuse to differentiate between gymnastics and ballet – or between a trampoline and the Broadway stage, or between the locker room and the bedroom. They are the inevitable outcome of the Me Generation, the fitness craze, diet beer and Tab; they are the ultimate narcissistic tools for a culture already high on what it sees in the mirror. They have one common message: they both preach that class barriers can be surmounted by self-love. Of all things. This must be the first time in history masturbation has shared marketing with Marxism.

Staying Alive, in which John Travolta once again essays the role of Italian stallion Tony Manero, never deals directly with the most remarkable change that has occurred in the life of its hero since we last saw him leaving Brooklyn at the end of *Saturday Night Fever* in 1977: he has turned into a hunk. Everyone watching the movie knows, of course, that the director, Italian stallion Sylvester Stallone, himself no stranger to hulk 'n' bulk, got hold of Travolta and transformed his soft teen curves into the hard stuff the little boys in *Blueboy* are made of (on the cover of the current *Rolling Stone*, Travolta comes across like gay America's altar boy) but the movie never mentions the metamorphosis.

When Manero goes to visit his mom in Brooklyn (in the picture's single believable scene), you expect her to gape at her son's new body but she doesn't even notice; maybe it's happening to all the guys on the block – first puberty, then pimples, then pecs and lats and Charles Atlas.

Stallone, Travolta and Co. have purposely turned the Tony Manero story into meta-cliché. *Saturday Night Fever*, based on Nik Cohn's article for *New York* magazine, "Tribal Rites of the New Saturday Night," was neon pop sociology with at least one foot on the ground, but *Staying Alive* never touches down. *Saturday Night Fever* was a wistful, clear-eyed celebration of how kids caught in the recession of the seventies organized a good time for themselves against all odds. *Staying Alive* is not about those kids: it's a fantasy made for them.

Presto chango, the sullen, sexist Tony Manero of '77 – a guy with about as much future as platform shoes – has become a gentlemanly, would-be Broadway hoofer elevated to stardom on the night an abominable modern dance show, "Satan's Alley," opens on the Great White Way. How does Stallone, who's only slightly less shameless but a hell of a lot more vulgar than Norman Rockwell, get away with it? He trusts the audience, pumped solid from the last go-round at Nautilus, to know what *Staying Alive* is really about, and it's not how talent can get you to the top, any more than *Flashdance*, the story of a female welder finally admitted to a chic ballet school, is about how immersion in dance culture equips you to make the grade. (The heroine of *Flashdance* learns to dance in her dreams; what she doesn't get there, she picks up on TV.)

"Satan's Alley," the show that makes Manero a star, is full of writhing but no dancing: when the audience applauds, the approbation is presumably intended for the film editor, the true choreographer of both these movies. Or, more likely, the applause is for Universal Gyms and protein powder. "Satan's Alley" is described as "the story of a man who journeys through hell to ascend to heaven at the end." That's as good a summation of tough, properly paced workouts and of the physical euphoria they engender as you're going to find in the Collected Works of Arnold Schwarzenegger, a guy who sure knew how to start something.

For all their novelty, *Staying Alive* and *Flashdance* are in the mainstream tradition of Hollywood musicals. Their books are wholly atrocious excuses to get from one number to another; the numbers

139

themselves usually have nothing to do with the action of the script and are presented in contexts in which they are laughable (the working-class *Flashdance* bar hosts kinky video-type routines that resemble Helmut Newton photographs on the move), and, more important, they celebrate the triumph of the worthy, noble working class over the snotty, unworthy upper class.

But in old Hollywood musicals, it was an ability to sing, dance or tell jokes that made the difference. Not here. Here, the chosen reach the peak because their muscles peak. We know Tony Manero will get picked for the lead in "Satan's Alley" because his body is in ace shape and he'll look great on the cover of *Rolling Stone*. We know that the *Flashdance* cutie – one of that movie's key sequences is of mighty but-tocks bouncing, warming their owners up – is going to make it because her hours of bum-bobbing have equipped her with a prole-tarian energy lacking in the exsanguinated ballet types she competes against. (The seat of her talent is in her seat.)

Flashdance and *Staying Alive* actually argue that body building is not an answer, it's The Answer. You can become a star if you look hot and you're hard as acrylic nails. You can become a dancing star even if you don't dance. These whorish, patronizing fantasy films do have their own weird integrity and they do practise the lowest common denominator democracy they preach: the star of *Flashdance* was dubbed, or whatever you call it when one body replaces another, so that the non-dancing star only had to look as if she might be able to dance, and Travolta, whose raunchy amateurishness on the disco floor gave *Saturday Night Fever* its soul, was merely asked in *Staying Alive* to jump a little, run a little, work the arms a little and work the pelvis a lot. These folks worked hard for their muscles; why should they have to do anything with them?

The cliché in popular entertainment used to be that the working class produced better lovers, and that blue-collar sexual prowess would sometimes open doors otherwise closed; now, workers success-fully battle through the barricades because they're built better.

"Guys like you," a girl tells Tony Manero in *Staying Alive*, "aren't relationships, you're exercise." She doesn't know it, but she's paid him the supreme compliment, and she's put her finger on the bulbous secret of his success.

At Fred Segal's in the heart of Hollywood, the Lee Grant woman is fully outfitted in her *Flashdance* flash by the time her retirement-age husband appears and awards her a long, low wolf whistle. Kids in the same store, dressed in the same clothes, smile charitably. Two realities are dovetailing. Kids hungry for success are witnessing the plight of aged fans nostalgic for aged movie myths. *Staying Alive* and *Flashdance* maintain that the firm of mind and young of body will reach heaven on earth; a corollary could be that the young of mind and firm of body can join up, too. For kids, the clothes reproduce the hot looks of hot movies; for the aged and successful fans, they are a talisman of the one thing they don't have: youth.

The husband of the Lee Grant woman is wearing a moulded German black leather jacket that seems vaguely familiar. It is. It's a duplicate of the jacket worn by Tony Manero and it's available right down the street at the Leather Locker. Making their way to their Rolls in their slum duds, the two wealthy groupies from Beverly Hills are almost too cute to be real and too bizarre to be true – a couple of aged babes in fantasyland, staying alive.

August 12, 1983

❖

The Lonely Lady

Directed by Peter Sasdy
Written by John Kershaw and Shawn Randall
Starring Pia Zadora

In Harold Robbins' *The Lonely Lady*, a movie about Hollywood, "actress" Pia Zadora, the stacked Munchkin with the rich husband, reads Sylvia Plath's *The Bell Jar*, loses her virginity to a garden hose, is rescued by a rich screenwriter in a Rolls-Royce, is made pregnant by a matinee idol, gets the brush-off, gets an abortion, is romanced by an Italian nightclub owner, is turned over to a Sapphic woman who likes to smooch and a fat man who likes to watch, has a best friend who's gay, gets hooked on drugs and booze and wicked sex, has a nervous breakdown, is sent to a mental institution, gets out, sells a script, is turned over by her gay friend to a lesbian who likes hot tubs, wins an Oscar – for screenwriting – and in her acceptance speech says, "I don't suppose I'm the only one who had to —— her way to the top."

October 3, 1983

❖

Testament

Directed by Lynne Littman
Written by John Sacret Young
Starring Jane Alexander

"Your children are not dead. They are just waiting until the world deserves them." – *The Pied Piper*

No shots of poisonous mushroom clouds, no gore, no hysteria: *Testament*, one of the most shattering movies ever made about mankind's rush toward oblivion, doesn't need the props of science-fiction or horror to make its point. This version of the aftermath of Armageddon is simple, and almost artless, and entirely believable, and utterly unforgettable.

One morning, a family in a bedroom community of San Francisco (the film was shot in Sierre Madre, Calif.) awakens. The mother, Carol (Jane Alexander), goes about the business of making breakfast while the father, Tom (William Devane), takes to the hills with his eldest son, Brad (Ross Harris), on a bicycle – Tom is obviously pushing Brad into an area of athletic activity the boy is bored with and intimidated by. Back at the house, the youngest son, Scottie (Lukas

Haas), appears to have been absorbed into the intricate circuits of his electronic equipment – he's a neurotic High Tech introvert. The daughter, Mary Liz (Roxana Zal), is at a difficult age – she's no longer a girl and not yet a woman.

Tom goes to work. Carol settles down for a few seconds to watch television. A bright light fills the room and in five seconds flat the world turns inside out. Carol rushes into the street to be greeted by other people on the block. The electricity is gone. There are no phone lines. San Francisco has been incinerated. What next?

The rest of *Testament*, derived from Carol Amen's short story, "The Last Testament," answers the question steadily and unblinkingly. Scottie, devastated by loss, buries his stuffed toys in the cemetery. "Tell it to go away," he orders his anguished mother, who whispers disconsolately, "I can't." There are attempts to keep civilization alive and, in one especially wrenching sequence, the children of the neighbourhood perform "The Pied Piper," a play that was in rehearsal when the holocaust walked in.

Director Lynne Littman, who has dedicated the movie to her family, has allowed great latitude to her actors – they are exceptional – and has unflinchingly done what we have been told is impossible: she has imagined the unimaginable. *Testament* is a terrifying movie, a whimper on the cusp of the end of time.

November 4, 1983

Star 80

Written and directed by Bob Fosse
Starring Mariel Hemingway and Eric Roberts

When Paul Snider met Dorothy Stratten at a Vancouver Dairy Queen in 1978, she'd been nowhere and done nothing. Two years later, she was a *Playboy* centrefold and the star of a real Hollywood movie, *They*

All Laughed, directed by Peter Bogdanovich. While *Playboy*'s publisher, Hugh Hefner, was "only" fond of her – in a paternal way, he said – Bogdanovich was madly in love. For Dorothy Stratten, the American dream was high-noon reality: she was famous, she was getting rich, she looked like a million. The sky looked like the limit.

But as Bob Fosse (*Cabaret*) illustrates unforgettably in his gruelling, breathtakingly intense exploration, *Star 80*, the dream metamorphosed fatally into a nightmare when Dorothy tried to dump the man who made it possible. Paul Snider (Eric Roberts) was a classless lounge lizard hustler smart enough to know a good thing when he saw it and clever enough to exploit it with a relentlessness that may have had something to do with love. At his behest, Dorothy (Mariel Hemingway) took her clothes off, first for him and then for the camera. In so doing, she entered a world she'd barely imagined, let alone dreamed of inhabiting. She liked it. When she wanted to make it her own, her lover killed her.

Fosse begins *Star 80* with mock *Playboy* stills of Hemingway as Dorothy and then cuts into and out of the murder with face-slapping regularity. (The cuts are heralded by melodramatic music recalling Bernard Herrmann's work for Hitchcock and Martin Scorsese.) In the most imaginative performance any actor has given this year, a performance to rank with the best of Brando and De Niro, Eric Roberts brings to unerring low-life an infantile narcissist (he adjusts his genitals in front of the mirror for maximum effect) who believes everything he reads, which isn't much. He believes, as he tells Dorothy's mother (Carroll Baker), that he and Dorothy "could be somebody. People would treat us the special way they treat stars." His dreams are simple: fast cars, girls and fame. The dreams are simple. The man is not.

His ticket to ride is a compliant hourglass figure of apple-cheeked beauty, a guileless creamy creature who can say in interviews that at *Playboy* "they go for art, perfect art," and believe it. Hemingway is radiant in the role. The transformation she has effected on her Minnie Mouse voice – it now has timbre, rather than squeak – is much more startling than the more famous augmentation of her breasts. Her

Dorothy is a pretty plaything, a bosomy babe in a toyland for jaded adults; under it all, she is a sweet girl who dies on the verge of becoming a woman.

Packed off to the *Playboy* mansion by Snider, she phones home flabbergasted: "They're going to give me $10,000 to have my picture taken!" Of Hefner (impersonated with exactly the right sleazy gentility by Cliff Robertson), she exults, "Oh, Paul, he's wonderful, like a father or something!" When Hefner finally meets Snider, he tells Dorothy her beau is bad news. "What's wrong with him?" she wants to know. Hefner blurts his assessment: "Well, he's got the personality of a pimp." Dorothy giggles, relieved: "Oh, Mr. Hefner, that's just the way he used to dress!"

Paul Snider shot Dorothy Stratten, raped her, and then put a shotgun in his face and blew his brains across the back wall. Although Fosse has been able to base most of *Star 80* on interviews conducted by Teresa Carpenter for her Pulitzer Prize-winning *Village Voice* account, the final twenty minutes of the movie, the agonizing and deadly confrontation between Dorothy and Snider, are necessarily fictional. Fosse carries the movie to its conclusion steadily and superlatively, with a directness that is devastating and with a depth of insight that ameliorates, if only slightly, the ghastliness of the carefully choreographed images.

In the end, *Star 80* raises more questions – about the nature of the American class structure, the media, commercialized sex and the problems between men and woman – than any one movie or minor deity could possibly answer. The same questions arose during the coverage of the Dorothy Stratten case, and they weren't answered then, either. Good for Fosse. The one sin *Star 80* cannot be accused of is reductionism. People anxious to exploit the picture to grind the axes of narrow ideologies are going to find the going tough.

And *Star 80* does transcend the sordid specifics with a subtle suggestion: throughout the film there is a hint, though it is no more than that, that in the story of Dorothy Stratten and Paul Snider is to be found the malevolent flower of the pathological seed that resides in all relationships. What *Richard III* is to rulers, Paul and Dorothy are to lovers. Their tragic fate is classic, in the Shakespearean sense, and it is compelling not because the events are outlandish and bizarre but because the psychology leading to the events is shockingly familiar and inescapably mundane. "Why would Fosse want to make this?" was the most often-asked question at the conclusion of a recent screening, followed by, "Some of the creeps are famous, but otherwise there's nothing special about them." Exactly.

November 10, 1983

The Wars

Directed by Robin Phillips
Written by Timothy Findley
Starring Brent Carver, Jackie Burroughs and Martha Henry

Marinated in melancholy and steeped in psychological and political scepticism, the immensely intelligent Robin Phillips film of Timothy Findley's equally intelligent novel, *The Wars*, begins what should be a long, exciting process of reclaiming the Canadian past. Set in 1914, this is one of the few movies to present the nation's forebears as something other than toque-bearing, plaid-coated, maple-sugared hams, and it may be the only major feature film to have examined in depth the Rosedale ruling class.

What is shocking about *The Wars* is that it wasn't made sooner. In terms of style and unapologetic self-absorption, it's the first Australian-Canadian film, arriving nearly a decade after the Aussies resolved to please and educate and enlighten themselves rather than cater to the phantom ciphers of the "international market."

Findley's cinematic transcription of his novel has inevitably lost texture – where the book was a kaleidoscope of complexity, the film is an inventory of incident. But what incident! In recounting the short and none too happy life of the hero, Robert Ross, the filmmakers are able to survey a panorama of colonial Canadian activity, ranging from the dark drawing rooms of the new world to the pretentious estates of the British gentry to the urine-drenched trenches of the frontlines. The survey is conducted with a moody reserve and an esthetic precision that sometimes suggests an Ingmar Bergman remake of *All Quiet on the Western Front*. That's a compliment.

The domestic sojourns in Toronto introduce Robert (Brent Carver), a soft and aimless boy – a nascent homosexual, in all likelihood, who might have reached happiness had he reached a life beyond confusion; Robert's sister Roweena (Ann-Marie MacDonald), physically maimed beyond repair; Robert's *grande dame* mother (Martha Henry), an alcoholic spiritually sodden beyond salvation; Robert's father (William Hutt), spiritually absent beyond reach; and the family's governess, Miss Davenport (Jackie Burroughs), a retainer whose eyes, black and sweet like fine chocolate truffles, have viewed endless upper-class conflicts beyond her ken. Each is a victim of the genteel repression *The Wars* defines as a national characteristic of the English-Canadian upper class.

There are great scenes showcasing great acting, and the greatest is Mrs. Ross' visit with her son in the family's arena-sized green bathroom. "A mother's prerogative, to visit the wounded," she says, the voluptuous exhalation of her cigarette smoke the last vestige of sensuality she permits herself. The interlude follows a death in the family; Mrs. Ross is irrationally incensed with her son, but she is also disturbed by their estrangement. And we can see, as she casts an agonized but appreciative eye over his body, that she is attracted to him on levels of which she is thoroughly ignorant. When the attraction threatens to reach consciousness, her defensive alter ago, the ice queen, intervenes. "We're all cut off with a knife at birth and left to the mercy of strangers," she hisses.

Almost as memorable is a scene in which Mrs. Ross furiously exits from a church one Sunday morning, the feathers of her black hat tall and stiff and imperious, like the smokestacks of a battleship. Trailed by Miss Davenport, bouncing a comically stuffed bird on her uncomprehending head, Mrs. Ross is disconsolate: "What does it mean to kill your children and then go in there and sing about it?" To numb the pain, she fingers a discreet flask. Meanwhile, a world away, her son is writing letters that express, but barely, his own increasing disillusion with the meaning of manhood.

Phillips is an awesomely gifted director of actors (these actors are awesomely gifted) but he does not have enough experience behind the camera to impart to sequences taking place far from the human face the cinematic three-dimensionality that comes naturally to, say, Steven Spielberg. More often than not, the spatial strategies in *The Wars* are static or lateral, and even intricate camera movements result in an oddly flattened *mise-en-scène* (the cinematography is competent – just). What we see of the actual war is neither plastic nor kinetic; it resembles a mural, or a diorama, and if the effect is intentional, it evokes little.

This sort of thing is minor, a shortcoming easily rectified with experience, but it does take its toll in the second half of the picture, when the audience should be overwhelmed by the affront to the senses that war represents. Instead, the knowledge is reached vicariously, through Brent Carver's finely shaded performance (a performance lacking only the indefinable magic that transforms actors into stars – the camera likes Carver, but it doesn't love him) and through the soundtrack's dextrous mix of martial songs, choral arrangements and the piano of the late Glenn Gould.

An inordinate amount of expectation has been attached to this film, and it is a pleasure to be able to report that it carries most of it without strain. Flaws aside, *The Wars* is a historically important event and, like so many important historical events of late, it bruises the heart.

November 11, 1983

❖

Terms of Endearment

Written and directed by James L. Brooks
Starring Jack Nicholson, Shirley MacLaine and Debra Winger

You may want to see *Terms of Endearment* right away; if you don't, you're going to have to hear about it second-hand from every third person you meet, because there's every chance this high, wide and handsome movie is going to turn out to be the adult hit of the year. It should. Compared already to *Ordinary People* and *Kramer vs. Kramer* – the comparison doesn't begin to do it justice – *Terms of Endearment* is the rare commercial picture that sets audiences to laughing hysterically and crying unashamedly, sometimes within consecutive seconds, and then shoos them out of the theatre in contented emotional exhaustion.

Deftly adapted by writer-director James L. Brooks from Larry McMurtry's sprawling novel, the film is in sharp contrast to the clinical *Kramer* and the antiseptic *Ordinary People* in that it is blessedly free of condescension, or thesis and antithesis; the characters are symbols only of themselves. Because they do not pretend to be universal, they are paradoxically more familiar than, say, the chic boutique clones of *The Big Chill*. Nobody has a neighbour like Garrett Breedlove (Jack Nicholson), the ex-astronaut who lives next door to *Terms of Endearment*'s *grande dame* heroine, Aurora Greenway (Shirley MacLaine). But before the picture is over, Garrett Breedlove has become a friend of the viewer's family.

The thirty years covered by this shaggy movie whiz by with the dizzying, disorganized rapidity of life itself. Emma Greenway (Debra Winger) is reared in Houston by her mother Aurora, a matriarch without portfolio – but with a Bostonian background – who thinks herself majestically superior to the uncouth Texans seeking her favours. When Emma marries Flap Horton (Jeff Daniels), an English major, Aurora warns Emma the union "will ruin your life and make wretched your destiny." When Emma wants to know why, Aurora is characteristically frank: "You are not special enough to overcome a bad marriage." Emma stubbornly goes her own way and moves to Des Moines, where extramarital affairs and Flap's shallow egotism do indeed threaten the marriage, now complicated by children.

Back in Houston, Aurora is facing her fifth decade with contradictory desires: she's yearning but aloof, puritanical but sensual, an unsteady combination of the remote and available. Eventually, she descends from her lonely pedestal to take up with Garrett, whose NASA days are commemorated by trophies in his living room and whose post-NASA nights are commemorated by his paunch. During his cat-fight courtship with Aurora, *Terms of Endearment* reaches its comic climax; a slapstick drive along the Gulf Coast is high hilarity.

The time-honoured Hollywood axiom for mixing the serious and the comic decrees that the latter precede the former; get 'em laughing, then get 'em by the throat. (It is astonishing how few movies toy with the formula.) But when one of the characters in *Terms of Endearment* develops cancer, the filmmakers knock Hollywood's homily on its ear by refusing to alter the picture's bubbly humanism – there is comedy in cancer, and *Terms of Endearment* finds it, along with the tears. The film's tactic throughout is to define a situation seriously and then to rescue the audience from depression via an unexpected and even shocking comic turn.

The method is intrinsic to Larry McMurtry's novel and to much of the rest of his work (*The Last Picture Show, Cadillac Jack, The Desert Rose*) because it is intrinsic to the westerners he invariably writes about, people for whom hard times call forth behaviour that would be tabbed tasteless and excessive in the east. Out west, bawdiness is sometimes next to godliness.

Shirley MacLaine has said that Aurora Greenway is "the best part I've ever had" and it's the best thing she's ever done: waist cinched by an enormous silver concha belt, hair stiffened by lacquer, breasts protected by a Wagnerian bra, Aurora is an independent woman in bondage to the illusion of self-sufficiency. MacLaine unerringly finds her vulnerability and exposes it, tremblingly, to the camera. Her makeup gone and her world in momentary ruins, Aurora is pitiable but not pathetic. It's a terrific performance.

As Emma, Debra Winger is a non-neurotic, conventionalized Elizabeth Ashley – the open, healthy optimism she has radiated in every role, along with her practically feverish love of performing, have made it possible for her to triumph over an alarmingly primitive and transparent technique (she does double takes in this movie that would embarrass Lucille Ball). The terms Emma places on giving and receiving endearment are generous to a fault, as they always have been for McMurtry's women (his first sketch of this character was in the novel *Leaving Cheyenne*; in the movie version, *Lovin' Molly*, she was played by Blythe Danner). McMurtry women are in the Tennessee Williams tradition, but they bear roughly the same relationship to Williams' women that Debra Winger's screen persona bears to Elizabeth Ashley's: they are no less sensual and no less loved, but they are younger, sturdier, more self-reliant, and they have sunnier and less sexist futures.

In the one role invented for the film, that of the astronaut, Jack Nicholson seduces the audience with the charisma that frequently makes his supporting appearances (the attorney in *Easy Rider*, Eugene O'Neill in *Reds*) more engaging than his full-scale portrayals. His work is supplemented by the artistry of Jeff Daniels as the understandable if unsympathetic Flap; John Lithgow as a Des Moines bank manager involved with Emma; Lisa Hart Carroll as Emma's best friend; and several child actors. The film's only major failing is the cinematography by Andrzej Bartkowiak, whose name on a movie – he shot *The Verdict, Deathtrap* and *Daniel* – has become synonymous with grainy gloom. The early scenes of *Terms of Endearment* are supposedly filmed through the mists of memory. In Bartkowiak's photography, the mists never lift.

November 23, 1983   151

❖

The Dresser

Directed by Peter Yates
Written by Ronald Harwood
Starring Albert Finney and Tom Courtenay

As the aged, curmudgeonly, emotionally infantile Shakespearean actor known only as Sir in Peter Yates' film *The Dresser*, Albert Finney plays the sort of artist who really ought to have died young, before he outlived his legend. And he gives the sort of performance that nowadays exists almost exclusively in legend – the contemporary emphasis on naturalistic acting has robbed film and theatre of portrayals that exult in artificiality and the grand gesture, portrayals that permit actors to leer at the audience happily as they unabashedly chew pieces of scenery in bovine contentment. Finney gives the most flamboyant, delightfully theatrical male performance of the year in *The Dresser*, but in fairness to his competition it should be noted that he has been granted the most flamboyant, delightfully theatrical role of the year, a role that rarely gets bogged down in alienating distractions like psychology and believability.

The subject of *The Dresser*, expansively adapted by Ronald Harwood from his claustrophobic play – the adaptation affords Peter Yates a splendid opportunity to tour a picturesque war-torn England replete with British versions of the memorable faces of Walker Evans' *Let Us Now Praise Famous Men* – is in the largest sense acting, and it is an ironic coincidence that it showcases two major performances, one that works and one that doesn't. As the valet ("dresser") who has travelled with Sir for sixteen years, Tom Courtenay's fussy, embittered queen, hands in constant buzzing flight, like worried hummingbirds, is technically impeccable, but entirely external. Those who have seen various incarnations of the play (Courtenay did it in New York, and there was a Canadian production in Vancouver) have reported that the title makes sense, but it seems a lame joke when attached to this very funny film, a film bracing in its exuberant embrace of theatrical hokum: because Finney is so strong and Courtenay is so weak,

Norman, the dresser, the ostensible centre of the play, is a mere gewgaw, an unstraight straight man to Sir and his flights of comic narcissistic fancy. Perhaps because he was too long on stage, Courtenay has found nothing to show the camera that could not be viewed in five minutes at the nearest watering hole catering to the flightily effeminate. (Maybe that's where Courtenay found the character.) In any case, Norman feels much more like an impersonation than anything Ed Harris does with John Glenn in *The Right Stuff*.

The only person Finney could be impersonating as Sir is Charles Laughton. Or the bronze majesty (so majestic it's nearly silly) of Rodin's *Balzac*. "I've been reduced to old men, cripples and nancy boys," Sir wails of his acting company, but Sir is in no great physical shape himself. In one of his rare moments of unsentimental self-awareness, he sees the writing on the theatrical wall: "I'm a spent force. My days are numbered." But when he numbers the days, he counts them with a roar, and his life's every quotidian detail is elevated self-importantly into high tragedy or low comedy. An encounter of extreme banality is reported by, "Now I know how Mr. Churchill will feel when he faces Josef Stalin," and instructions to a young actress consist of, "You must be prepared to sacrifice what most people call life." Sir is a wreck and he's so senile he can't plan more than five minutes in advance ("Two hundred and twenty-seven performances of *King Lear* and I can't remember the first line," he cries), but he has taken Dylan Thomas's advice and is raging like hell against the dying of the (spot)light.

It would be possible to record Sir's demise naturalistically, to illustrate what wartime England, so beautifully and so nostalgically photographed here by Kelvin Pike, really looked like, and to outline realistically the smallness and meanness of spirit written into Sir's character. It would be possible, in other words, for a film of *The Dresser* to live down to Courtenay's waspishly realistic Norman. But Finney is a marvellous theatrical actor (his skills have all but obliterated with staginess the roles he has been assigned in naturalistic films such as *Shoot the Moon*) who plays Sir as only a terrific actor could play him, as a protean and stylized metaphor for the race's desire to entertain itself. His sentimentality pulls out the stops, his comedy runs to slapstick and back, and his bitchiness ("I saw his Lear," he says of another actor. "I was pleasantly disappointed") is to Norman's nastiness as the wit of Oscar Wilde is to the wisdom of Richard Simmons.

Toward the end of the film, we watch a few minutes of *Lear*. In Finney's delineation of Sir performing the part, there is a glimpse of greatness, a greatness that provides ballast to this movie's wonderfully wayward, wind-tossed fluff: there is a farcical – but nonetheless sad and truthful – glimpse of the monsters we make of the talented, and of the monsters they make of themselves. Wilde said that people should confine themselves to appearances because their real natures were too soon found out. Most actors do confine themselves to appearances, and call it realism. In *The Dresser*, Finney arrives at truth by exploding appearances. Sir's real nature is found out by artifice, a paradox that would have pleased Wilde, the man who fervently believed, as any theatrical artist must, that the real world is profoundly artificial.

December 2, 1983

Silkwood

Directed by Mike Nichols
Written by Nora Ephron and Alice Arlen
Starring Meryl Streep, Kurt Russell and Cher

The actress: in *Silkwood*, the movie biography of Karen Silkwood, believed to have been murdered in 1974 when she was preparing to blow the whistle on what she saw as serious safety infractions at a Kerr-McGee nuclear plant in Oklahoma, Meryl Streep does something she hasn't done for a while now – she portrays an American woman – and she's mighty fine at it. She reminds you that before she became La Streep, diva of dialects, in *The French Lieutenant's Woman* and *Sophie's Choice*, she had offered appealing, unmannered performances in The *Deer Hunter* and *Kramer vs. Kramer*. But *Silkwood* is easily her most admirable outing: this is the first time she has been completely satisfying in a lead. And this is the first time Kate Nelligan couldn't have done it better.

The movie: as invisibly directed by Mike Nichols, *Silkwood* is a small-scale, *Norma Rae*-ish political statement that is not quite as political as it pretends to be, probably because Nichols' preference is for behaviour rather than beliefs – you can feel the film's reluctance to return to the plutonium plant, to the business of *Silkwood*, when it means leaving the laconically comic shanty where Karen, a manic Okie who might have been invented by novelist Tom Robbins, lives in a turbulent ménage with her mechanic boyfriend Drew (Kurt Russell), her severely plain housemate Dolly (Cher, who has become a glorious actress) and that housemate's exceedingly odd and far from plain girlfriend Angela (Diana Scarwid), a beautician who "puts lipstick on stiffs." Nichols and his screenwriters, Nora Ephron and Alice Arlen, adore these people, and their love shines through every overture of affection, every belligerent battle, and every drop of spilled milk.

Comparisons to *Norma Rae* are inevitable in that Karen, a sleep-walker in her own life, experiences a raised political consciousness – she joins and becomes instrumental to a union – and even has an affair with a Jewish union organizer (Ron Silver), an affair that recalls Sally Field's liaison with Ron Liebman in *Norma Rae*; Karen's boyfriend, Drew, meanwhile objects to the time Karen devotes to her political activities. He and Beau Bridges, Norma Rae's hubby, would have a lot to talk about.

But if *Norma Rae* could have been made in almost any decade (the closing tune, "Bless the Child of the Working Man," might have been sung by Paul Robeson forty years ago), *Silkwood* is determinedly a product of the hard-headed, spare-nothing eighties. The working man, theoretically sympathetic *en masse*, is not glamorized individually, and the film is sharp about the cultural and moral realities of blue-collar life in the Southwest – one of Karen's co-workers, Thelma

(Sudie Bond), confides that her daughter, a cancer victim, is being made to die in the hospital "next to a coloured person." In the factory (the holocaust is a nine to five, assembly-line job) the filmmakers are careful to delineate the full range of positions possible to employees, from the intransigent rebellion embodied in Karen's protests to the slavish adherence to company policy represented by her superior, Winston (Craig T. Nelson). The movie is populist but not mindless, anti-élitist but not anti-intellectual.

It departs even further from standard progressive melodramas by raising the stakes. In traditional leftist movies, bosses oppressed and endangered only their own workers; here, corporate shoddiness can lead to Armageddon. The film subtly suggests that Karen was "accidentally" exposed to radiation leaks, a process workers at the plant term with brutal accuracy "getting cooked." (Knowledge of the Silkwood case is assumed and because the film is shot through the heroine's eyes, the audience is never privy to the wealth of material that became public after her death.) Karen Silkwood, the picture whispers, knew too much and may have been killed because of it. But while the picture treads delicately – it intermittently feels as if it had been written by libel lawyers – the imprints taken by its tiny steps stick.

There are misses. The music by Georges Delerue is organized around an Uncle Remus banjo (the cast talks about Willie Nelson; why don't they play him, or the obstreperous Hank Williams Jr.?) and several scenes – a lullaby on a porch swing, for example – are unnecessarily protracted. But other potentially wild swings – deep focus, a self-effacing camera, Streep's a cappella rendition of "Amazing Grace" – hit the target smoothly and soundly. Silkwood is a friendly, kooky and caring film, about a courageous, friendly, kooky and caring woman, a rough-neck, red-neck, chain-smoking cowgirl saint. Saint Joan of the Honky Tonk.

December 9, 1983

❖

La Balance

Written and directed by Bob Swaim
Starring Nathalie Baye and Philippe Leotard

Thanks to the wisdom bestowed through hindsight, it is easy to see why *La Balance* (the title is slang for informer or snitch) became a hit in France and why it is doing well in North America: American expatriate director Bob Swaim, thirty-nine, has blended the crisp violence of Clint Eastwood's *Dirty Harry* with the moral uncertainties of French *policiers* and the lurid low-life romanticism so many Americans find in Paris (or want to find). It's a triple-threat combo, an explosive mixture that makes for one of the fastest, most entertaining melodramas around, and Swaim's dexterity with the camera makes everything old seem new again. Almost.

By European standards, *La Balance*, outfitted with a bluesy, acidic, Algerian-influenced score and a title tune belted by Eleonore Lytton, the Gallic Janis Joplin, whistles by like a bullet, but Swaim takes his time in unexpected ways. The two stars, Nathalie Baye, as the whore Nicole, and Philippe Leotard, as her pimp, Dede, don't show up for half an hour; the long first movement of the movie is given over to an intricate exploration of a Serpico-like undercover cop squad. These guys might be a different species from the thickly-accented *gendarmes* so helpful in American musicals and so inept in American comedies – they are hip, fast-talking kids, the rock 'n' roll arm of law enforcement, and their finger-snapping repartee brands them as dramatic descendants of the surgeons in Robert Altman's *M*A*S*H* – punchlines under pressure – instead of the stolid, sadistic burghers of the Los Angeles Police Department according to Joseph Wambaugh.

Although *La Balance* is sympathetic to the dilemmas faced by its quasi-counterculture cops (they are the people they warned themselves against, back in '68), it does not always approve of the tactics they employ, a fine but important line the movie treads with the misleading effortlessness of an accomplished tightrope walker. To balance

La Balance, Swaim relies on the considerable charms of Baye and Leotard, and they arrive just as the film is in danger of becoming a doting *billet doux* to the boys in blue.

Nicole is a thoughtful, resourceful and efficient hooker going about her lucrative business when she is leaned on by the cops. They want her to persuade her pimp and lover, Dede, to snitch on the activities of a drug smuggler, Massina (Maurice Ronet, arguably the best-known face with the least-known name in all of French cinema), but Nicole has her own fiercely defended code of honour and refuses. "I'm a whore, not a tramp," she snaps. The cops pay no attention and proceed vigorously – viciously – to blackmail both her and Dede. The bulk of the picture contrasts the single-minded and sometimes disastrously incompetent undercover investigation with the effect collaborating has on the lives of these two petty criminals.

Swaim is slightly heavy-handed in his desire to get us to care for Nicole and Dede (does the sloe-eyed pimp have to sniff roses?) but he need not have worried: cast against type, the squeaky-clean Baye is a kinky revelation in skin-caressing sleaze, and Leotard is equipped with a wonderfully battered bulldog face, a physiognomy so photogenic in its decay its owner could be half the actor he is and still engage the audience's interest.

Swaim's script for the film was prepared in the wake of months of research with Paris's rock-on cops. The writing has the gritty texture of undeniable authenticity and the directing gleefully turns the esthetic screws: this is a smart, slick neon tour through the tough new Paris of Big Macs, cocaine and couscous. *La Balance* is like "Starsky and Hutch" transformed into something like art.

December 23, 1983

❖

Slapstick of Another Kind

Written and directed by Steven Paul
Starring Jerry Lewis and Madeline Kahn

It is from the novel by Kurt Vonnegut. *Slapstick*. It is called *Slapstick of Another Kind*. So it goes.

Jerry Lewis is in it. Madeline Kahn is in it. They play two parts. Each. Hi Ho.

The book was written in short sentences.
Like this.
With lots of colons.
Like: this.
With lots of paragraphs.
Like this.

The movie is done in short scenes. They are directed by Steven Paul. Written by him, too. He is twenty-five. He is young. But he is not a prodigy. He may have talent. But not here.

The book is about twins. Boy and girl. Extraterrestrials. "Mork and Mindy" with two Morks. And also about love and common decency. Love and common decency are not twins. Vonnegut says: "Love is where you find it. I think it is foolish to go looking for it, and I think it can often be poisonous." Vonnegut says: there should be less love and more common decency. For some reason, Laurel and Hardy get mixed up in this.

Vonnegut likes Laurel and Hardy. They might have been able to do something about this movie.

The book uses things Vonnegut has used before. The phrases "nation of two." "So be it." "Hi ho." "So it goes." Hi ho. So it goes. So be it.

The movie is about make-up. The make-up that gives Madeline Kahn and Jerry Lewis big heads and long legs: when they are playing the twins. The make-up that makes them pretty: when they are playing the parents of the twins. There is nothing they can do: no matter who they are playing. They try hard: no matter what they are doing. They have: common decency.

The movie is also about the Americans. Hard times have happened. There is no oil any more. Cars are run on chicken poop. Air Force One is run on chicken poop. Jim Backus is the President. The President is run on chicken poop.

The movie is also about the Chinese. The Chinese are two inches high. They come to America in a small spaceship that looks like a fortune cookie. They want the secret of gravity. The twins discover it. The twins are geniuses. When the twins are together, their big heads throb. Their big heads pulsate. Their big heads emit coloured special effects. The big heads think Big Thoughts. They are Hot Stuff.

This is all true.

This movie is not about love and decency. This movie is about other movies. Most of all it is about: *Close Encounters of the Third Kind.* It is not funny. Ever. There is a word for this. No. Two words for this: (1) rip, (2) off.

March 17, 1984

❖

Die Erben (The Inheritors)

Written and directed by Walter Bannert
Starring Nikolas Vogel

In American films, kids deprived of love at home and discipline at school turn to rock and roll, vandalism and sex on the beach. Mistreated children in French films turn to Marx and fast food. Scandinavian children kill themselves. German children buy heroin. And Austrian children? Austrian children, according to the evidence in *Die Erben* (*The Inheritors*), a controversial film screened at the Cannes Film Festival as part of the Director's Fortnight series, turn to Nazism. *The Inheritors* is a youth-in-revolt movie with a difference: it makes the skin of everyone who sees it crawl.

Its forty-year-old director, Walter Bannert, investigated the neo-Nazi movement in Austria by gaining the trust of the leaders of the ultra-right-wing National Unity Party. He said he was first attracted to the idea out of revenge – in 1979, he was sitting in a restaurant frequented by leftists when a group of neo-Nazis, dressed in their semiofficial uniform of leather jackets and ties, berets and boots, entered and beat up the clientele. (The scene appears in the movie.)

Bannert approached the party and told its leaders he was interested in making "an objective documentary" about the movement. He was taken into confidence and found a strange, paramilitary world devoted to the deification of the memory of Adolf Hitler and to the protection of the Aryan people against debilitating influences – Jews, immigrant workers, leftists and homosexuals. "The family," says the neo-Nazi leader in the film, "is the basic unit of society. It is the family we seek to protect and preserve."

Bannert was forced to dismiss the idea of a documentary – too much of the truth of the movement, he felt, would be hidden by its leaders from the camera. The official neo-Nazi attitude toward the death camps, for instance, is that they were merely prisoner of war installations. The neo-Nazi leader in the movie even claims that

161

Eichmann was relocating Jews purely as a means of giving them their own country, "out of Europe." But in private, the Holocaust is celebrated and in one of the film's particularly horrifying sequences, an elderly Nazi, entertaining fifteen- and sixteen-year-old converts, points proudly to a lamp giving off a soft yellow glow and smiles, "This lampshade is very rare, very beautiful and very rare. From Auschwitz. This is of skin, of a Jew." He pauses as the boys stare speechlessly at the obscenity. "It is so fine, this skin," he continues, "so unmarked, and you can see here the identification number has few digits. It must have been of a beautiful young girl. Or a child."

After gathering similar material, Bannert crafted a script that compressed his years of research and hired performers to enact the scenes he had observed. He invented nothing, he said a few days ago. "I did not need to. The truth is enough." When the film opened last year in Vienna, the neo-Nazis arrived on opening night and disrupted the showing with screams of "lies, lies" as the picture progressed. A discussion that was to have been held afterward was cancelled because of the heckling. Other screenings in West Germany and Austria were identically besieged and just four months ago a theatre in Mannheim exhibiting the picture was burned down in the middle of the night.

Although the response to *The Inheritors* in Cannes has been extremely positive, and although the picture has achieved American distribution, and although the insights it sheds on some of what is happening in Europe right now are of an importance that would be difficult to underestimate, Canadian distributors are so far steering clear of the film for one reason: the Ontario Board of Censors. There is a good chance the board would ban the film, were it to be submitted, and there is no chance it would pass uncut.

The problem, as usual, is juvenile sex. The protagonist of *The Inheritors*, called Thomas, is played by Nikolas Vogel, who was fifteen when Bannert shot the picture, and the performers who play his cohorts, male and female, are equally young, which is, of course, part of the picture's point, and part of its horror. Thomas's father in the film, Bannert said, "is a successful social climber who cannot understand that his son is missing. The atmosphere in the family is so frosty the younger brother, sensitive and gentle, commits suicide." Thomas's best friend, transformed by neo-Nazi training from an obstreperous rebel to a coldly efficient killer – the same thing happens to Thomas – is reared in a family that is a psychopathological sideshow: the father is a drunk who beats the mother and commits incest with the daughter.

The sexual experimentation undertaken by Thomas and Charly is depicted with what Gerald Peary, writing about the movie for the *Los Angeles Times* from the Berlin Film Festival in February, termed "post-Bertolucci [director of *Last Tango in Paris*] explicitness," and it is an explicitness the Ontario censor board has never allowed – in one scene, for example, Thomas, dressed only in his Nazi hat and a black belt, persuades the family's domestic to have sex with him while he watches himself approvingly in a mirror.

Bannert's analysis of the attractions of the neo-Nazi movement to children who are products of difficult economic times and self-involved parents is as exact as it is frightening. Schoolteachers turn away from Thomas as soon as his first tentative involvement with the neo-Nazis is discovered and his friends deride him unmercifully. Instead of aiding him, they ostracize him, and he later tells a TV crew that he has found within the party the first true camaraderie he has ever known.

The charms of the party to kids such as Thomas and Charly are seductive, which is the reason the sexual sequences are both explicit and idyllic, and Bannert does not shrink from viewing those charms through the eyes of his two major characters. (The New York film distributor Ira Deutschmann found the film to be of unimpeachable intentions and expertly made, but he commented, "You see just how seductive it is and it scared the hell out of me to think of young kids all over Europe watching this and thinking it looks great.") The picture is *in toto* an eerie artifact, an object lesson in what can happen to the innate romanticism of adolescence if it is thwarted and then manipulated. At the neo-Nazi Jugend Club, a kind of fascist YMCA, Thomas and Charly absorb ideology masked by affection, and they embark on a series of raids – the wreaking of havoc at the leftist club, the bombing of a statue in memory of the Holocaust, the beatings of countless liberal enemies who have spoken out against the party – that seem to them no more than a series of missions impossible, like the adventures of the TV programs invariably droning in the background of their loveless living rooms.

North Americans with no direct experience of the kind of racism on view here are apt to find the picture unbelievable and perhaps to suspect it of exploitation, but the packed house of mostly French men and women at an afternoon showing in Cannes nodded gravely and knowingly as the descent of Charly and Thomas into the pit of ideological terrorism was outlined. The experience of watching the movie is unique, as if the "Tomorrow Belongs to Me" sequence in the musical *Cabaret*, the sequence in which all the beautiful young blond boy and girl Nazis display their good teeth and their swastikas for the camera, had been extended from five minutes to two hours.

"I am pleased but not surprised that Europeans everywhere have taken this seriously," Bannert remarked. "There are probably more fascists right now in England and France than in West Germany or Austria, you understand. Wherever they are, they are waiting, and if economic conditions get bad, if there is even worse unemployment among the young, I am afraid you will see everywhere the rise of strong fascist movements. Of course it can happen here again." *The Inheritors* is about people to whom it has happened already.

May 22, 1984

Marianne and Juliane

Written and directed by Margarethe von Trotta
Starring Barbara Sukowa and Jutta Lampe

Marianne and Juliane, which won first prize at the Venice Film Festival in 1981 under the original German title, *Die Bleierne Zeit* (Leaden Times), and first prize later the same year at the Chicago Film Festival under the title *The German Sisters*, is, whatever it chooses to call itself, a near masterpiece. The passage of three years has diminished its stature not an iota; what seemed merely timely in 1981 now seems in 1984 not only timely, but prescient. For example: long before Germaine Greer got there, writer-director Margarethe von Trotta was wondering where childbearing and maternal responsibility fit into the women's movement, and where the women's movement fit into the task of improving everything for everyone.

Von Trotta's framework for a hundred thoughts and a thousand questions is the sad but instructive real-life story of the Ensslin sisters, a story inexorably enlarged into a metaphor for post-war Germany and its "leaden times," its refusal, in the director's words, "not to admit feelings of guilt at all." The methodology is Proustian: von Trotta cuts with effortless clarity back and forth through the sisters' lives, from scenes of childhood (air raids under Hitler) and adolescence (a chilling vignette when the girls come face to face with the death camps in the form of a documentary screened in the classroom) to sequences in modern West Germany (where feminism and family are at first viewed as mutually exclusive).

(Von Trotta is the wife of Volker Schlöndorff, director of *The Tin Drum*, *Circle of Deceit*, and most recently, *Swann in Love*, from Proust's novel, *Swann's Way*.)

Christiane, to whom *Marianne and Juliane* is dedicated, was and is the elder Ensslin sister, and for a time worked at a progressive women's magazine, *Emma*. Gudrun, the younger sister, was rounded up with the Baader-Meinhof terrorist group, three of whose members, including Gudrun, died mysteriously in prison. Gudrun becomes Marianne in the movie and is played with a perfection that must be seen to be believed by Barbara Sukowa, who undergoes a complete psychic transformation, from dutiful daughter of a Protestant minister to haughty, intransigent terrorist. Sukowa was the star of Rainer Werner Fassbinder's *Lola* and was the doomed, innocent Mieze in his *Berlin Alexanderplatz* and, although she looks like that actress, she acts not at all like her: her own transformation is as total as her character's.

Equally arresting is Jutta Lampe as Juliane, the fictional name assigned to Christiane, the liberal journalist whose sibling rivalry with Marianne assumes political and philosophical dimensions as the sisters grow older. The film's fulcrum is the ambivalent relationship between the two, dramatized with extraordinary immediacy in the confrontations that take place in the visiting rooms of the two prisons where Marianne is incarcerated.

Marianne argues that in becoming a terrorist and in having given up all pretence of bourgeois existence, including the care of her son, Jan, she has expunged her past and has discharged a social responsibility higher than slavish adherence to corrupt codes of conduct; she is confident history will justify her. Juliane, while admitting the justice of many of Marianne's criticisms, maintains that both sisters are trapped in their personal and national histories, and that no positive steps to freedom can be taken until the size of their cell has been surveyed.

Von Trotta sympathizes with both. She passionately communicates Marianne's outrage at the way things are, but she shares Juliane's concern with understanding the past so as to illuminate the present. (And to avoid the excesses of self-righteousness: when Juliane screams that thirty years earlier Marianne might have been a Nazi, von Trotta does nothing to signal disagreement.) *Marianne and Juliane* is a document that struggles to come to terms with an impossible past in a barely feasible present, and its director appears to realize that her film, like its heroines, is trapped by history, which is why she avoids pretending to be definitive – either about the sisters, or about the agonies of the nation she has presumed to concretize in their story. "I'll tell you all I know," Juliane says to Marianne's son when he asks about his mom, "but it's not everything." *Marianne and Juliane* is not everything, either, but it's more than any reasonable filmgoer might expect. If von Trotta finds few causes for optimism, she must know that the existence of her own movie is one of them.

June 29, 1984

❖

Sheena, Queen of the Jungle

Directed by John Guillermin
Written by David Newman and Lorenzo Semple Jr.
Starring Tanya Roberts

In the depths of darkest Africa, two American scientist-explorers killed in a cave-in leave behind a little blonde girl in her underpants. "A golden god child!" cries the local wise woman, who goes by the handle of Shaman, and who informs her incredulous tribesfolk that the orphaned tyke is going to grow up and save them from evil outsiders. Prophecy, says Shaman, says so.

It comes to pass that the little blonde one grows straight and strong and bosomy on the African veldt and comes to be called Sheena, Queen of the Jungle, and comes to be played by Tanya Roberts, the last angel begat by Charlie unto the tube. From Shaman, Sheena learns all things African – how to greet and call the pink flamingo, how to converse with (and order about) the lion, the elephant and the rhinoceros, and last but certainly not least, how to apply make-up to look like that greatest of all golden god children, Marilyn of Monroe.

It is only fitting that Sheena should learn all manner of beauty aids and aerobic skills and sartorial tips from Shaman, for Shaman is played by Princess Elizabeth of Toro, once a lawyer, once a model, once Minister of Foreign Affairs for Idi Amin. "Her diplomatic career ended, however," saith the *Sheena* press kit, "when she refused Uganda President Amin's proposal of marriage and she took exile in Kenya." A wise woman, indeed.

As Sheena grows in amplitude and pulchritude, there are evil machinations in the cities to the South. The tribe to which Sheena is attached roams across valuable land, the dust of which is miraculous even unto the curing of cancer, and the evil men of the South would seek to conquer that land and retain the dust of that good earth. One of the evil men is, in fact, an evil woman, an evil black woman, wife of the evil black King Jabalani (Clifton Jones), who is brother to the even more evil Prince Otwani (Trevor Jones), a sports hero who would be king now that his career in professional football is kaput.

The evil black woman, Princess Zanda (France Zobda), teams up with the evil Prince Otwani to kill the less evil and therefore more reprehensible King Jabalani, the better to conquer and market the magic dust of the North. "I am the most wicked woman in Tigora," exults Princess Zanda, clicking her false fingernails together, and giving even the legendary Joan of Collins a run for her rhinestones as Wickedest Bitch on This or Any Other Earth.

In the meantime, two American journalists, a thin and sexy one, Vic Casey (Ted Wass), and a fat and funny one, Fletcher (Donovan Scott), catch a glimpse of Sheena swinging her T & A through the trees. (Fat 'n' funny is a bit much, but thin 'n' sexy's Wass is an expert comic leading guy who could've given Kathleen Turner a run for her talent in the Michael Douglas part in *Romancing the Stone*.) "Back when we played doctor, that's what we called a girl! A blonde!" So says fat 'n' funny, but it is thin 'n' sexy who later smooches up Sheena, Q. of the J., from her callused toes to the tips of her burnt umber eyeliner, and causes her to sigh wonderingly as she rubs her raspberry Elizabeth of Toro lip gloss: "Mouths we were given to eat with, why did you touch yours to mine?" Forsooth she finds out forthwith and becomes Sheena, Siren of the Jungle, Slutress of the Bush, and in her sexualized euphoria is able to save her people merely by putting hand to head and ordering about three and a half million flamingos, a dozen rhinos, a scattering of elephants and a collection of chattering chimpanzees to attack the minions of wickedness that up from the South come, in uniforms, driving Land Rovers, throwing hand grenades and bad acting hither and thither. But she is not able, magnificent creature that she is, rustic and wild centrefold though she may be, to summon all the king's horses and all the king's men to put her movie together again.

August 10, 1984

❖

The Woman in Red

Written and directed by Gene Wilder
Starring Gene Wilder

Twenty questions to ask while watching *The Woman in Red* (written, directed by and starring Gene Wilder), a comedy that is much less painful than a walk in the summer heat, but not quite as pleasant as a swim in a cool pool:

1. Why is Gene Wilder, who plays a philandering husband living in San Francisco, wearing so much eyeliner?

2. Why is Stevie Wonder singing mushy love duets with Dionne Warwick on the soundtrack, when the movie is full of middle-aged guys cheating on their wives?

3. Why is Stevie Wonder turning into Neil Diamond?

4. Why has Dionne Warwick turned into Dusty Springfield?

5. Why has Judith Ivey, who gets such good reviews on Broadway and who plays Wilder's wife, been wasted by Hollywood?

6. Why has Gilda Radner, who's the funniest thing in *The Woman in Red*, been made to look like a particularly unattractive Nancy Walker (Rhoda's mummy)?

7. Why has Gilda Radner been given a role smaller than a chick pea?

8. Why does the discovery that one of the guys is gay – the movie is about four buddies played by Wilder, Joseph Bologna, Charles Grodin and Michael Huddleston – elicit virtually no comment?

9. Is San Francisco really this blasé?

10. Can you really tear a bar in San Francisco apart, as Charles Grodin does, and not go to jail or get a fine?

11. Does everyone in San Francisco live in mansions and drink all day?

12. Is San Francisco really this rich? This clean?

13. What time is the next flight to San Francisco?

14. Why do homely middle-aged comedy directors think there is nothing funnier than adultery?

15. Why do homely middle-aged comedy directors all want to be Woody Allen?

16. Why do homely middle-aged comedy directors always let themselves get the girl?

17. Why does the girl they get – her name is Kelly Le Brock in this case – always look like a goddess?

18. Where can I meet a girl like this?

19. Why do sex farces make adultery look great and then say: no, no, stay home, stay married, stay faithful?

20. And why – *The Woman in Red* is a rewrite of a French sex farce *Pardon Mon Affair* – do the wrong kind of movies travel?

August 15, 1984

❖

Annie's Coming Out

Directed by Gil Brealey
Written by John Patterson and Chris Borthwick
Starring Tina Arhondis

"Failure is no crime. Failure to give someone the benefit of the doubt is." – *Annie McDonald*, in her memoirs

Until Rosemary Crossley came along, no one gave Annie McDonald the benefit of the doubt. Annie had been placed in St. Nicholas, an Australian hospital for the profoundly retarded, by her parents when she was three years old. Because she was a victim of athetoid cerebral palsy, she appeared to be misshapen and she had little muscle control. Because she was difficult to feed, she was fed very little. At the age of eighteen, she resembled a child of nine. "The hospital was the state garbage bin," Annie wrote later. "Very young children were taken into permanent care, regardless of their intelligence. If they were disfigured, distorted or disturbed, then the world should not have to see or acknowledge them. You knew that you had failed to measure up to the standard expected of [such] babies. You were expected to die."

When *Annie's Coming Out*, the movie of what happened to Annie McDonald when she met Rosemary Crossley, was screened this week at Montreal's World Film Festival, there were a lot of people who didn't want to give it the benefit of the doubt. Another movie about a handicapped child and a miracle worker? Another well-meaning "problem" picture? Another *One Flew Over the Cuckoo's Nest*? "Oh, I'm sure it's worthy," one festival goer said, "but we've all seen it, haven't we?"

Not quite. The evening première concluded to a spontaneous standing ovation; the film's director, Gil Brealey, was besieged by questions and congratulations; at least five North American distributors were in competition for the rights to the movie. "Our greatest problem has been resistance from people who think they've seen it already, or from people who don't want to see it at all," Brealey observes dryly over breakfast one morning. "But once they get there, they seem to quite like it."

"Death lived in the wards at St. Nicholas. He was often more friendly than the nurses. Death walked around my cot, but he never felt that my ribs were well covered enough to stand the worms a feed. For much of the time I spent at St. Nicholas, Death would have accorded me the greatest pleasure by paying me a visit."

Annie's Coming Out is likeable, to be sure – there are more laughs in the grim tale of Annie's battle to be recognized as human than might have been thought possible – but that is not all: it is one of the best movies about a handicapped person ever made, and it is authentically inspiring, without electronic music, big stars or jazzy cinematographic effects. "The film is extremely simple," the bear-like, gregarious Brealey agrees. "It cost $1.4-million and was shot in twenty-four days. The crew never complained. If you've got a difficult crew, put them on a film where they work with the disabled – you soon feel you've nothing to complain about. I thought the story should be told simply because the emotional impact would be infinitely greater. It took a bit of guts to be as simple as we were, but I'm glad we did it."

With remarkably little dramatic compression, *Annie's Coming Out* recreates the events recorded in the book of the same name, an autobiography by Crossley and Annie that is published by Penguin only in Australia, though a North American edition is contemplated. Crossley, a teacher of the handicapped, arrives at St. Nicholas and is instantly drawn to the frail child, whom a nurse says has no more than six months to live because her body is twisting in a fashion that will make feeding her impossible. "Rosie," as Annie comes to call her teacher, performs a number of experiments that lead her to believe Annie might not be profoundly retarded after all. She is pleased with the short-term results and dares hope that her pupil might even have the glimmerings of a sub-normal intelligence.

"I often thought about ways of communicating while I was incommunicado. Using letters had always seemed better than using symbols or words. When Rosie said she thought she could teach me pictures or symbols, I was worried that that would be all she would try. I worked so hard because that was my only way of showing her I was brighter than she thought."

In less than a year, Annie was reading *Catch-22* with an automatic page turner, and she had so far outstripped Rosie's mathematical abilities a special tutor was provided. But Annie's amazing progress was greeted at first by scepticism and then by outright denial on the part of the institution's director, who in diagnosing her as profoundly retarded had consigned her to years of living hell. While she was institutional-ized, her parents loved her and visited her often, but they too resisted the revelation that she might have normal intelligence; most of the movie is devoted to the incredible perseverance both student and teacher displayed in getting the authorities finally to grant Annie's wish to live with Rosie and her boyfriend Chris.

Today, the real Annie, played phenomenally well in the film by another child with athetoid cerebral palsy, Tina Arhondis, is an ironic and even bitchy young woman who reports, "Since leaving St.

Nicholas I have grown forty centimetres. Now I sit in an ordinary wheelchair and use a pointer mounted on a headband to operate a mini-typewriter or a voice-synthesizer. In 1981 I sat a public exam in English and passed. In 1983 I started a Humanities degree and completed two units. At the end of 1983 I was given a grant by the Australia Council to work on a book about the ethics of the decisions the community makes about its disabled members. I no longer receive a pension but am a taxpayer entitled to complain about my hard-earned money being used to support severely disabled children who will never contribute."

Annie wanted to play herself in the movie but realized she had grown too large ("She loves cakes," Brealey grins) to be convincing and settled instead on advising the filmmakers – she attended the dailies and made comments, "some of them quite caustic," according to the director, on what she saw. In the end, she approved enthusiastically of the movie, although she may well regret that in the interests of brevity some aspects of her story have been left out – there is no discussion of the fact that the disabled children on Annie's ward developed their own language, for example. "We spoke," Annie remembered in her book, "a mixture of Yugoslav and English we later called Yuggish." The strange combination was the result of a primarily Yugoslav-speaking staff at the lower levels of the institution and it meant that the children – all diagnosed as profoundly retarded – "could understand everybody, but no one understood us. Because the adults could not understand us they shut us up every time we tried to talk."

"Some things have not changed. I still feel I should not have been resuscitated given that I was destined to be institutionalized. My parents do not visit. I think they refuse to see me type for fear that this book may all be true.

"From the floor at St. Nicholas to chatting with a Minister of State is a long jump, and I seemed to have missed the ground in between. I have been expected to behave either like an animal or an ambassador when better casting would give me the part of an adolescent.

"Being a disabled person is not all bad. At twenty-three I have probably done more than I would have had I grown up as a normal girl in a country town. Soon a film based on this book is to be released. I have met some remarkable people and made some wonderful friends. And no one ever asks me to do the washing up."

August 24, 1984

A Soldier's Story

Directed by Norman Jewison
Written by Charles Fuller
Starring Adolf Caesar, Howard E. Rollins, Jr. and Larry Riley

It is foggy in the fields near Fort Neal, La., the night Master Sergeant Vernon C. Waters (Adolph Caesar) is shot to death. The grey vapour that instantly shrouds the deed in mystery is more than a simple physical fact: throughout *A Soldier's Story*, the featurelessness of fog, its ability to obscure sharp colours and to soften rigid definitions, is used as a metaphor for the complicated, stormy reality of relationships between the races in the United States – and for the equally complicated and even stormier reality of relationships within the races.

Directed by Toronto's Norman Jewison (*Best Friends*) utilizing a script adapted by Charles Fuller from his Pulitzer Prize-winning play, *A Soldier's Story* brings to the screen for the first time in a major Hollywood film a particularized black milieu, and a new point of view. There have been black Hollywood films that purported to dramatize everyday life (*A Raisin in the Sun*) and there have been black musicals (*Porgy and Bess, Carmen Jones*) and there have been dozens of black exploitation films and a few comedies, but not until *A Soldier's Story*, set in 1944 and featuring the men of the fictitious 221st Smoke Generating Unit's "C" Company, has there been a black movie that examines seriously and without sentimentality the effect of prejudice not only on blacks, but among blacks. Jewison's powerful picture is a look at blacks who would be blacker, at blacks who would be grey, at blacks who would be white.

Sgt. Waters, expertly played by Caesar with a hissing James Cagney malevolence that hides a galaxy of insecurity and self-hatred, despises "geechees," by which he means the kind of Southern "niggers" – his word – without which he feels "white folks wouldn't think we was all fools." Waters would like to be liked by whites, and he is determined to expunge all traces of "yassur" from his vocabulary and all traces of Uncle Tom from his life. But Sgt. Waters is not a simple man. He also hates whites: the fellow soldier who says of him, "Any man who ain't sure where he belongs gotta be in a whole lotta pain," says volumes.

In an unconscious, eerie echo of Hitlerian racism, the thing he is supposed to be going to war to fight, Waters rejoices when "geechees" come to a bad end. "One less fool for the race to be ashamed of," he crows. But he paradoxically experiences soul-destroying fury when confronted by white racists. Drunk, before his death, he moans, "I ain't doin' nuthin' white folks say to . . . look what it's done to me . . . I hate myself . . ." In the fullest sense of the concept, the eminently dislikeable but oddly empathetic Waters is a tragic figure.

His death is investigated by Captain Richard Davenport (*Ragtime* star Howard E. Rollins, Jr.), a Howard University-trained military attorney, also black, who is the first "colored" officer ever glimpsed by most of the whites or blacks in the godforsaken Louisiana outpost. Rollins does his best with a remote role that requires him to function primarily as a sounding board for the men he investigates. It is those men – black men as variegated, for once, as any group of white men – who give *A Soldier's Story* its depth and, sorry to say, its novelty. That it should be novel to see blacks interact on screen is close to criminal, but you may find watching the film that you suddenly become transfixed by the way dark skin looks in stylized light, or by the cadences of speech overheard on street corners but never in movie theatres. A whole population on this continent is as alien to its most popular art form as any of the aliens that take up so much of that art form's time and resources.

Actors who demand compliments include Art Evans, David Alan Grier, David Harris, Dennis Lipscomb, William Allen Young, Denzel Washington, Robert Townsend and, above all, Larry Riley, whose portrait of C. J. Memphis, a happy-go-lucky "backwoods nigger," is virtually an anthropological essay. Congratulations are also due Herbie Hancock, whose score is brassy and bluesy and unabashedly vulgar; cinematographer Russell Boyd, who has transformed atmosphere into character; and to Jewison and his co-producers, Ronald L. Schwary and Patrick Palmer, for undertaking what must have seemed an unrealizable project.

There are flaws – the flashback structure creaks with theatricality, and the camera is not always as fluid as one might wish – but they are minor in comparison to the film's virtues. Fuller has altered the play's ending by removing a notation that the company was killed in Europe, a change that has been seen by some writers as a sop to the audience, an attempt by Jewison to "commercialize" the piece. Well, the only way to commercialize the script of *A Soldier's Story* would be to give it to Eddie Murphy and tell him to eat it on camera. We don't need to be told what happened to the men in this movie: their fates are worn on their faces. We know how the Second World War came out. And we know what it meant on an individual basis, which is what *A Soldier's Story* is about – individuals. In the end, the soldiers' stories were all the same. Everybody who didn't live lost.

September 13, 1984

Amadeus

Directed by Milos Forman
Written by Peter Shaffer
Starring F. Murray Abraham and Tom Hulce

Amadeus, the Milos Forman film of Peter Shaffer's hit play, has as much to do with the historical Wolfgang Amadeus Mozart as Mika Waltari's novel *The Egyptian* had to do with real life along the Nile, but that doesn't stop it from being a smart and vastly enjoyable exercise in camp.

The Egyptian was made into a thoroughly ridiculous and anachronistic but consummately entertaining 1954 costume drama with Edmund Purdom and Victor Mature. Something very similar has happened to Shaffer's play in Forman's film, which features a foul-mouthed Mozart who looks and sounds like Paul Simon on a bender, a perky Mrs. Mozart so West Coast she'll probably go back to windsurfing and coke-snorting in Santa Monica when her beloved "Wolfie" dies young, and an Emperor Franz Joseph who carries on as if he were John Turner in knickers, the newly appointed chairman of the board of Austria, Inc. The movie is a parade of witty caricatures, deftly drawn on thin air.

Shaffer, a middle-brow playwright with a savvy commercial sense, specializes in "metaphysical" explanations of the inexplicable. *The Royal Hunt of the Sun* purported to explain why the Inca empire fell, and *Equus* went after the psychological roots of the idea of the holy. The press kit for *Amadeus* includes a modest comparison of Shaffer's "fantasia" on Mozart's life to George Bernard Shaw's *Saint Joan*; both plays are said to be rooted in the tradition of the Shavian Theatre of Ideas. The "idea" in *Amadeus* is that God, for reasons known only to Him, has decided to make "an obscene child" – the scatologically-obsessed and sexually impish Mozart (Tom Hulce) – the "instrument" of His divine voice.

Court composer Antonio Salieri, a good but not great Italian musician and (until the advent of what he calls "the creature") a good but not great man, is at first perplexed and then saddened and finally outraged by the perversity of Himself in affixing the ultimate talent in music to a rutting runt. In a line cut from the film, Salieri compared himself ruthlessly to Mozart: "From the ordinary he created legends, whilst I, from legends, created only the ordinary." (No wonder Shaffer sympathizes with Salieri.) In the theatre, *Amadeus* strained to depict the tragedy of the second-rate; Forman has magically turned the material into a farce for the unfulfilled.

The play's momentum was hampered by Shaffer's intellectualizing and by the fact that the villain, Salieri, was where the protagonist, Mozart, should have been – *Amadeus* was *Othello* told from Iago's point of view. Forman has given Mozart equal screen time and has refused to treat Shaffer's metaphysical mewlings regarding God's perversity as anything but a parody of a play of ideas. The film recognizes that, in the skewed scheme of things, implanting the immortality of genius in the mortal flesh of a horny hell-raiser is a pretty piddling example of divine mysteriousness next to, say, the slaughter of innocent babies in any war or natural disaster you'd care to mention.

Shot mostly in Czechoslovakia, decorated with a powdered-sugar sweetness and creamy lavishness unseen since the days of Josef von Sternberg, and performed by an eager to please, rootin'-tootin' American cast that would be comfortable in *Oklahoma!*, *Amadeus* is a junk food *par excellence*. (There is nothing junky about the music, of course, and there is a lot of it.)

In elderly make-up as the mildly senile Salieri, F. Murray Abraham is a courtly, rubbery old demon with a nose that wrinkles beneficently at the camera, like the faces of the Phase One cuddlies in *Gremlins*, the Mozart of Tom Hulce (pronounced Hulse) is a cackling, gleeful gargoyle, an ithyphallic cherub and, in a small role as Salieri's opera-singing wife, Christine Ebersole is a rococo gumdrop, all heaving pastel bosoms – Dolly Parton on a time machine tour.

Elizabeth Berridge is somewhat disappointing as the common-as-dirt Mrs. Mozart, however (too much method, too little madness), and Roy Dotrice, the composer's overbearing father, cuts a self-effacing hole in the screen.

Amadeus begins in a madhouse borrowed from Ken Russell circa *The Music Lovers* and *The Devils*, but Russell is merely one of the many directors Forman (*Hair, One Flew Over the Cuckoo's Nest, Ragtime*) sends up in his catalogue of cinematic excess – *Amadeus* ceases to be entertaining only on the occasions it forgets to be excessive. That's not often.

People who bought Shaffer's line about a "theatre of ideas" will probably be affronted by this film, which offers one of the most astonishing internal critiques of its own mechanisms in the history of movies – it's as though von Sternberg had been conscious of making twaddle when he was making *The Scarlet Empress* – but everyone else will no doubt be delighted. Speaking of the relationship between court composers and their rulers, Salieri said (in another line cut from the film), "We sacramentalized their mediocrity." Forman's sacrament is as enjoyable as the mediocrity is profound.

September 19, 1984

❖

The Terminator

Directed by James Cameron
Written by James Cameron and Gale Anne Hurd
Starring Arnold Schwarzenegger

The casting of bodybuilder Arnold Schwarzenegger as a Cyborg Terminator – a computer gunslinger encased in an envelope of "living human tissue" – who pops into 1984 from 2029 to kill the mother of a hero of the future so the hero can never be born, is brilliant. With his various bulbosities and protuberances shoved into leather and tied off, his diction chopped off, his eyebrows blistered off, his hair hacked off and his attitude ticked off, Arnie is a walking punchline – a joke that kills.

And *The Terminator*, in which Arnie does his Heavy Metal thing, is an efficient, cold-blooded sci-fi splatter movie that never makes the mistake of forgetting that on some level it is deeply ridiculous. The Ontario Board of Censors, which should be taking baskets of food to the poor or correcting spelling papers or doing something else socially responsible, has instead spent its time lately by outfitting *The Terminator* with an advertising man's dream slogan, a statement sure to provoke all the little kids the board has ruled can't see the movie into sneaking into it any way they can: "BRUTAL VIOLENCE. HORROR." It's not that good, but it does dish out the steaming stuff the audience comes for in pile-high helpings.

Arnie arrives in the L.A. of 1984 on shafts of lightning, resplendent in his beefy nakedness, and promptly slugs a punk who won't give up his pants when Arnie asks nice. Thing of it is, when he slugs the punk, Arnie's fist goes right through the guy, and Arnie has to pull it back out with a wet sucky noise, skwooch. Arnie is real, real unpleasant: he shoots up a whole cop shop, he keeps putting his hands through people's persons, and he goonily runs over a kid's toy with his car. (Wonder if there'll be Terminator Dolls for Christmas: "The Gift That Keeps On Killing.")

Sent from the future slightly later than Arnie is Kyle (Michael Biehn), who also arrives on a shaft of lightning and is well-built but is not going to give Arnie a run for his muscle. Kyle needs to protect the mother of the future, Susan (Linda Hamilton), and does, chivalrously, while trying not to answer her questions about what will happen to the future if the present changes. "God," she says with the gallows good humour that runs through *The Terminator*, "a person could go crazy thinking about this."

There's not much time to talk, though; like Yul Brynner as the robot gunslinger with the ball-bearing eyes in *Westworld* – that was the last time an actor kidded his image so cleverly – Arnie keeps on coming, until there's not much left but chrome bones. In *The Terminator*, a lot of the action takes place in a dance bar, Tech Noir. That describes the bar, the action and the movie.

October 26, 1984

Stranger Than Paradise

Written and directed by Jim Jarmusch
Starring Eszter Balint, John Lurie and Richard Edson

The new American film *Stranger Than Paradise*, which deservedly
won the award for best first film at the Cannes Film Festival and is in
black and white and probably didn't cost as much as Dolly Parton pays
for a dress, is filmed in short scenes. The scenes are

separated

by blackouts

that give the movie

a ragged

rhythm

that is unique.

More than the rhythm of *Stranger Than Paradise*, written and
directed by New Yorker Jim Jarmusch, is unique. This is a plaintive,
intelligent, laconic New York comedy – almost avant-garde, certainly
avant-garde in comparison to major feature films – that owes nothing
at all to Woody Allen. What Woody Allen owes to Ingmar Bergman
and Charlie Chaplin, Jim Jarmusch owes to Samuel Beckett and Bus-
ter Keaton.

Stranger Than Paradise, like Gaul, is formally divided into three
parts. Part the first, "The New World," is in New York. Part the second,
"One Year Later," is by far the best part, and is in Cleveland in winter.
Part the third, "Paradise," is in Florida, and has an ending worthy of
Guy de Maupassant, O. Henry and Daphne du Maurier.

In *Stranger Than Paradise*, a Hungarian girl, Eva (Eszter Balint), comes to visit her New York cousin, Willie (John Lurie), then goes to Cleveland to visit her aunt Lotte (Cecillia Stark), then goes to work in a hot dog stand. Then Willie and his friend Eddie (Richard Edson) come to Cleveland. Willie and Eddie are dimwits; they're like Martin Scorsese characters with the rough edges rubbed off. They're existentially absurd, but individualized; they're like Beckett characters, with the personality traits glued on. Like good graffiti, they're funny in a scrawly, creepy-crawly way – the guys are punk versions of Jackie Gleason and Art Carney, *circa* "The Honeymooners," and the girl is an East Europe Patti Smith, tired of living and bored with dying.

Stranger Than Paradise is put together with magisterial formal austerity. Within each scene the camera occasionally moves, but not by much, and there is no editing whatever – only once in the film does Jarmusch use rack focus (where the background becomes indistinct as the foreground hardens, or vice versa). For the most part, the camera's eye pops open, takes in a scene and slams shut. The technique is daring, and not one you'd want to see often, though it seems certain every third college filmmaker in North America is destined to use it – it's ideal for artists without money. But from beginning to end, Jarmusch carries it off. His vision is stranger than paradise, and his talent is odder than hell.

November 16, 1984

❖

The River

Directed by Mark Rydell
Written by Robert Dillon and Julian Barry
Starring Mel Gibson and Sissy Spacek

If you see only one farm film this year, let it not be *The River*, a meretricious piece of populist propaganda that patronizes the salt of the earth so thoroughly the screen is awash in a sea of crocodile tears. Let's get the comparisons out of the way: next to Mark Rydell's *The River*, Richard Pearce's *Country* is *Citizen Kane* and Robert Benton's *Places in the Heart* is *Gone With the Wind*.

While John Williams' music toots its flutes in a Prokofiev mode, things get mighty wet down at the Tom Garvey farm. *The River's* barely run a second when there's a shot of a dead cow artfully draped over a branch in the drink: it's the first phony-looking shot in the film, but it's not the last. The next honest image doesn't show up until the end, when the Garveys roll around in a vat full of corn.

The farm wife is Mae Garvey, played by Sissy Spacek, who looks more at home in a kitchen than Jessica Lange, and since I can't say nuthin' else nice, I won't say nuthin' at all. The farm husband is Tom, played by Mel Gibson, who has nice eyes. There is also a bad man who wants to take away the Garvey place, and he's played by Scott Glenn, and he's not nearly as odious as he's supposed to seem, probably because Tom Garvey is a pretty inept farmer: he owes the bank more money than his place is worth. (In *Country*, they explained how this could happen; in *The River*, things happen because the script says so.)

"Sometimes I think we'd be better someplace else, away from the river," quoth Mrs. Garvey thoughtfully (and under the circumstances reasonably), to which hubby hollers, "This is our home place, Mae. My people are buried here!" Now can you imagine Aussie actor Gibson delivering that speech in a Tennessee drawl? Neither could Gibson, I guess.

Slow as sap to rise in a rotting tree, *The River* goes by. Mae makes bread, a cow gets sick, the Sears bill comes, Mae turns down the advances of the bad man by saying, "It's too late, you chose Emily, I chose Tom" (don't they get "Dynasty" in Tennessee?), then Tom goes to work in a factory as a scab. This is a factory where the striking union members beat up the scabs when they try to stop working. It is here that Tom gets right perplexed when a man asks, "Howcum you grew all that food and people are still hungry?" Tom thinks about that, then says, "I don't know. There's somethin' wrong somewhere."

Mae comes to visit Tom at the factory and they go to a motel but his manliness has been all messed up by his troubles, so she kisses his cuts and that gets him hot and everything's fine. He goes back to the factory long enough for a big poetic scene – a deer comes in one day, probably looking for the sign that read SYMBOL that dropped off its neck. The deer represents Tom and all the other Vanishing Americans, and it probably couldn't get a bank loan, either. Taking a leaf from SYMBOL, Tom gets out of the factory and there is a big show-down at his farm with bulldozers and he says, "I ain't leavin', 'cept in a box." But somehow you can't help thinking he's already got a plan for the future right there in the pocket of his bib overalls: a return ticket to Australia.

December 21, 1984

❖

Sam Peckinpah (1925-1984), An Appreciation

At the beginning of his career, he was fired from Liberace's television show – he was a prop assistant – because he refused to trade his blue jeans for the business suit mandated by his glittering boss. At the end of his career – he had become by then a significant American film-maker, in the tradition of John Ford – he directed a video starring Julian Lennon, son of John. Between the bizarre bookends, Sam Peckinpah, who died Friday of a heart attack at fifty-nine, amassed a unique body of work that celebrated machismo, glorified violence, praised independence and worshipped individuality, a body of work that simultaneously denigrated machismo, criticized violence, mocked the possibility of independence and treated individuality as an illusion. Peckinpah never resolved the paradoxes. It was the paradoxes that elevated his finest films into art.

He was the product of a wealthy and extremely correct California ranching family – his father and his grandfather were judges, and when he died, his brother Denver Peckinpah, another judge, revealed the details of the death to the press – so it was perhaps inevitable that authority would become anathema to him. The family sent him to a military school, but the attempt to impose discipline failed; not until a stint at Fresno State College, where he joined the theatre department, did he settle down. Relatively speaking. His life was marked by abrasive relationships, personal and professional: he was involved in countless disputes with studios, actors and screenwriters, and several of his major films, including *Pat Garrett* and *Billy the Kid* (1973) and *Major Dundee* (1965), were removed from his creative control and mutilated by producers prior to release.

Others were not. In *Ride the High Country* (1962), *The Wild Bunch* (1969), *The Ballad of Cable Hogue* (1970) and *Junior Bonner* (1962), Peckinpah explored the fierce lyricism of the West, old and new. The first two were notorious for their violence, and *The Wild Bunch* did indeed conclude with a slow-motion ballet of brutality that became a cliché in the hands of less gifted directors, but *The Ballad of Cable Hogue*, with Jason Robards as a prospector, and *Junior Bonner*, with Steve McQueen as a rodeo rider, were elegiac and introspective, ample illustration there was more to Peckinpah than gore.

The key film, the picture that pulled everything together, was *Straw Dogs* (1971), a movie that sent Vietnam-era American critics into a state of shock. (For *The New Yorker's* Pauline Kael it was both "fascist" and "a work of art.") Set in a village on the Cornish coast, the film is about a man with, as Toronto critic Robin Wood put it in the best essay on Peckinpah ever written, a growing determination "to defend a 'home' that doesn't really exist." During a violent and brilliantly edited climax (it had audiences in the theatre howling in blood lust) he succeeds, but destroys in the process the very home the violence was meant to protect.

"I made that movie," its star, Dustin Hoffman, reminisced years later, "because I was interested in repressed violence in liberals. I had strong left-wing friends who would be ringside at fights, or who would be screwing everybody they could. I wanted to show the duplicity in that kind of person. When I sat in the audience, the women would scream at my character every time he didn't defend himself. 'Kill him!' they'd scream."

"The effect of the violence," Wood wrote of *Straw Dogs*, "is as much exhilarating as horrifying: when Dustin Hoffman swings the man-trap down over his adversary's head, most of us (unless we have deliberately rejected the film's hold on us) are in there swinging with him. This is what our 'moralistic' critics can't stand – the film's reminder that the violence is not in the action but in them . . . Peckinpah sees life as, inevitably, a bloody struggle for survival . . . His films implicitly accept violence as a metaphysical fact, a condition of our existence, and go on from there at times equivocally to celebrate it, though the celebration is never simple or complacent, never free from an accompanying sense of horror."

Straw Dogs, the most horrific film, was followed by *Junior Bonner*, the gentlest, in turn followed by movies – *The Getaway* (1972), *Pat Garrett*, *Bring Me the Head of Alfredo Garcia* (1974), *The Killer Elite* (1976), *Cross of Iron* (1977), *The Osterman Weekend* (1983) – of diminishing quality. *Alfredo Garcia* was an embarrassment, an emulation in part of the surrealism of Sergio Leone; *The Getaway* was miserably compromised by the writing of Ali MacGraw's character and her performance of it; *The Killer Elite* and *Cross of Iron* came to life only during sequences about death; and *The Osterman Weekend* was a plot-besotted mess, though Peckinpah's ability to orchestrate violence was so awesome audiences didn't care who was killing whom, or why. The underrated exception during this period was *Convoy* (1978), a cheerful cartoon of a film about truckers, an eighteen-wheeler *Wagon Train*. ("I can't live in the Old West, so I re-make it," Peckinpah said.)

He was at work on an independent film, *On the Rocks*, to be shot in San Francisco, when he died, but his reputation as a cinematic outlaw fighting the repressive forces of convention was already secure. He was an odd kind of outlaw, however, one with a nostalgic attraction to a mythical homestead. Given Peckinpah's on-screen world, it makes sense that off-screen he would marry a Mexican actress, Begonia Palacio, divorce her, marry someone else, divorce her, marry Palacio again, divorce her again – and that she would be with him at his death. Wood declared Peckinpah's work to be an example of the conundrum faced by "the artist who is vociferously anti-Establishment yet lacks any defined ideological alternative," and the director's favourite motto, used in *Ride the High Country*, was: "All I want is to enter my house justified." The motto was taught to him by his father. Sam Peckinpah never gave the impression he found justification difficult to come by; it was the location of the house that eluded him.

December 31, 1984

❖

Witness

Directed by Peter Weir
Written by Earl W. Wallace and William Kelley
Starring Harrison Ford, Lukas Haas and Kelly McGillis

Australian director Peter Weir's first American film, *Witness*, begins with a visual joke. Across a *National Geographic* landscape of undulating wheat fields and clear blue skies, dour men and women dressed in the plain black clothing of nineteenth-century farmers travel in horse-drawn carriages. Idyllic music plays. A title appears at the bottom of the screen: "Pennsylvania 1984." Welcome to Amish country, home of the cultural time-warp.

Despite its playful opening, *Witness* is not a comedy, though it's full of humour; and it's not exactly a thriller, though it's full of thrills; and it's certainly not a sex film, though it's full of steamily suggestive sexuality; it's not a documentary, but there is a raft of ethnographic insight; it's anything but a musical, but its exultant respect for rural

187

American values harvests the corn of *Oklahoma!*; and while it may prove to be as commercial as Michael Jackson's glide, it is designed as an art film – it occasionally puts its plot on hold and wanders casually through the Vermeer environment it has painstakingly constructed. *Witness* is satisfying on so many levels it stands with *Cabaret* and *The Godfather II* as an example of how a director in love with his medium can redeem its mainstream clichés.

That *Witness* should come from the director of *Picnic at Hanging Rock*, *The Last Wave* and *The Year of Living Dangerously* is not altogether unexpected – Weir is a wizard with the camera, a magician at summoning hallucinatory cinematic power – but there is nothing in his previous work to rival the lucidity of *Witness*. The opposite, in fact: his weakness has always been an attraction to the pretentiously ambiguous, the metaphysically pompous. In *The Last Wave* and *The Year of Living Dangerously*, flimsy melodrama was freighted with a cargo it couldn't carry – *The Last Wave* promised aboriginal enlightenment and wound up a disaster picture, *The Year of Living Dangerously* posed as a demanding trek into the heart of Indonesian darkness and emerged with a remake of *Casablanca*.

The *Witness* script by Earl W. Wallace and William Kelley has no such pretences; it has an absorbing story to tell, it tells it, and that's that. Because the premise (in witnessing a murder, an eight-year-old Amish boy places himself and the cop who questions him in danger) is straightforward and strong, Weir has the latitude to wobble artily without irritating the audience, and he uses the periodic intermissions from the story to impart to the picture the multiplicity of life itself.

Take the scene where the boy, Samuel (Lukas Haas, Jane Alexander's youngest child in *Testament*), shuffles through a Philadelphia police station, the camera perched on his shoulder. Samuel's adventure results in a plot payoff, but what the sojourn is mostly about is how strange the people in the cop-shop appear to an isolated Amish child for whom a drinking fountain is an exotic experience.

Or take the scene in an Amish barn when the cop, John Book (Harrison Ford), dances with an Amish woman, Rachel (Kelly

McGillis), to a crackly car radio rendition of the Sam Cooke tune "(What a) Wonderful World." Amish taboos against pre-marital sex afford Weir the opportunity to return the yearning to sex without becoming ridiculous or coy – as he shoots the smouldering looks of longing that pass between Rachel and John Book, he electrifies the screen with the erotic charge Meryl Streep and Robert De Niro must have hoped they were generating in *Falling in Love*.

Finally, take the scene in which the Amish community erects a barn for a recently married couple – Weir transforms the event into a rhapsodic depiction of communal effort that carries the unabashed sentiment (and the cinematic expertise) of the farmers digging the irrigation ditch in King Vidor's 1934 *Our Daily Bread*.

The Amish are treated with respect in *Witness* – their values are appreciated, if not condoned – and the impossible love that develops between the mildly rebellious widow and the wildly profane cop is irresistible, as impossible loves usually are. In fiercely difficult roles, Ford and McGillis approach perfection. Other actors assigned the daunting task of portraying living relics include Toronto opera singer Jan Rubes, as Rachel's stern father, and expatriate Russian ballet dancer Alexander Godunov, as her would-be beau; both skirt caricature in favour of characterization and both are convincing. Back in heathen Philadelphia, Danny Glover, the reliable black handyman Moze in *Places in the Heart*, is unrecognizable as an evil cop, and Patti LuPone, Broadway's treacherous Evita, has a memorable minute or two as John Book's sister. They round out the admirable ensemble of a film that never exploits the community it explores – a community that ironically cares less about the quality of *Witness* than the fleeting appearance of a single white cloud in an otherwise sunny sky.

February 7, 1985

❖

Mask

Directed by Peter Bogdanovich
Written by Anna Hamilton Phelan
Starring Cher and Eric Stoltz

"I stood at the window and looked out at a grassy park and I saw three people. A woman dressed all in black with bright red hair, a man with a bowie knife and a teenage boy with a bizarre, deformed face who held himself with the most tremendous sense of dignity I'd ever seen."

The speaker is Anna Hamilton Phelan, a screenwriter who was working as a genetics counsellor in a California hospital. The woman in black was Rusty Dennis, a bikers' moll who drank too much booze, smoked too much dope and ingested a pharmacy whenever she had the chance. The man with the bowie knife was Rusty's current biker beau. And the teenage boy with the bizarre face deformed by craniodiaphyseal dysplasia, a congenital condition in which calcium is deposited in lumps around the skull – a condition which had heretofore killed every one of its victims by the age of eight – was Rusty's sixteen-year-old son, Rocky.

It took Anna Phelan eight years to transform the sense of "sympathy and morbid fascination" she felt in Rocky's presence into the screenplay of the Peter Bogdanovich film, *Mask*. Rocky had in the meantime died and Rusty had vanished. But Phelan found the red-haired woman in black and with her co-operation researched the details of Rocky's short life. "Rusty sat me down and gave me a list of names of friends, relatives, schools, where Rocky went to camp – everything," Phelan reports. "Then she looked me in the eye and said, 'You're going to hear a lot of bad things about me and . . . all of them are true.'" But Phelan discovered something else about Rusty. "Most people with a child like Rocky do one of three things, they overprotect him, institutionalize him or kill him. Rusty, for all her problems, was never late for a doctor's appointment and never treated him differently than anyone else."

More than anything else, *Mask* communicates that extraordinary relationship, the love between a woman who chose her outsider status proudly and the boy whose exoticism was forced on him. Bogdanovich's film begins with a long shot of L.A. freeways in blinding light and then enters the Rusty/Rocky home, a tract-shack that houses Springsteen posters, a sound system that's a perpetual motion machine, and a gaggle of teddy bear bikers. In her red, pre-Raphaelite curls and cruelly tight jeans, Rusty (Cher) is a one-woman crusade on behalf of her kid: when the local high school principal tells her he'd like to talk to the boy's father, she tartly replies, "Perhaps you should speak to the Pope, too, he'd be easier to find." And then Rocky (Eric Stoltz), whispering in a high-pitched voice through an Elephant Man face that does, in fact, resemble a mask, says, "Don't worry, Mr. Simms, I look weird but otherwise I'm real normal."

And he is. And that's a testament to the one thing Rusty did right. "All you care about is getting loaded and laid," Rocky hollers at her, but he knows there's one more thing she cares about: him. A scene in which she helps him overcome his persistent headaches by having him talk to her as she holds him in her arms is one of the tenderest depictions of parental love ever filmed. "My mom," Rocky tells a girl proudly, "is very . . . modern."

The time Bogdanovich spends with Rusty and Rocky, and the time Rocky spends at a summer camp for the blind with a gorgeous blonde (Laura Dern) who falls in love with him, is time that is priceless. The time Bogdanovich spends with the cuddly bikers, especially the time he spends with Sam Elliott in a dismally ingratiating, cockeyed performance as Rusty's boy friend, is time that exacts a terrible toll: credibility. It may well be that Rocky's graduation caused a mute biker to speak, just as knocks to the head have been known to cure amnesia, but if it did, it ought to have been left out – truth is sometimes less believable, and much sappier, than fiction. The one thing this tough but inspiring story does not need is pathos, and Bogdanovich is for the most part content to proceed without it, masterminding a movie that is in justifiable love with its two leads.

Stoltz's Rocky probably couldn't be better and Cher continues her amazing career as one of the most exciting natural actresses in contemporary movies. Rusty is raunchy but insecure, affectionate but defiant, hard-boiled but self-destructive, and Cher is with her every swaggering step of the way. Rusty is a woman who, unable to face her always-critical father, Quaaludes herself into oblivion, but then rises to the occasion on another occasion with an outburst of maternal fury that sends her out into the streets to find drugs as a salve for her own pain and a prostitute as balm for the aching needs of her lovelorn son. Because Rocky's hair is red and long, and because his face is broad and flat, Rusty says he "was a lion in a past life and it got left over." It's only fitting he should be the cub of a lioness.

March 8, 1985

❖

The Hit

Directed by Stephen Frears
Written by Peter Prince
Starring Terence Stamp

Blood Simple

Directed by Joel Coen
Written by Joel and Ethan Coen
Starring John Getz and Frances McDormand

A Private Function

Directed by Malcolm Mowbray
Written by Alan Bennett
Starring Michael Palin and Maggie Smith

The Hollywood blockbuster mentality, which decrees that a movie is either *Indiana Jones and the Temple of Doom* or nothing, has rendered the modestly scaled independent film an endangered species. And, given the cost of an evening out at the movies, casual theatregoers would just as soon stay home and rent a cassette unless they are convinced the biggest biggie in town – at one point it was *Terms of Endearment*, now it's *Amadeus* – will not only show them a good time but will impart a life-changing experience once thought to be the prerogative of religion (or drugs).

Because so few films, even the biggies, can possibly live up to their advance billing – all those "stupendous!" "magnificent!" "monumental!" quotes – audiences emerge from almost any highly touted movie that has been around more than a month or two chirping a chorus of disappointment.

In the case of tiny perfect movies that do not set out to be religious experiences, the dangers of raising expectations destined to be dashed are compounded. Three cases in point: within their self-imposed limits, *The Hit, A Private Function* and *Blood Simple* are well-nigh perfect films, but avoiding the oversell is all but impossible. The best bet is to rush to see them before anyone has a chance to tell you how terrific they are.

The Hit, a British comedy directed by Stephen Frears, must be the only gangster movie in history to owe a portion of its inspiration to Elisabeth Kubler-Ross' *On Death and Dying*. In that volume, the doyenne of death doctors outlined the five states that the terminally ill and their loved ones are said to pass through. *The Hit*'s screenwriter, Peter Prince, has used the stages (denial, anger, bargaining, depression, acceptance) as the framework for an extraordinary fable in which Willie (Terence Stamp), a London gangster now living in Spain, is sought out by a couple of repulsive professional killers, Braddock (John Hurt) and Myron (Tim Roth), to even the score – Willie turned snitch years ago and now it's time for him to pay with his life.

The catch is that Willie has already worked through his death and is ready to go. He's as resigned to his fate as a Sunday school saint, a beatific state contrasted poignantly with the desperate desire to live at all costs displayed by Maggie (Laura Del Sol), a resourceful young slut who is taken hostage during the journey.

Eventually, the film, shot on location in Spain by a director with an innate understanding of how to stylize without becoming self-conscious, asks to be seen as a comic but moving meditation on the ways we do, or do not, go gently into that good night.

The style in *Blood Simple* is entirely self-conscious, and good for it. This rewrite of James M. Cain by way of the grottiest splatter movie around is a triumph of artificiality in which the owner of a Texas roadhouse (Dan Hedaya) hires a reptilian private eye (M. Emmet Walsh) to murder his adulterous wife (Frances McDormand) and her lover (John Getz).

Written by Joel and Ethan Coen, and directed by Joel, the deadpan script is salty with mock Texanisms such as, "You thought he was coloured; you're always assuming the worst." Meanwhile, the visuals play sophisticated games with clichés – to reveal any of them would be to spoil the surprise.

Devotees of splatter movies will be unfazed by the Gothic violence toward the end, but for people who quail at *Friday the Thirteenth* movies and won't even consider Clint Eastwood, *Blood Simple* may prove gory going, despite the fact that the carnage is staged intentionally as baroquely unbelievable.

Over all, with its equal emphasis on mendacity, bloodletting, high style and avarice, *Blood Simple* suggests what might have resulted had playwright Sam Shepard been hired to write a parody of horror films for Brian De Palma.

Avarice and mendacity are the subjects of *A Private Function*, set in a ravaged and rationed postwar England of 1947 where a bit of bacon is capable of bestowing social status. Gilbert Chilvers (Michael Palin) is a hard-working chiropodist who is married but doesn't wear a ring – "Tiny bits of skin from people's feet tend to collect under it," he tells one of his clients cheerfully.

Gilbert's wife, Joyce (Maggie Smith), is as restless as her husband is content. Joyce, a matinee Lady Macbeth, puts on airs and has ideals. "Mrs. Rhoades' ingrown toenail has turned the corner," reports Gilbert, engaging in small talk after his day at work. "Please, Gilbert," Joyce recoils airily (as only the magnificently mannered Smith can recoil), "don't bring feet to the table."

Director Malcolm Mowbray and writer Alan Bennett (*An Englishman Abroad*) take their time in introducing the inhabitants of the Chilvers' Yorkshire village and in making the basic premise (an illegal pig is being fattened for "a private function") clear, but the wait is worth it, and when the pig, having become even more incontinent than usual as the result of a diet that included ginger cookies, rodents and toenail snippings, pays an extended, odiferous visit to the Chilvers' household, *A Private Function* becomes a public cause for comic celebration.

The image that sticks is not, however, essentially comic: it's of the tartily attired Joyce Chilvers with her dreams of "making this town sit up and take notice," telling herself wistfully, "I want a future that will live up to my past." She is speaking for herself, for her people, for her era – and for her Empire.

April 5, 1985

Prizzi's Honor

Directed by John Huston
Written by Richard Condon and Janet Roach
Starring Jack Nicholson, Kathleen Turner and Anjelica Huston

Darker in implication but funnier in execution than *The Godfather* saga, seventy-eight-year-old John Huston's burnished, processionally paced film of Richard Condon's comic novel, *Prizzi's Honor*, is a rogue's gallery in which every picture is, morally speaking, mute.

This is a movie in which the "hero" is a hit man who takes pride in his work. For all his virtually congenital criminality and his well-nurtured misogyny, Charlie Partanna (Jack Nicholson) is the best of his very bad lot. Practising Catholics his people are; good Catholics they are not. Sicilians they once were; Borgias, they might become – and all-American they already are.

Into gangland Charlie's baroque Brooklyn life, *circa* the early sixties, strides a high-thighed Beverly Hills ash blonde named Irene Walker (Kathleen Turner), a "tax consultant" who advises her clients that ransoms paid as the result of kidnappings are deductible. Charlie has already been burned by woman trouble – a mess-up with the boss's daughter, Maerose Prizzi (Anjelica Huston), led to her exile – but that doesn't stop him from playing with the potential conflagration Irene carries around with her casually, like a clutchbag. (She's got a secret like Nevada's got sand.)

Catching sight of the torch Maerose is still carrying, Charlie tells her to settle down with some guy and "practise your meatballs." He adds kindly that he had no way of knowing, years ago, that she was going to keep her shape, that she was going to turn out to be a looker: "You coulda been a fat wop broad." He is serious and, he thinks, reasonable; the surreal logic of his excuse is Condon's trademark as a writer and the glory of the script he has produced for Huston in collaboration with Janet Roach.

Having doused at last Maerose's flame – or so he thinks – Charlie chases Irene out to L.A. and proposes marriage. Irene wonders how Charlie can afford to invest so much so fast. "I look at you and see what I wanna see," he replies. "That's what love is." Charlie may be no genius, but his definition of love proves he's no fool. As Nicholson sees him – complete with Italianate Brooklyn accent ("Maybe youse went to Marymount wid da bride or somethin'";), protruding upper lip and an expression of stunned disbelief that is summoned by the obvious but never by the excessive – he's a canny Sicilian cousin to J. J. Gites, the private eye of *Chinatown*, the film that *Prizzi's Honor* resembles in its delight at taking the temperature of a species colder than crushed ice.

"Straight-arrow Charlie, the all-American hood," in the words of another hood, meets his intellectual, amoral match in Irene; their reptilian relationship is the device that allows the plot several classic Condon twists that lead obliquely to a climax that deserves the designation. As in *Winter Kills*, the film William Richert made of a previous Condon book, the grotesques are never allowed to cozy up to the audience, and the satirical subtext is never softened.

Andrzej Bartkowiak's cinematography is unfortunately incapable of differentiating Brooklyn from Las Vegas and Beverly Hills – with the exception of *Terms of Endearment*, everything Bartkowiak has done, including *Daniel*, *The Verdict* and *Death Trap*, has had an identical green sheen – but in all other areas, *Prizzi's Honor* is a work of crazed distinction.

The excellence of the leads is reflected by the supporting cast, especially Anjelica Huston as the jealously brittle Maerose (she's an interior decorator into Art Deco – "Art who?" asks Charlie) and William Hickey as the withered, wheezing and repugnantly childish eighty-four-year-old don, a parody of Huston. *Prizzi's Honor* is not about nice people, but these are Mafiosi, after all, and not Mennonites.

Condon and Huston are soundly subversive: they use their profiteering monsters to argue that organized crime has found a snug fit in the well-fed belly of the American beast – the death-dealing businessmen in *Prizzi's Honor* are hit men at the heart of the American dream.

June 14, 1985

Mad Max Beyond Thunderdome

Directed by George Miller and George Ogilvie
Written by Terry Hayes and George Miller
Starring Mel Gibson and Tina Turner

Pale Rider

Directed by Clint Eastwood
Written by Michael Butler
Starring Clint Eastwood

Silverado

Directed by Lawrence Kasdan
Written by Lawrence and Mark Kasdan
Starring Kevin Kline and Kevin Costner

"I'm wild again, beguiled again, a simpering whimpering child again."
— *Bewitched, Bothered & Bewildered*

Australian director George Miller's *Mad Max Beyond Thunderdome* does what Lawrence Kasdan's *Silverado* wants to do: it reinvents the Western for the eighties. Now that the *Mad Max* cycle is complete, it seems obvious that the laconic Max (Mel Gibson) was always a classic Western hero, and that his quest for an illusory home and hearth neatly reproduced the evolution of the genre itself. From the primitive morality-play melodramas of the early Westerns, to the modernist, nihilistic Westerns of Sam Peckinpah and Sergio Leone, to the most recent (and utterly bizarre) development, the post-modernist Western that expresses nostalgia for the moral certainties of the United States in its infancy and for the simplicities of its pre-McCarthy childhood and for the unfailing pubertal potency of its pre-Vietnam adolescence ("May The Force be with you," indeed), Max has seen and summarized it all.

Probably because Australia had no Western tradition of its own, and possibly because the country is closer nowadays in spirit to the mythology of the Wild West than the United States is, and certainly because the Aussies lagged behind the Yanks in expressing themselves,

George Miller was able in the first *Mad Max* (1979) to do what no American director since Sam Peckinpah had been able successfully to bring off: a non-elegiac Western that was not a mournful statement (*pace The Grey Fox*) about the decline of the West. And to do it, Miller went back to the beginning, to the most basic Western of all, the primal revenge parable. Max (Mel Gibson) was a good man who surrendered himself to the imperatives of vengeance when his family was destroyed by the modern equivalent of Indians; the tragedy transformed him into a loner, a cold-blooded killer on the epic scale of Jeremiah Johnson or Nevada Smith.

(That leather and chains replaced chaps and Stetsons in the *Mad Max* movies, and that motorcycles and airplanes replaced horses and stagecoaches, and that musclemen and their fey consorts replaced bad cowboys and dangerous Indians, and that the dramas were played out in a mythically mountainous and dusty future instead of a mythically mountainous and dusty past, amounted to little more than a fashion statement, similar to designer stunts such as a punk *Measure for Measure* or an Art Deco *Julius Caesar*. But it was a fashion statement that cleverly enabled audiences to enter Max's world without having to tote the *Gunsmoke* baggage that clear-cut Western iconography would have piled on them.)

In the second chapter of the trilogy, *The Road Warrior* (1982), Max entered the nihilistic and surreal society familiar from the amoral, existentialist Westerns of Peckinpah, Leone and the Clint Eastwood who directed *The Outlaw Josey Wales*. Throughout the sixties and seventies and into the eighties, these end-of-the-West Westerns flourished intermittently, but they led the genre down the same cul-de-sac into which painting was pushed by abstract expressionism. Variations on the melody might be possible, but the ideology mandating the melody itself (in Westerns, that the Western had died; in painting, that representation was *verboten*) vitiated against the introduction of any new songs. Peckinpah's *The Wild Bunch* took the Western as far as it could go – in the end, it literally blew its heroes apart – and in *The Road Warrior*, Max was taken as far as he could go – in the end, he literally blew his villains apart, and he was left alone, a stranger and afraid, in a world he mostly made.

Enter Clint Eastwood's *Pale Rider*, Kasdan's *Silverado* and Miller's *Beyond Thunderdome*, three films about rebuilding rather than wrecking – about rebuilding not only a genre, but civilization itself. *Pale Rider* and *Silverado* virtually take Reagan at his word when he says the United States could win a nuclear war and set out to show what might happen after. (The answer: exactly what happened before.) In *Pale Rider*, the land has been stripped by ecologically unsound mining practices and hooliganism; all that's needed to set things right (in more ways than one) is a display of mighty rather than mousey muscle (this picture says: "The United States should nuke the Shiites"). In *Silverado*, a town is terrorized by a paunchy authoritarian; all that's needed to set things right (in more ways than one) is for the good guys to get together and form a vengeful family (this picture says: "NATO should nuke the Shiites").

Beyond Thunderdome is superficially similar, fundamentally different, and far more progressive politically. Whereas *Pale Rider* and *Silverado* are nostalgic retro artifacts anxious to reproduce the situations that gave the filmmakers mindless good times when they were in Davy Crockett caps, and are even more anxious to demonstrate that the values of those times – the values of the American Midwest of the fifties – still apply (talk about *Back to the Future*), *Beyond Thunderdome* is authentically utopian. The film is about a form of primitivism that Miller believes humankind must go beyond, a primitivism conveniently exemplified by *Pale Rider* and *Silverado*. In *Beyond Thunderdome*, primitivism is symbolized by the eponymous Thunderdome, the major form of entertainment in Bartertown, the single outpost of civilization in Max's world. Thunderdome is a Buckminster Fuller building in which two men, armed with their choice of weapons, decide a disagreement; the only rule is that the decision involve the death of one or both of them. (You can read this as a metaphor for everything from a bar brawl to a bad marriage to the Cold War to nuclear annihilation.)

What can be beyond all this, beyond Thunderdome? Mad Max IV's version of Walden II: Communards in Leather. On the far side of Thunderdome is a desert whence Max flees after his combat in Barter-town; in that desert is an oasis sheltering a society of children; those children, whose ancestors perished in the Third World War, have awaited the return of the pre-Holocaust world (Eden) and have constructed around its detritus – an abandoned jetliner, a View Master machine – a complicated cosmology of hope, a religion of renewal. Max, a man who understands odysseys, aids the kids by getting them to the ruins of Sydney, but along the way, he teaches them that he is not the Messiah they seek; he teaches them that the Messiah they seek may not exist; and he teaches them that while the society they seek may well exist, they will have to make it happen themselves, free from outside assistance.

Pale Rider preaches salvation through the destruction of other men and women, and posits a world in which mysterious events – personified by the stranger, played by Clint Eastwood, who descends like Jesus to reveal The Way – can be exploited to advance the cause of one's own family. *Silverado* preaches salvation through co-operation and posits a world in which derring-do and insane risks – personified by the film's heroes, who charge into town to reveal The Way – can be exploited to advance the cause of one's own family. In both cases, the future is faced by galloping into the past. *Mad Max Beyond Thunderdome* preaches salvation through hard work and knowledge, and posits a world in which co-operation – personified by the children who decide to rebuild Sydney, without knowing The Way, or even the way – can be exploited to advance the cause of the family of man. *Pale Rider* and *Silverado* celebrate force as a means of imposing lawfulness – the ideal it envisions is fascist; *Beyond Thunderdome* celebrates knowledge and understanding as an antidote to lawlessness – and if the unattainable utopia it envisions is tribal, the reality will no doubt turn out to be democratic. *Pale Rider* and *Silverado* are a product of the America of Reagan and Rambo, desperate to strike out and back; *Beyond Thunderdome* owes its ecumenical good cheer and optimism to a culture yet to become bitter or defensive.

But all three films join forces in hewing to the time-weathered romantic line: all three centre on romanticized individuals – Eastwood in *Pale Rider*, the gang of good guys in *Silverado*, Max in *Beyond Thunderdome* – who are in the last analysis classic Westerners, guys who know that no place they hang their hat is home. A community springs up in *Pale Rider*, a town is civilized in *Silverado*, and a metropolis is domesticated in *Beyond Thunderdome* – and Eastwood, the Silverado gang and Max all get the hell out of there. The family Eastwood inspired, the townsfolk the gang protected, the orphans Max fostered – all three communities are left tossing their gratitude onto the wings of the whistling wind, are left fondly remembering gods whose pre-eminent commandment was, Don't fence me in.

July 12, 1985

❖

Kiss of the Spider Woman

Directed by Hector Babenco
Written by Leonard Schrader (from a novel by Manuel Puig)
Starring William Hurt and Raul Julia

The structure of Manuel Puig's novel *Kiss of the Spider Woman* is dialectical simplicity itself: two men, Molina, a homosexual arrested on a morals charge, and Valentin, a revolutionary arrested for political reasons, share a jail cell and come to see the world in part through each other's eyes. Written in the form of non-stop dialogue and footnoted with bizarre digressions, the book is a love story that attempts a synthesis of Latin dichotomies: the puritanism of revolution and the anarchism of sexuality, the virility of machismo and the fragility of sensitivity, the push of optimism and the pull of pessimism. It's a stunt, but an extraordinary one, and the novel is a compulsively entertaining and speedy, if ultimately sentimental, read.

The film version, adapted by Leonard Schrader, is entertaining and ultimately sentimental, but there's nothing speedy about it, and it's stymied by the novel's structure. Molina was a creature of the movies and in the book he "told" the plots of several real films, including *Cat People*, to Valentin; in the movie, those films must be re-created through Molina's eyes – to include real movies would be unenlightening, in that we would learn nothing about Molina's attitudes toward them. The Molina of the novel loved and respected the films. The Molina of the movie condescends to them – as energetically reproduced by director Hector Babenco (*Pixote*), the films he "tells," a Nazi melodrama and a lush tropical fantasy, are camp.

That's not the only alteration in the film or even the most damaging. Far more significant is William Hurt's interpretation of the flamboyantly nellie Molina, a Latin answer to Albin, the transvestite of *La Cage aux Folles*. In the novel, Molina, a loser, learns to be a man by taking proud political action. (Valentin, meanwhile, learns to incorporate into his persona what the novel sees as female traits – he learns sensitivity and sensuality.) But because Hurt is in command of the character from the first moment he is on screen, and because the character is equally in command of himself, there is no psychological progression, no movement from loser to winner: this Molina is not an unsuccessful man, he's a wildly successful screaming queen.

Combine Hurt's excesses with Raul Julia's numbed interpretation of Valentin – the movie keeps telling us his personality is expanding, but what we see is the same dyspeptic scowl – and you end with something on the order of Mister Laurel and Miss Hardy; the biggest surprise of *Kiss of the Spider Woman* is just how enjoyable that can be, once the film's pretensions to greatness are laid to rest. Schrader has reproduced some of Puig's best bitchery and has added a few scathing *bons mots* of his own: it's worth the price of admission to hear Molina, whose offer of food to Valentin has been rebuffed, wonder what kind of revolution demands that its acolytes forgo avocados.

The camp films, which feature the madly photogenic Sonia Braga in various form-fitting fashions, are also a fair bit of fun, and the ending does send a light mist scudding across the eyeballs. *Kiss of the Spider Woman* may be yet another demonstration that great books seldom make great movies, but it also illustrates that, if judged on their own terms, adaptations of great books can fail with satisfying style: this one goes down with all hands on deck dancing.

September 11, 1985

Mishima

Directed by Paul Schrader
Written by Paul and Leonard Schrader
Starring Ken Ogata

Can a film that raises more questions about its subject than it answers be considered a masterpiece? If it can, that film is Paul Schrader's innovative cinematic biography of the Japanese novelist, essayist and actor Yukio Mishima, the man who in 1970 committed public seppuku (hara-kiri) in an unprecedented, grandiloquent attempt to turn his life into art.

Mishima has been conceived academically in four parts; each part has a story to tell and a thesis to advance. The technique is reductionist, to be sure, but the only way to begin to approach Mishima, whose most revealing novel was entitled *Confessions of a Mask*, is to take each pose at face value. Ergo, Schrader presents fundamentally without comment Mishima in his many guises – literary figure, loving family man, sadomasochistic homosexual, militaristic *poseur* – and he does it by using the artist's work; three of the film's four "chapters" are centred on highly stylized dramatizations of Mishima's novels (*The Temple of the Golden Pavilion, Runaway Horses, Kyoko's House*). The fourth and final "chapter" does not utilize a novel: by then, Mishima is writing his fiction in fact.

The stylized sequences have been photographed in a variety of pastel palettes by cinematographer John Bailey, have been plushly underpinned by an appropriately Wagnerian score from Philip Glass, and have been designed with exultant theatricality by Eiko Ishioka, whose tenure as art director at the Parco shopping centres in Tokyo altered advertising in the seventies. (And not only advertising: she and one of her collaborators, fashion designer Issey Miyake, were responsible by example for the over-all look of the Talking Heads concert tour reproduced in Jonathan Demme's film *Stop Making Sense*.) Because Schrader was forbidden by his agreement with Mishima's widow to make use of certain materials (missed the most: the novel *Forbidden Colors*), there is an odd indirection in many of the sequences – the film suggests rather than demonstrates, infers rather than depicts. The limitations imposed by the widow have ironically turned out to be salubrious, in that Mishima lived much of his life in disguise, and it seems only proper that his biography should present his life as if seen from behind a scrim.

Never before has the problematic director of *Cat People* and *Blue Collar* been so confident, so in control of his material – *Mishima* is so tight it comes close to strangling on its own schema. But it doesn't. Unified by Mishima's final day – he delivered the manuscript for *The Decay of the Angel*, the last instalment of his greatest achievement, *The Sea of Fertility* tetralogy, on the morning of his death – the four "chapters" survey directly his childhood (photographed in black and white), his youth and his literary career; the family life and the homosexuality are rendered elliptically. (In addition to the homosexuality, Schrader was not permitted to include on screen representations of the family.) Ken Ogata, familiar from *The Ballad of Narayama*, looks nothing like Mishima and fails to communicate the sinewy, effeminate silkiness of the man as seen in period kinescopes, but he is otherwise effective, and the actors who impersonate Mishima at younger ages are flawless. For students of Japan and Japanese film, the picture is a treasure trove: the pop star Kenji Sawada appears as a narcissistic actor in the Kyoko's House sequence, for example, and the legendary Sachiko Hidari, star of Shohei Imamura's *Insect Woman* (1963), is his preening mother.

Eiko Ishioka has said that Mishima became a non-person after his death in Japan because he held up "for all the world to see" the contradiction of what it meant to be Japanese in the last half of the twentieth century: he wanted, vaingloriously, to restore the Empire, but he also wanted the best of the West, and was proud of his international stature and his Occidental associates. Schrader has said that for him Mishima was "a bookend" to Travis Bickle, the character he created in *Taxi Driver*, the movie he wrote for Martin Scorsese. "I feel most congruent with him when he's talking about not being there, about not existing, about the things that don't work for him: the social unit doesn't work, family life doesn't work, sexual life doesn't work, fame doesn't work and finally art itself doesn't work," Schrader revealed last year on the set in Tokyo. "That's where I feel congruent and that's where the film finds its centre. I also feel rather comfortable with his day-to-day schizophrenia, both sexual and professional, the way he drifts and is not really anything, the way he avoids dealing with himself by putting on masks. He was afraid there was nothing under them. I think probably there was nothing. And yet this nothing, this black hole, sucked everything in. Nothing becomes everything."

With equal parts integrity and dementia, Mishima intransigently moved toward his fate and predictably found himself stranded in the cul-de-sac at the end of the romantic road. Schrader's film follows him each sturdy step of the way and becomes in the process a metaphor for one of the salient paradoxes of the age, expressed personally by Mishima's seppuku and globally by the Bomb: the insane need to authenticate existence by eradicating it.

September 12, 1985

❖

Jagged Edge

Directed by Richard Marquand
Written by Joe Eszterhas
Starring Jeff Bridges and Glenn Close

Jeff Bridges has always had one thing working against him in the superstar sweepstakes: he's too good. When Dustin Hoffman becomes Willy Loman, the effort is up there for all to see, but when Jeff Bridges takes on a character, he disappears with an effortlessness that seems magical only in retrospect. He's the Fred Astaire of acting, and in the ingeniously artificial courtroom thriller *Jagged Edge*, he gives a performance that barely grazes the ground.

A wealthy San Francisco newspaper publisher, Jack Forrester (Bridges), is accused on primarily circumstantial evidence of having brutally murdered his wife – the accuser is a district attorney (Peter Coyote) who has good reason to have it in for the guy. Forrester hires an attractive female attorney, Teddy Barnes (Glenn Close), to represent him, but she warns him that if she decides he's guilty, she'll drop the case. (Any lawyer that unprofessional should be automatically open to suspicion, but never mind.) He convinces her of his innocence and together they embark on constructing both his case and their love affair. The film winds up in court and brings back with vigorous and entirely satisfying over-acting the peculiar charms of Perry Mason, complete with a wily Hamilton Burger in the person of the wily prosecuting attorney. The only difference is that this time Della Street is in charge of the defence.

For *Jagged Edge* to work, the audience must be kept in doubt as to Jack Forrester's innocence, and Bridges is masterful at keeping everyone in the picture – and everyone watching it – off guard. The scene in which he re-enacts for Teddy Barnes his discovery of his wife's body is an acting masterpiece, the full scale of which cannot be appreciated until the denouement. (The climactic revelation is handicapped by a sloppily composed shot of the murderer that makes the guilty party look for a confusing moment like someone else in the film who could not possibly have committed the homicide.) Bridges' Jack Forrester is vital, seductive and guarded; he's the kind of man who can attract one woman and scare the hell out of the next.

Bridges is excellently supported by the menacing Coyote, and Close's scenes are jazzed up by the foul-mouthed Robert Loggia, who plays her researcher. But Close herself, the Midwest Meryl Streep, is adequate and nothing more. In *Jagged Edge*, she's the smooth cookie, and even when she's meant to be hysterical, her tantrums can't cut warm butter. Della Street, who sometimes drank acid for breakfast, would be disgusted.

October 4, 1985

Colonel Redl

Directed by Istvan Szabo
Written by Istvan Szabo and Peter Dobai
Starring Klaus Maria Brandauer

Colonel Redl, directed by Istvan Szabo with Klaus Maria Brandauer (the star of Szabo's previous film, *Mephisto*) in the role of Col. Alfred Redl, a lower-class homosexual Jewish functionary in the army of the Austro-Hungarian Empire, is a magisterial movie about betrayal, set in an epoch when betrayal was "a national virtue." The film has the sweep and depth of a great novel, and in Brandauer's subtle delineation of Redl, a man who denies his nature at every turn, it has a performance that ranks among the landmarks of modern cinema.

Szabo and his co-screenwriter, Peter Dobai, open the account when Redl is a child and for a time see his world through his eyes. What Redl, even as a small boy, most wants is to escape censure, in some vague way to succeed, to rise above his station. It's not easy: he is in the wrong class and of the wrong race, and as Szabo lets us know via a scene extraordinary in its economy – a piano teacher places a lustful hand on the boy's knee – he also harbours sexual desires that have been absolutely forbidden by the Emperor. Nonetheless, his talent for organization, which in his case amounts psychologically to a talent for repression, is sufficient to allow him to be accepted by a military academy normally reserved for the élite.

Redl prospers. But his desires remain. In an oddly erotic scene filmed in close-up, Redl smokes a cigarette with a homosexual officer who is preparing for a duel – nothing is stated, everything is suggested. Publicly, Redl separates himself from his past and from himself. "I've always noticed the soldiers who complain of privilege," he says contemptuously of his own kind, "are only of average ability." Stupidly, but understandably, he believes that by appearing to be anti-proletariat, anti-Semitic and anti-homosexual he can secure his place in the Empire's great adventure.

Much later, he will see his error and will defensively quote Montaigne: "It is no sin to be involved, it is a sin to remain uninvolved." The real Alfred Redl committed suicide on May 25, 1913; in 1924, a Prague journalist, Egon Erwin Kisch, concluded that Redl was forced to act as a spy for the Russians because his homosexuality had been discovered; the historian Robert Asprey followed the same interpretation in a 1945 book; as did Stefan Zweig, in *The World of Yesterday*; as did John Osborne in his play, *A Patriot for Me*. Szabo does, yet he doesn't: this is the most complex interpretation of the case yet presented, and for Szabo, homosexuality is merely the obvious means to Redl's destruction, the final nail in the coffin that had been constructed for him from birth.

Lavishly filmed and paced with a stateliness that allows welcome moments for introspection, *Colonel Redl* stands with Elsa Morante's shattering masterpiece, *History: A Novel*, in its intelligent analysis of the effect of great events on small people. But Morante's novel, laid in Rome during the Second World War, took as its heroine the part-Jewish schoolteacher Ida, whose sorry life (raped by a German soldier, she gave birth to a son she strove valiantly to protect) had no effect on the outcome of anything; without Morante, she would have been forgotten, a nameless life consigned to an anonymous grave. The irony of Szabo's attitude toward Redl, whose life was far from anonymous and whose death continues to inspire speculation, is that for all Redl's subsequent infamy, he was no less a powerless tool in the service of a cause he could never fully comprehend.

October 25, 1985

❖

One Magic Christmas

Directed by Phillip Borsos
Written by Thomas Meehan
Starring Mary Steenburgen, Gary Basaraba and Harry Dean Stanton

Three-quarters of the way through *One Magic Christmas*, a small-town wife and mother who has lost the Christmas spirit finds a letter she wrote as a child to Santa Claus. The letter, a scrawl on Ramada Inn stationery, initiates a pure Proustian experience – her memory is flooded with the warmth and optimism of childhood, and she remembers in an instant what innocence was. Because she has already lost most of what she once held dear, the effect is devastating; she is overcome with nostalgia for a world that will never be, and perhaps for a world that never was.

One Magic Christmas is a children's movie for adults, a one-of-a-kind classic. The debts to *A Christmas Carol* and *Miracle on 34th Street* are obvious, but not important: this is the darkest, most straightforward and realistic vision of the holiday season ever committed to celluloid. Canadian director Phillip Borsos (*The Grey Fox*), working from Thomas Meehan's script, has faced up to the reason so many people find Christmas depressing as they grow older – instead of being a reminder of how much is to come, it is a reminder of how much has been lost. For children who have never known death, Christmas exists as a celebration of the universe's benevolence, with the jolly fat man standing in for God; for adults reminded by Christmas of loved ones no longer there, the season can become symbolic of the abyss.

How can a film distributed by Disney cope with all this? Ginnie (Mary Steenburgen), the wife and mother, works in a grocery store. Her husband, Jack (Gary Basaraba), is a dreamer who may never amount to much. Her children, Abbie (Elizabeth Harnois) and Cal (Robbie Magwood), are looking forward to Christmas along with their father, but Ginnie, the realist, feels no reason to get excited. Enter Gideon (Harry Dean Stanton), an angel in a long black coat and black hat – Gideon looks like The Exorcist. He tells the kids that they must trust him and that he thinks he can restore their mom's Christmas spirit. The next day, their father is shot in a bank robbery.

From there on, it is impossible to discuss the plot without destroying the film. Borsos and Meehan combine realism with outrageously entertaining magic – there is a full-dress visit to the North Pole with opera singer Jan Rubes as Santa – and their version of Ginnie's Christmas-yet-to-come makes the dismal future painted for Scrooge by the ghost in *A Christmas Carol* seem comparatively rosy. (Scrooge, after all, had nothing to lose but money.) The lesson Ginnie is taught for failing to have the Christmas spirit is almost sadistic, in fact (alternate title: One Hell of a Christmas), and the film comes dangerously close to winding up in a pessimistic cul-de-sac.

But it gets out of it, with the help of that leathery old angel Gideon. In a film of fine performances, Harry Dean Stanton's is the finest: perched in a tree and playing his harmonica, he looks more like a child molester than a harbinger of season's greetings, but his weathered face and his sparkling black eyes become a metaphor for how it is possible to reach great age and, against all odds, hold on to a twinkle of innocence.

Starkly and effectively shot by cinematographer Frank Tidy, *One Magic Christmas* is in the end an existential parable based on the fable Colin Wilson tells of the fairy in the vinegar bottle. A dissatisfied fairy promises that she will stop complaining if only she can live in surroundings a bit more spacious. Put into a small hut, she is happy for a time, but then starts feeling cramped; put into a mansion, she is happier for a longer time, and then starts feeling cramped; put back into the vinegar bottle, she finally appreciates what she had been given.

Most children's movies promise heaven for good behaviour on earth; *One Magic Christmas* does not. It looks honestly at the pain Christmas can bring and advises those in pain to concentrate not on what they have lost but on what they have gained, or at least retained. Offered the hut once more, the sadder but wiser fairy feels she's recovered the mansion.

November 22, 1985

❖

Dreamchild

Directed by Gavin Millar
Written by Dennis Potter
Starring Coral Browne and Ian Holm

In *Dreamchild*, a glorious memory and mood piece directed by Gavin Millar and written by Dennis Potter (*Pennies From Heaven*), Alice is once again in Wonderland. Alice Liddell Hargreaves (Coral Browne), the seventy-nine-year-old woman who at the age of ten inspired the Rev. Charles Dodgson, also known as Lewis Carroll, to commit to paper *Alice's Adventures in Wonderland*, has been invited to New York to celebrate the centenary of the writer's birth. The year is 1932, and Mrs. Hargreaves, an imperious Victorian, is thrown, much against her iron will, into a new kind of Wonderland: America in the Depression.

She brings with her a gem in the form of a beautiful and unworldly young orphan employed as her maid, Lucy (Nicola Cowper), and a treasure chest of memories, not all of them sparkling. *Dreamchild* opens with a fantasy sequence in which the aged Alice is on a fabulist seashore with Carroll's Gryphon and Mock Turtle, both created, along with the rest of the creatures in the film, by Jim Henson, and both fiendishly faithful to John Tenniel's original illustrations. Throughout the film, as Mrs. Hargreaves thinks back on events of the summer of 1862 when she coaxed the shy and stuttering Dodgson into telling her his tales, the past and present, along with fantasy and reality, become confused in Mrs. Hargreaves' mind.

Landing in New York, she is met by a phalanx of reporters – an editor at the *New York Herald Tribune* has told his staff, "Any old dame who fell down a rabbit hole and had tea with the Mad Hatter is going to cheer me up" – but she is instantly put off by their rudeness and vulgarity. She dismisses them by snapping of Dodgson, "I can scarce recall him after all these years." She is lying.

The truth is that she remembers Dodgson all too well. She remembers his stories, she remembers her love for him, she remembers his love for her, and she remembers that there was something not quite right about that love. In one extraordinary flashback, the ten-year-old Alice (Amelia Shankley) has joined her mother (Jane Asher) and Dodgson (Ian Holm) for an afternoon boating excursion. Dodgson stares at Alice with a love that imperceptibly transforms itself into lust. Alice splashes him – quickly, viciously. "He was looking at me," she explains, not fully conscious of what she means. Then she rushes apologetically to embrace him.

Potter and Millar have caught perfectly the repressions of the era and they have dealt sensitively not only with Alice's anguish as an object of tainted desire, but with Dodgson's anguish at feeling that desire. "It's an emotion I've always been frightened of," the elderly Alice confesses of love, and when we see the young Alice with Dodgson, we understand why. But Dodgson, for all his pathetic pedophiliac longings, is not presented as a pathetic figure: he sublimates his desires

213

and in so doing creates a masterwork of children's literature. The scenes in which that masterwork is unveiled for Alice are elegiac and civilized, with a disturbing and potentially malevolent underside – rather like the Victorian era itself.

In New York, Mrs. Hargreaves and Lucy fall in with an ambitious reporter (Peter Gallagher) who merchandises the Alice connection with a verve Mrs. Hargreaves comes to admire. She is pushed into accepting commercial endorsements ("Not think about what I'm saying?" she trumpets when a radio director advises she not fret about the message of a soap commercial, "I've never heard of anything so reprehensible in my life") and into condoning a "talking picture" based on *Alice's Adventures* that has not yet been made. At the same time, in her dreams, the dying woman – she knows she is about to die, and muses, "Now that I am very old, I find the Grim Reaper has a smile on his face, after all" – is back in Wonderland: at the tea party in her nightmares, the Mad Hatter taunts her with, "You should be dead, dead, DEAD."

Browne brings to the aging Alice the pathos of a woman surviving on strengths gleaned from times long gone. This unimpeachable performance reaches epiphany when Alice accepts an honorary degree at Columbia University. As she reads Dodgson's words, the failing figure on the Columbia stage looks back across the years to the man she loved (with justification) and to the man she feared (with reason). She tells the audience she was too young to realize the extent of his gift, too naive to accept it, too uncaring to appreciate it. Then Millar cuts to Dodgson, distraught and awkward and guilt-ridden that day on that river opalescent with sunlight and greenery and promise, and Dodgson smiles at the little Alice; across the miles and across the years, the dying Alice smiles back – with gratitude, forgiveness and love.

December 13, 1985

❖

Ran

Directed by Akiro Kurosawa
Written by Akiro Kurosawa, Hideo Oguni and Masato Ide
Starring Tatsuya Nakadai

"This is the end, my friend ... beautiful end." – *Jim Morrison*

Francis Coppola used those lines from one of the most famous of The
Doors' compositions in *Apocalypse Now*, but the picture to which they
apply is Japanese director Akiro Kurosawa's *Ran*, which means Chaos,
and which is the greatest nihilistic film in the history of movies. No
other director of Kurosawa's age has ever released a statement of such
magisterial, uncompromising bleakness, and no other director has
ever made destruction seem so inevitable, so esthetic, so seductive.
Most nihilistic films are made by dyspeptic pessimists in their
twenties. Kurosawa is seventy-five years old and is working at the
peak of his considerable powers; his age and his stature impart to *Ran*
an authority that may be possible to argue with, but is impossible to
dismiss.

Although *Ran* is based loosely (very loosely) on Shakespeare's
King Lear, there is never a sense in *Ran*, as there is occasionally in *Lear*,
that the protagonist's fate is too harsh – Kurosawa is careful to present
a warlord who has earned the chaos he has created. The bulk of the
contemplatively paced first hour deals with the decision by Lord
Hidetora (Tatsuya Nakadai) to divide his kingdom among his sons (to
divide a kingdom among daughters in sixteenth-century Japan would
be inconceivable) as a method of guaranteeing the kingdom's survival.
The sons think the decision insane and the youngest, Saburo (Daisuke
Ryu), is blunt: "What do you think this world is? This is a world where
men's evil, cruel instincts are exposed, where you cannot live unless
you throw aside your humanity and all better feelings. You spilled an
ocean of blood, showed no mercy, no pity. But, father, we too are

215

children of this degraded age, weaned on strife and chaos. 'My dear children,' you think. You do not know what we are thinking: to me, father, you are an old, senile madman."

That speech is from Kurosawa's version of Shakespeare's Cordelia – Saburo is the child who cares enough to tell the truth. Hidetora, protrayed brilliantly by Nakadai with a ravaged Kabuki stylization that makes him more sympathetic than he may have any right in Kurosawa's mind to be, pays no attention and banishes the boy. The stubbornness of Hidetora, Lord of the House of Ichimonji, written ironically with the Japanese character for One, leads to the splintering of the oneness symbolized by the family name, and to a wholesale carnage that for Kurosawa exemplifies the conduct of human beings. "Nature takes good care of her appearance," he wrote several years ago in his autobiography. "What makes nature ugly is the behaviour of human beings." Even in the blasted, post-nuclear landscapes Kurosawa employs for much of *Ran*, there is eerie beauty; in the actions of the figures in that landscape, the beauty that exists is too little too late.

But beauty there is. *Ran* contrasts the malevolent actions of the Lady Kaeda (Meiko Harada), wife of the first son, with the compassionate actions of the Lady Sue, wife of the second son. Hidetora long ago destroyed the families of both women, but whereas Lady Kaeda reacted by turning to revenge, Lady Sue reacted by turning to religion. Kurosawa applauds her alternative, even as he dismisses its ultimate efficacy – in *Ran*, the only ultimate is the void.

The unparalleled ability at staging battles which the younger Kurosawa brought to *Yojimbo*, *The Hidden Fortress* and *The Seven Samurai* – movies that influenced virtually every American action director – surfaces halfway through *Ran*. Kurosawa's own description in his unpublished *Ran* screenplay of an eight-minute apocalypse cannot be topped: "From this point, a terrible scroll of Hell. There are no real sounds during this scroll. It unfolds like a daytime nightmare. It is a scene of human evil-doing, the way of the demonic Ashura, as seen by a Buddha in tears. The music superimposed on the pictures is, like the Buddha's heart, measured in beats of profound anguish, the chanting of a melody full of sorrow, that begins like sobbing and rises gradually as it is repeated like Karmic cycles, and finally like the wailing of countless Buddhas."

In *Ran*, Buddha is absent, or reduced at most to the role of an impotent onlooker (the final, heart-stopping image is unequivocal). Humanity is in turn summarized by a ghastly joke made by the fool (Peter, a Tokyo transvestite performer): "Man is born crying. When he's cried enough, he dies." All the jokes in *Ran* are philosophical: "I'm lost," moans Hidetora, having taken the wrong road. "Such," cracks the fool, "is the human condition."

On no account is any of this self-pitying, self-indulgent or even depressing: in *Ran*, the only account Kurosawa settles is with existence itself, and he is determined artistically to even the score with fury, precision and grandeur. In 1981, he wrote, "There is one person I feel I would like to resemble as I grow old: the late American film director John Ford . . . Of course, compared to these two illustrious masters, [Jean] Renoir and Ford, I am no more than a little chick." Well, neither Ford nor Renoir, for all their genius, would have been capable of the scene in *Ran* in which Hidetora descends from a burning castle and sleepwalks through soldiers who part in horror at the spectacle of a man whose madness has at last enabled him to see existence whole. ("The failing mind," says the fool, "sees the heart's failings.") For all its revulsion at human behaviour, *Ran* is an act of sublime empathy: it views the world through eyes that have seen everything, through eyes that have refused to look away. The eyes are Kurosawa's own.

December 20, 1985

❖

Aliens

Directed by James Cameron
Written by James Cameron, Walter Hill and David Giler
Starring Sigourney Weaver

Conventional Hollywood wisdom has it that to work, sequels must actually be re-makes of the original, only bigger – the thinking is that audiences go to sequels to reproduce the experience of seeing a movie they already know they love. By that standard, *Aliens*, Canadian writer-director James Cameron's sequel to Ridley Scott's *Alien*, the movie in which nasty things emerged from people's tummies – the movie that critic Roger Ebert said was really about the fear of cancer – should be one of the monstrous hits of the year.

It deserves to be. It is a re-make of *Alien* (Sigourney Weaver even goes back for the cat again, in a manner of speaking), but it is bigger, better and – at about two hours and twenty minutes – longer. Although it remains faithful to the thoroughly grotesque cosmos Ridley Scott devised for *Alien*, it is a far more traditional exercise in scaring and thrilling the moviegoer; essentially, it re-constitutes the war movie, and in so doing marries a feminist *Rambo* to *Star Wars*.

You'll remember that, having bested the ugliest beasties the universe had to offer, Sigourney Weaver at the end of *Alien* climbed into her hyper-space sleep-chamber with her kitty and set off for homeplate. At the beginning of *Aliens*, she gets there, only to find that her journey took fifty-seven years and that in the interim the corporation for which she worked has blithely colonized the planet that gave birth to the beasties. She is not amused: "Did IQs just sharply drop while I was away?" she wonders acidly.

Zap. All communication signals from the colony cease and she is asked by Burke (Paul Reiser), a corporate representative, to accompany a group of "colonial Marines" on a rescue mission as "a consultant." The parallels to various real-life rescue missions undertaken by the Americans are obvious, but perhaps because Cameron is

Canadian, the movie is far from gung ho about militarism; it argues that informed civilians might know something, and it argues against the indiscriminate, vengeful slaughter that *Rambo* celebrates. The Marine company is, in fact, virtually a copy of the slap-happy, foul-mouthed, working-class cretins of *Alien*, except that this time, they're slap-happy, foul-mouthed, working-class killers, and they include several female "grunts." "Have you ever been mistaken for a man?" one of the guy-grunts asks Vasquez, a tough-as-taco-sauce Puerto Rican woman who likes to waste enemies while wearing a red bandanna and flexing her biceps. "No," she snarls, "have you?" Also along for the journey is Bishop (Lance Henriksen), called variously an "android" and a "synthetic," though he says with a straight face – the only kind of face he has – "I prefer the term artificial person, myself."

On the beastie planet, the Marines land amidst much profanity and the deployment of much hardware. (Cameron previously directed *The Terminator*; he has a love of vehicles and guns that Scott did not share. That love gives the first forty-five minutes of *Aliens*, minutes consumed by an elaborate set-up for what is to follow, their own kind of tension and bizarre beauty.) It transpires that the beasties are still about and that a small blonde child, Newt (Carrie Henn), has managed to repel their drooling onslaught.

Enough plot. From here on, Cameron, whose talent is considerable – his use of close-ups, for example, is both incessant and eloquent – piles one peril on another, shamelessly and effectively: you may giggle at yourself for sitting on the edge of your seat, but the backrest will remain untouched. Up against the wall with time running out (the situations are nothing if not clichéd – there's even a kid hanging from a high-tech cliff), Sigourney Weaver is given two reasons most pacifists accept as justifications to kill – self-defence and the protection of the young – and when she moves into murderous gear, she makes the Schwarzeneggers and Stallones of the movie world look like posturing male pinups. She is, in fact, a complete adventure-film heroine, able to beat the men at their own (war) game while expressing love and maternity on the side. (As an actress, Weaver has left her resemblance to Jane Fonda behind; in *Aliens*, she's more like Mercedes McCambridge as Luz Benedict, the self-sufficient matriarch of *Giant*.) The final showdown is mother to mother – all barrels blazing, Weaver goes up against what has to be the meanest mother of all time, and in the process she and her film turn audiences into screaming, cheering children. If all mothers were like this one, Freud would have kept his trap shut. Or had it shot off.

July 19, 1986

The Fly

Directed by David Cronenberg
Written by David Cronenberg and Charles Edward Pogue
Starring Jeff Goldblum and Geena Davis

In David Cronenberg's astounding remake of *The Fly*, a scientist puts himself in a pod, "teleports" himself to another pod and in the process is combined, molecularly and genetically, with a common housefly that accidentally entered the apparatus when it was switched on – the film is about a man's fight to remain a man while his flesh insists on turning into an insect.

The film also acts as a metaphor for its creator: Cronenberg, who is based in Toronto, has spliced his own extremely idiosyncratic obsessions into a Hollywood format, resulting in a movie that is a battle between Cronenberg the Canadian artist and Cronenberg the Hollywood entertainer.

In the end, the Canadian wins. *The Fly* is a mass-market, horror-film masterpiece that is also a work of art; it is the very movie the timorous feared *Aliens* would be – a gruesome, disturbing, fundamentally uncompromising shocker that accesses the subconscious.

From the beginning of his controversial career (controversial because most of his films are gross beyond belief), Cronenberg has been fascinated by the flesh and horrified by the ills to which it falls heir. (A line from *The Fly*: "That's why old ladies pinch babies' cheeks. It's the flesh. It makes them crazy.")

In Cronenberg's cancerous universe, anything that alters the flesh can be transformed into the material of dread. In *Shivers*, it was venereal disease; in *Scanners*, telepathy; in *The Brood*, pregnancy, and in *Videodrome*, the electronic media, by virtue of the film's assumption that television could somehow reorder the neurology of the human body. Now, in *The Fly*, it is cancer itself, with a strong, if subliminal dollop of AIDS panic – or, as the scientist himself describes his condition, "a bizarre form of cancer and general cellular chaos."

The scientist, Seth Brundle (Jeff Goldblum), meets a reporter, Veronica (Geena Davis), at a convention at the Art Gallery of Ontario. He is working on something, he tells her, "that will change the world." To prove it, he invites her back to his place for cappuccino and a peek at the device. "I have a Faema of my own," he adds boyishly, pushing his proficiency with espresso. "You know what that is?" She does.

The teleportation pods don't impress her – "designer phone booths," she sniffs – but once their capabilities are demonstrated, she is hooked, on them and on him. As he slowly, surely, excruciatingly is metamorphosed into an unimaginably grotesque mutant (the make-up is magnificent), she finds herself unable to abandon him, in part because she is pregnant with his baby. (There is an abortion sequence that contains several of the most terrifying, repugnant seconds ever shot; Cronenberg appears in the vignette as the doctor in charge.)

At first, the scientist considers himself "born again" in his "new flesh" (a motif carried over from *Videodrome*) and is ecstatic about the baptism. "Am I different somehow?" he asks. "Is it live or is it Memorex?" But when the metamorphosis, which begins with stout hairs on the back and purplish spots on the face, changes all that, he resolves first to cure and then to kill himself. "I won't," he vows, "be just another tumorous bore."

The film's concession to Hollywood structure arrives in the person of the reporter's editor, Stathis Borans (John Getz), who is basically around to give the plot a kick in the impetus every so often. His clankingly clear-cut function as a catalyst is exacerbated by the dreadful performance of Getz – the maladroit scenes between the editor and the reporter feel as though they've been dropped in from an earlier era in Cronenberg's career. (His films were not famed for their kindness to thespians.)

But Goldblum gives a peerless portrayal of a man watching his body turn itself inside out, recalling in the process everything from Frankenstein's monster to Spencer Tracy's Jekyll and Hyde to one of James Cagney's oddly witty gangsters to Charles Laughton's Hunchback of Notre Dame.

Underneath its melodramatic horror-film disguise, *The Fly* is a classic tragedy ("I was not pure," says the scientist of the reason for his fate) with a hero who comes to the ugly, pathetic demise he engineered for himself with a dignity – with a grandeur, almost – that is the last, transcendent vestige of his humanity.

"The challenge," Cronenberg has said, "was to do it straight, to do it without parody and to do it for real. And to say, well, there's a period in everyone's life when he or she is going to be a monster, whether it is because of old age or death or weirdness or senility or whatever, and so I'm going to play it as a metaphor for that, play it absolutely straight and not pull any punches, and hope it works."

It does: a movie about a man who gets changed into a fly has become a universal statement, an unforgettable explication of what its maker sees as the horror of the human condition.

August 15, 1986

The Decline of the American Empire

Written and directed by Denys Arcand

Starring Dorothée Berryman, Louise Portal, Pierre Curzi, Rémy Girard,
Yves Jacques, Dominique Michel, Genevieve Rioux, Daniel Briere
and Gabriel Arcand

Dancing in the Dark

Written and directed by Leon Marr (from the novel by Joan Barfoot)
Starring Martha Henry and Neil Munro

On a rudimentary level, the contrast between the two Canadian
films *The Decline of the American Empire* and *Dancing in the Dark*
is the contrast between stereotypical Canadian solitudes – the ebulli-
ence and *joie de vivre* of Quebec bloom comically in one while the
dourness and repression of Ontario dankly fill the other.

In Quebec director Denys Arcand's *Decline of the American
Empire*, the large and talented cast discusses past and present sexual
relationships in a detail that is sometimes joyful, sometimes poignant,
and invariably dirty; in Toronto director Leon Marr's *Dancing in the
Dark*, a lone woman, in hospital for reasons initially unknown, discusses the single sexual relationship of her life in exhaustive detail – a
detail that is sometimes literary, sometimes lyrical, nearly always
poignant, rarely joyful and never dirty.

The central situation of *Decline* is quintessentially contemporary:
while the men make dinner and talk about the women, the women
work out in a health club and talk about the men. *Decline* is all talk,
but it's talk that hits home, at least in Quebec. The speechifiers
include:

• Rémy (Rémy Girard), married twenty years, but an unregener-
ate rake ("I once visited a brothel on the way to see my mistress. Try
explaining that to a woman");

• Claude (Yves Jacques), a gay teacher who confesses the only time
he feels alive is when he's on the prowl – and that the only thing he

regrets about his nights in bars, baths and parks is that he's too tired to teach the next day;

• Mario (Gabriel Arcand), a sadistic punk who acts as the film's symbol of unfettered working-class id;

• Diane (Louise Portal), the cultured woman with whom Mario is involved. She worries about her involvement because she is not worried ("Then he tied me to the radiator," she recalls in the health club. "It's me I'm afraid of. I'm the one who always wants to go further. The power of the victim is incredible");

• Dominique (Dominique Michel), an academic who has developed a thesis to explain the scarcity of commitment and surfeit of hypocrisy she sees around her – she has concluded that as the "American Empire" has declined, the emphasis on individual happiness has resulted in collective misery.

And yet, the only time the people in *Decline* are truly happy is when they are with their friends. The film argues that if the romantic dyad has failed to live up to expectations, and if the nuclear family has proved disastrously susceptible to fission, comfort can still be found in the communality of friendship. Arcand himself does not share Dominique's nay-saying: "After I had written three-quarters of the script," he has said, "I had to invent a thesis and justify all the blue language I'd written. It's not a real thesis, it's a thesis for movie purposes."

Decline, photographed in warm autumnal colours, is open-ended enough to absorb varying interpretations. Despite Arcand's disclaimer, it can be seen as a demonstration of Dominique's thesis, or as nonjudgmental, supercharged naturalism (few people are this funny this often), or as a vicious satire of the self-absorbed. (Mostly, it should be seen.) For Arcand, "It's a film about my friends. I love them, even if I see what they are." A lot of people, even people in grim Ontario and points west, are likely to find their friends – and themselves – in Arcand's company.

Leon Marr's *Dancing in the Dark*, from a book by Joan Barfoot, has been repeatedly described as Bergmanesque, and it is: Scenes From a Moribund Marriage. When the film had its world première at the

Cannes Film Festival last May, the reaction was split along cultural lines. The French loved it, many of the Americans hated it, English-Canadians respected it, and French-Canadians were amused by it.

It was invited to the New York Film Festival, but even there the reaction was far from uniform. One member of the selection committee, aghast that another member liked it so much, was told by the admirer that the movie was a comedy, "a parody of that kind of film." (Martin Knelman has already longed in print to see Andrea Martin send it up on SCTV.) Love it or not, few Canadians are apt to share the U.S. position that the picture is a parody; it's an admirably straight-ahead exploration of a tidy perfect Ontario life that falls apart (even the pieces are tidy).

After twenty years of marriage, housewife Edna Cormick (Martha Henry) is asked by husband Harry (Neil Munro) if she's happy. This woman, who spends her days in a frenzy of housecleaning and cooking – she has no life away from the scouring pad and the food processor – has never thought about herself in those terms. In the literary, voice-over narration that glueily binds the film together like cornstarch, Edna, who has just turned forty, dismisses the question with the bald statement, "This is it. This is what I'm doing." Only when a crisis intervenes does she seriously reassess her narrow, hermetically enclosed universe. "I spent twenty years unwittingly," she says in a perfect diction that bespeaks the control she practised so long and so well, "and did a lifetime's thinking in a mere twelve hours."

The stark, uncompromising style developed by Marr and his cameraman, Vic Sarin, for *Dancing in the Dark* is an optical correlative of Edna's bleak interior existence: small rooms seem smaller, cleanliness becomes antiseptic, and everything is drenched in a fuzzy golden light that may be Edna's last-ditch effort to "see pretty."

A crippled and all too replaceable appendage to an uncaring husband, the poor creature could have been ridiculous – her story could have been a parody of that kind of film – without Martha Henry. But her performance is unimpeachable, a paradoxically expansive portrait of a constricted woman with no options. Even the furiousness of her obsessive floor-scrubbing, risible at first, becomes a soberingly objective indication of her doomed attempt to make sense of the senseless, to wipe up a mess impervious to the cleanser of the most perfect housekeeper. Should the troubled but fun-loving souls of *Decline of the American Empire* ever see *Dancing in the Dark*, they may realize how lucky they are.

September 5, 1986

Blue Velvet

Written and directed by David Lynch
Starring Kyle MacLachlan, Isabella Rossellini and Dennis Hopper

Red roses against a white fence against a blue sky: writer-director David Lynch's metaphysical mystery *Blue Velvet*, the oddest Hollywood film of this or any other year, begins its tour through trauma in beauty. In a suburban backyard – Anytime, Anywhere – a man watering a lawn falls to the ground, clutching his ear. A dog drinks from the spume of water issuing from the hose that the man continues to clutch in his hand. The camera moves across the grass, into the grass, and settles on large black beetles fighting or mating; that the activity is indefinable – that combat and coupling are indistinguishable – is *Blue Velvet*'s opening statement of what will become a barrage of interlocking themes.

Young Jeffrey Beaumont (Kyle MacLachlan), home from college, finds an ear in the lawn and takes it to a detective; meets the detective's blonde, innocent daughter Sandy (Laura Dern); meets the dark chanteuse Dorothy (Isabella Rossellini), whose favourite song, a song she performs execrably at The Slow Club, is Bobby Vinton's hit "Blue Velvet"; watches from a closet as Frank (Dennis Hopper), a psychotic hooked on the inhalation of nitrous oxide, performs with Dorothy an impure Oedipal act of love that is an act of pure misogynist hate;

continues to investigate the "mystery" of the ear; and concludes, "I'm seeing something that was always hidden."

In his most disturbingly disorienting films (especially in *Psycho*), Alfred Hitchcock ripped the scrim from the American dream and exposed an American nightmare that threatened to break free of the director's carefully constructed thriller formats. But Hitchcock always retained commercialized control; though audiences were titillated and repulsed, they were never required to confront their voyeuristic yen to vicariously experience pleasure and pain – Hitchcock never asked his fans to think about the reason they wanted to witness the horror of other human beings. In *Blue Velvet*, which owes an incalculable debt to Hitchcock but intellectually transcends him, David Lynch does. The "mystery" is never solved on any real level: the entire film exists, like Lynch's earlier cult hit *Eraserhead*, in fantasy, in a place Lynch would no doubt argue is the most real level of all, the interior of the human mind. (Or at least the inside of David Lynch's mind.)

The two women Jeffrey meets are obvious embodiments of the madonna-whore syndrome – the light woman who brings life and the dark woman who brings death – while the character of Frank can be read psychoanalytically, as the Oedipal father from whose influence Jeffrey must escape in order to assert his identity. Other interpretations are possible: because *Blue Velvet* is not motivated by naturalism (the dialogue is intentionally clichéd and hilarious, utterly at odds with the horrific happenings), its vision of America as a sore festering beneath a bandage can also be taken as political or sociological satire. What defies interpretation is Lynch's talent, already familiar from *The Elephant Man* and *Dune*, for manufacturing sequences of unsurpassed ugliness. Not even David Cronenberg – not even the David Cronenberg of *Shivers* – has ever topped, if that's the proper term, the viciously decadent *Dune*.

Yet *Blue Velvet* represents for Lynch an evolution: rather than exulting in ugliness, he self-critically analyzes the desire to exult in it. Hidden things, he implies, become attractive things; that which is repressed becomes monstrous – he has repeatedly given vent in interviews to his fear that the United States is engaged in a massive act of collective repression that imperils its survival. "I don't know if you're a detective or a pervert," says the light woman to Jeffrey, who is the ultimate expression not only of Hitchcock's passive heroes, but also of those of his imitator, Brian De Palma. "That's for me to know and you to find out," Jeffrey coyly replies, but it's for him to know and for him to find out; at the beginning of *Blue Velvet*, he is in no position to know because his suburban backyard has insulated him from the "trouble in the world," as he phrases it, and from the trouble in himself. By the end of the film, he does know. The exterior "detective" has discovered the interior "pervert." The mystery *Blue Velvet* actually solves is the mystery of its hero's identity: with an ear to the ground, so to speak, Jeffrey finds the self-knowledge without which wisdom is powerless to begin.

September 20, 1986

Sid and Nancy

Directed by Alex Cox
Written by Alex Cox and Abbe Wool
Starring Gary Oldman and Chloe Webb

"If I asked you to kill me, would you?" – *Nancy Spungen wonders if Sid Vicious really loves her* . . .

Sid and Nancy, director Alex Cox's realistically scabrous yet weirdly lyrical autopsy of the "romance" between Sex Pistols bass player Sid Vicious and American groupie Nancy Spungen, is like getting a tooth filled without benefit of Novocaine: the relief when the pain has passed is so great it's possible to look back on the experience with nostalgia. But it's more than that: it's like getting a tooth filled sans anesthesia by a dentist who's a deadpan black comic – every time he pushes the drill through the enamel, he delivers a sidesplitting sick joke that leaves the patient howling in pleasure and twisting in pain. Sid and Nancy would, no doubt, approve.

Largely the invention of boutique owner Malcolm McLaren (David Hayman), the Sex Pistols flourished as the most *outré* of punk groups during the movement's brief efflorescence in the seventies. McLaren recruited John Lydon, who would become Johnny Rotten (Drew Schofield), and John Ritchie, who transformed himself into the anorexic and ferally charismatic Sid Vicious (Gary Oldman), and encouraged them to record a venomous version of "God Save the Queen" – this was during the Queen's Jubilee celebration in 1977 – that made the Sex Pistols and their album (*Never Mind the Bollocks, Here's the Sex Pistols*) infamous.

In the meantime, Vicious, harshly but truthfully summed up by McLaren as "a fabulous disaster" who embodied "the dementia of a nihilistic generation," met Nancy Spungen (Chloe Webb), a screaming id in leather, satin and high heels whose moon face bore a slight resemblance to Deborah Harry. ("It's a bad deal, lookin' like an established star, let me tell you," Nancy screeches.) Sid and Nancy were fêted by friends on champagne, baked beans and heroin. ("I wonder," sighs a drug addict as a stone shatters a window, presumably announcing the arrival of another guest, "who that is?") Nancy awakened Sid's slumbering sexuality (he lived what the Marquis de Sade could only write) and Sid provided Nancy with a sense of worth (toward the end of their lives, she said, "At least you used to be something, I've never been anything"). Before long, they settled into a grotesque slapstick parody of marital bliss and bathos; the vignette in which he vacuums the floor in a posing strap and then takes five to whack her evokes Maggie and Jiggs in hell.

Singly, Sid and Nancy were strange – she worked as an s/m hooker in London as he was touring Texas, slicing himself up with razor blades in his hotel rooms – but as a pair, they were indescribable. During a visit to her grandparents in Pennsylvania, Grandpa Spungen (Milton Selzer) turned a beady eye on Sid and asked, "What are your intentions?" Sid: "First, we're going to go down to the methadone clinic . . . then we're going out in a blaze of glory." Cox, director of *Repo Man*, presents Sid as a boy who knew his own mind. What there was of it.

The one thing Sid and Nancy could not be convicted of was compromise, and Cox has created a film true to that part of their spirit, but he has created something much more, a send-up and critique of the kind of cautionary celebrity biography exemplified by *Lady Sings the Blues*. Hypocritical Hollywood tracts squirt crocodile tears over awesome wastes of talent while revelling in every sordid step of celebrity decline, but in Cox's film, performed by his leads with an acting fervour that borders on demonic possession, Sid and Nancy begin at the bottom and burrow through the floor – Sid can feel neither the pleasure of his fame nor the pain of losing it, while Nancy is incapable of reacting to anything beyond the sensation of each given second. (Strung out, she compares herself self-pityingly to a famous fashion doll: "I'll never look like Barbie. Barbie doesn't have bruises.") It's as if Scott and Zelda, having been lobotomized – or perhaps having grown weary of the need to impress through excess – had decided that living badly was the best revenge; that Sid and Nancy did not try to shock is what makes their *amour fou* so shocking. A social worker at the methadone clinic remarks perceptively, "You guys got no business being strung out on that stuff, you could be selling healthy anarchy." But Sid and Nancy were selling nothing; they somehow slipped through the cracks of society and found a bottomless pit of . . . negation. Not only was Sid a fabulous disaster, he was a fabulous casualty, which is what makes the picture's high point, his rendition of the chestnut "My Way" – a bloodstained Nancy joins him on stage in an eerie simulation of their fate – so unsettlingly poignant, and so blackly funny. Nancy used to worry that Sid didn't really love her, but he did; hell, he killed her to prove it.

October 31, 1986

❖

Something Wild

Directed by Jonathan Demme
Written by E. Max Frye
Starring Jeff Daniels and Melanie Griffith

Something Wild is something else, a love story and a satire and a road movie and a fantasy that thuds to the soft heartbeats of a hippie and is knocked around by the hard head of the SoHo avant-garde: it's one of the finest, funniest American films of the year.

Its director, Jonathan Demme, a specialist in American eccentrics (*Handle With Care*, also known as *Citizens' Band*; *Melvin and Howard*; *Stop Making Sense*), has said that when he received the script from E. Max Frye, a recent college graduate, he began reading it as a courtesy. "But in the first few pages, I was hooked. I had no idea where the story was going. But I wanted to go along with it. And every time I thought I had it figured out, it veered off in another direction."

It does. Charles Driggs (Jeff Daniels) is a white-bread yuppie who works for a tax consultancy firm in Manhattan – he's just been appointed a vice-president. At lunch one afternoon, he walks out without paying and is accosted by Lulu (Melanie Griffith), a free-spirited stunner (hair by Louise Brooks, jewelry by all of Mexico) who had dined in the same restaurant while reading a copy of a biography of Mexican painter Frida Kahlo. Lulu informs Charles that "he's a closet rebel," invites him to accept a lift back to the office, kidnaps him, and takes him to New Jersey, where: (1) she handcuffs him to a bed and vamps him, (2) introduces him to her mother as her husband, and (3) invites him to her tenth high school reunion. "I like you, Charlie," she explains, "you're a really nice guy. Maybe a little too nice."

But Charlie isn't what he seems and neither is Lulu, and therein lies *Something Wild*'s dramatic method: it's a love story between put-ons who at last take it off, who see the truth about each other and themselves. Nothing else should be revealed, except to report that

Frye's ingenious script combines elements of *Irma La Douce, It Happened One Night, Desperately Seeking Susan* and *After Hours* into its own vision of an America that is comic yet violent, giddily entertaining yet frighteningly dangerous.

As Lulu, Melanie Griffith, daughter of Tippi Hedren, combines elements of Sigourney Weaver, Molly Ringwald, the early Shirley MacLaine and even – at the end of the film – Peggy Lee, into a sultry yet childish woman, both madcap and sociopath. "She's got some strange notions about life," her mother, Peaches (wonderfully played by Dana Preu), warns Charles. Mother says a mouthful.

Jeff Daniels, the matinee idol in *The Purple Rose of Cairo* and Debra Winger's husband in *Terms of Endearment*, does not combine familiar elements to emerge with something new: from beginning to end, his performance is a comic masterpiece reminiscent of no one else, even if the character type – the nerd who casts off his nerddom – seems at the outset to be a cliché. Daniels does everything from pratfalls to sex to dancing (he looks as though he's invented something called Funky Mt. Rushmore) with a klutzy energy that becomes its own kind of panache; other actors this year – Sean Connery in *The Name of the Rose*, Paul Newman in *The Color of Money* – have been as good, but none has been better.

Demme not only gives the script's nuttiness its due, he adds to it by filling the frame in virtually every scene with silliness – a motorcycle-riding dog, a harpsichordist, a man wearing a T-shirt that reads, "I don't love you since you ate my dog." The musical soundtrack is equally full, equally strange – reggae star Sister Carol does the old hit by The Troggs, "Wild Thing," and David Byrne, the lead singer of *Stop Making Sense*'s Talking Heads and director of *True Stories*, has contributed the title song. Demme recently contributed to Byrne's mystique by heaping praise on *True Stories*; he predicted that Byrne would be able to extricate narrative cinema from its "rut." Compared to the eccentricity of *Something Wild*, however, Byrne's *True Stories* is precious and exsanguinated. In terms of structure, Demme is more conventional than Byrne, but he's deeper and more imaginative. Byrne's got something chic; Demme really does have something wild.

November 7, 1986

Platoon

Written and directed by Oliver Stone
Starring Charlie Sheen, Tom Berenger, Willem Dafoe and Forest Whitaker

It was an ugly little war, but until now most of the admirable or at least memorable films made about it – *Apocalypse Now* in the first category, *The Deer Hunter* in the latter – have been big, beautiful movies, attempts to transform the experience of Vietnam into the stuff of epic, to record the sordid misadventure from the point of view of God. Oliver Stone's *Platoon*, an ugly little movie free of vistas and Wagner but stinking with verisimilitude, is a vitriolic view of the war from the point of view of a worm – specifically of the worms conscripted to fight and die for a cause that has not yet, and will never be, justified to the satisfaction of the survivors.

Stone, a master of filmic purple prose (*Midnight Express*) and sometimes of racism (*Year of the Dragon*) and sometimes of a grittiness that achieves its own kind of courageous grandeur (*Salvador*), is the first Vietnam veteran to make a feature fiction film about the war in Southeast Asia. He offers no context or overview – surely by now none is necessary – but what he does provide is immediacy and authenticity; to go any deeper into the belly of the militaristic beast than *Platoon* plunges the audience is probably impossible for art.

The film sticks bravely to the blinkered, callow perspective of its hero, Chris (Charlie Sheen), a nineteen-year-old enlistee who is unquestionably the young Stone: hoping to escape a boring, pampered past and find an exciting, self-reliant future, Stone signed up for

Vietnam exactly as Chris does. Chris's flights of romantic fancy, his naivety and his inexorable disillusionment are communicated via a narrative that is both embarrassing and valuable, a narrative that is valuable because it is embarrassing. Stephen King has forgotten nothing of what it meant to be fourteen; Oliver Stone remembers everything there is to remember about being nineteen.

Once in Southeast Asia (the base is photographed in ochre, the jungle in obscene green), Chris explains to a black draftee why an affluent white boy who could have avoided the army altogether would enlist and ask for a Vietnam assignment – Chris wanted to be an egalitarian American. "You gotta be rich in the first place to think like that," the black grunt grunts. Unfazed, Chris writes home of his comrades: "They're poor, they're unwanted, yet they're fighting for our society and our freedom . . . they're the best I've ever seen, Grandma." He's talking about guys who fit the description, sure, but he's also talking about Bunny (Kevin Dillon), who takes bites out of Bud cans and gets a sexual charge out of blowing civilians to bits, and about a sergeant who refers to a dead American soldier as "a lump of shit."

More than anything else, *Platoon* presents in an assaultive fashion (how else could it be presented?) what happened when the network news cameras were turned off: the film is alive to impending death, to the fear, lethargy, energy and euphoria that characterize men in groups trying to kill other men in groups. A mini-My Lai massacre, staged with a machete-wielding reality, causes the platoon unwittingly to take the same sides that were being taken stateside as the Vietnam debate raged on. The only narrative structure Stone imposes on the picture is this microcosmic civil war, and the only time the structure feels like an imposition is at the end, when he wraps up the interior war between the grunts with a neatness that the wrap-up of the exterior war never had. The denouement is Stone's single theatrical betrayal of the material, material he otherwise serves with an honour that does men so long deprived of honour proud.

December 19, 1986

The Morning After

Directed by Sidney Lumet
Written by James Hicks
Starring Jane Fonda, Jeff Bridges and Raul Julia

My name is Alexandra Sternberg and I've got problems. I'm pretty –
I've got frosted hair, a good face and a great body – but I'm a lush who
goes out on the town and picks up strange men and wakes up next to
them and can't remember who they are or what I did with them. I
don't even know until I look in my pocketbook if I've got the cab fare
to get home. I live in Los Angeles. Cabs are expensive.

So far, I guess it doesn't sound like I've got it all that bad, but it gets
worse. I used to be a movie star, semi-well-known, so that adds to my
self-hatred, which adds to my drinking: I mean, I was SOMEBODY.
Now, I'm nobody, just another middle-aged boozer with frosted hair,
a good face and a great body. Thank God I'm played by Jane Fonda in
the movie about me, *The Morning After*. If I had been played by somebody who looked like they'd actually been drinking for ten years, it
would be too depressing.

I'm married to Jacky, a heterosexual hairdresser. (Yes, they exist in
Hollywood – the other one was the model for the guy in *Shampoo*.)
Jacky's played by Raul Julia. We've been married ten years, but we
don't sleep together anymore. We don't even live together anymore. I
think Jacky wishes I'd been Julie Christie, who probably could have
played me better than Jane Fonda does. As I said, I'm glad that Jane
looks so good, but she does seem to think that I think I'm Bette Davis.
When Jane Fonda, playing me, says, "I used to be an actress," it sounds
like Jane Fonda talking, not me. Jane Fonda is still an actress, and a
good one, but it's certainly hard to tell from *The Morning After*.

On one especially gruesome morning after, I wake up with a dead
man in the bed. I should point out that this is not the first time this has
happened to me, except that this one stays dead. (Of course, some
people would call this luck: no need to make bacon and eggs and small

talk until you can get away from the bozo, leaving behind a phone number that is not your own on a matchbook from a bar you have no recollection of entering.) I make a double and then call my husband from the scene of the crime. He says, "Why are you boozing at ten in the morning?" I quip, "Breakfast of champions," and tell him about my dead trick. He says, "He had a heart attack?" I say, "Yeah, from a knife in his chest." Then I say to the corpse, "If I did that to you I didn't mean it, I swear. I'm not a bad person."

I meet another guy. This one is named Turner Kendell and he's a redneck (he calls Hispanic Americans "beaners" and says they "spend disproportionately on transportation and also dressing their young") but he's cute – he's played by Jeff Bridges – and so of course I fall in love with him, even if he is a teetotaler. He may also be the murderer, but my husband could also be the murderer. I suppose if you read the script without knowing who plays me, you might think I could be the murderer, too, but nobody is going to make Jane Fonda a murderer in a Christmas movie.

I do say one thing in the movie I like: "They were grooming me to be the next Vera Miles. I was supposed to replace somebody the audience didn't even know was missing." And I do like Jeff Bridges. Otherwise, I don't like anything about *The Morning After*, which was directed by Sidney Lumet, who has never made a movie in Hollywood before – so I suppose he should be forgiven for not knowing how to make a Hollywood movie, which is what *The Morning After* needed to be if it wanted to be anything at all. I noticed that the audience didn't like it very much (thank goodness I don't take things personally) and I also noticed that although the movie is supposed to make everybody think long and hard about the evils of alcoholism, the first thing everybody wants to do when they get out is run to the nearest bar for a good stiff drink.

December 26, 1986

❖

Thérèse

Written and directed by Alain Cavalier
Starring Catherine Mouchet

The Sacrifice

Written and directed by Andrei Tarkovsky
Starring Erland Josephson

In the modern world, canonization has been secularized – there's Saint Genet (so dubbed by Sartre), and there's Saint Joan (of Baez), and there's Saint Nostalgia (everyone's grandmother), and now there's Saint Warhol (the pope of Pop). However, secularization has nothing to do with the sort of sanctity explored in two new films that deal with the meaning of spirituality in a mechanistic and materialistic world. In Andrei Tarkovsky's *The Sacrifice* and in Alain Cavalier's *Thérèse*, the saints – one male, one female – are bona fide holy persons, icons whose lives are presented as exemplars of self-sacrificial transcendence.

In 1897, Thérèse Martin died of tuberculosis in a Carmelite cloister in Lisieux, France, without amounting, in any accepted saintly sense, to anything. She entered the convent at the age of fifteen and she devoted a fair bit of the time not spent cheerfully mortifying herself to a diary, later published as *The Story of a Soul*. This eventual bestseller recorded in breathless and even panting detail her distinctly erotic attraction to her boyfriend, one J. Christ. "Jesus saw that I was ripe for love," she wrote. "He plighted His troth to me and I became His." In Cavalier's austere yet perversely sensual adaptation of Thérèse's memoirs – the perverse sensuality is contained in the original material, which is why the picture has been embraced by Catholic critics for *Commonweal* and other religiously oriented publications – Thérèse swoons over crucifixes like high school girls faint at the sight of George Michael's earrings. "Fondle him," Thérèse orders an acolyte. "That's how I snared him."

Why in 1925 did Pius xi canonize this apparently unremarkable woman, calling her in the process "the greatest saint of modern times?" Was it perhaps because there was a dearth of saints "of modern times?" Too easy. Cavalier's film, shot elegantly in a studio against an opaque, pewter-coloured backdrop, suggests that Thérèse is a paradigm of passive holiness, as opposed to the active variety represented by her antipode, Mother Teresa. Thérèse's almost giddy attraction to Christ additionally serves to communicate, in blithe guise, the sadomasochistic fetishism that forms a portion of so many accounts of the lives of the saints. One nun in the film divulges the rapture she felt when a scale from a leper's skin found its way accidentally into her mouth – it was like taking communion, she says – and another ecstatically tastes Thérèse's tubercular, red-stained phlegm. Cavalier's attitude toward a subject so often the source of farce and dirty jokes, the sublimated sex lives of nuns, is admirably objective. He gives Thérèse (acted with sweet insouciance by Catherine Mouchet) respect, if not unconditional approval. But how could he? Only God can make a saint.

Maybe only God can make a saint. Andrei Tarkovsky's *The Sacrifice*, the overwhelmingly moving final film by the Russian émigré writer-director who died last year of cancer and who dedicated it, in "hope and confidence," to his young son, is an epic "poetic parable." Similar in content but not in style to Paul Almond's *Act of the Heart*, it attempts to canonize its lead character, Alexander (Erland Josephson), an ex-actor whose birthday celebration on an isolated Swedish island becomes a mystical odyssey into a dark night of the soul that is clearly a metaphor for what Tarkovsky sees as a dark age of the planet.

In the justly famed opening shot, a single ten-minute take, each of the film's many themes is stated while Alexander plants with his boy, "Little Man" (Tommy Kjellqvist), a "Japanese" tree (stylishly barren) on a blasted coast. The two are joined by a holy fool, a loquacious postman named Otto (Allan Edwall) who rides circles around them both literally – on a bicycle – and figuratively – he sets their minds to spinning with his sometimes potted and sometimes profound insights.

Discussing the themes of *The Sacrifice*, a film that at its peak depicts the living that is done while dying with a directness that verges on the intolerable, is unprofitable. Without the images to which they have been yoked by Tarkovsky and his nonpareil cinematographer, Sven Nykvist (who rightly considers this the best work of a distinguished career that has included the majority of Ingmar Bergman's films), the messages piled on the cart constitute a banal and perhaps reactionary cargo. We are told, for example, that our entire civilization is sinful because sin is "that which is unnecessary" (Puritans will approve), that we are "living like savages" (the New Right will approve), and that "every gift involves a sacrifice" (Solzhenitsyn will approve; acolytes of the late Ayn Rand will not be amused).

What Tarkovsky does with this philosophical hybrid (Christological and Oriental) is a wonder to behold. A key image, Leonardo da Vinci's *Adoration of the Three Kings*, backs the credits: with its presentiment of ultimate sacrifice in the roly-poly person of the Christ child, it is an apt and therefore recurring motif, and it's no accident that several significant moments are mirrored in the glass placed over the reproduction. Then, in what can be seen as the film's second (or maybe third) movement, an unspecified holocaust (at this point, the picture is briefly reminiscent of Bergman's *Shame*) is utilized as a powerful cosmic projection of Alexander's angst regarding his own mortality. After Alexander's servants and family gather at the manse, the women dressed in gowns that echo da Vinci, the men stuffily self-confident in their suits, Alexander dreams the end of the world. The film stock, leached of reds and blues, becomes an iridescent khaki. Alexander's sister, Adelaide (English actress Susan Fleetwood), succumbs to hysteria of an intensity virtually never encountered on screen, the cabinets open and spit crockery, and the picture reaches a surprisingly conventional climax. For Tarkovsky.

But this is Tarkovsky, director of *The Mirror*, *Andrei Rublev*, *Stalker*, *Solaris* and *Nostalgia*, and the film is far from over: the

239

penultimate movement, in which Alexander visits a nearby witch, is intentionally anticlimactic. The same cannot be said of the final sequence, however, a symmetrical single take of about six minutes during which Alexander performs his liberating and insane and unexpectedly comic act of sainthood.

The Sacrifice is long (approximately two and a half hours), loaded with *longeurs* (viewers fight over which bits are boring, just as they fight over what the movie means), rarely rational and – except for the journey-into-a-soul superstructure – almost never linear. Despite those reservations, it is a magnificent experience: watching it, you can feel Tarkovsky's life ebbing, but with vitality, dignity, candour, concern and, most of all, artistry – "with hope and confidence." *The Sacrifice* may not persuade you that Alexander is a saint, but it may convince you that Tarkovsky was. The breezy, wheezy diaries of the little nun of Lisieux are blown away by the hurricane howls of Tarkovsky's final days.

March 20, 1987

Working Girls

Directed by Lizzie Borden
Written by Lizzie Borden and Marusia Zach
Starring Louise Smith, Amanda Goodwin and Marusia Zach

Lizzie Borden, the director of *Working Girls*, the most sophisticated fiction film ever made about prostitution in the United States, set out to "de-mystify" and "de-romanticize" the profession as practised in a middle-class milieu, and she has done so handsomely; her midtown Manhattan brothel is claustrophobically unsexy. But she has done something more; she has depicted a so-called "degrading" profession without degrading the women who practise it. The real subversiveness of *Working Girls* is that you can't watch it without beginning to think of working boys and of other working girls, of boys and girls working in professions that carry fewer of the social stigmas of prostitution, and fewer of the financial rewards. Lizzie Borden has done for whores what Bruce Springsteen has done for factory workers; she has unsentimentally authenticated the angst of the assembly line.

"If it is asserted that prostitution degrades women, what does that say about women who choose to work in the sex industry, that they are degraded?" Borden asked recently in an interview in *Afterimage*. "The issue began to come up during the Women Against Pornography marches and also around the Canadian documentary *Not a Love Story*. Many of the women who worked in strip joints and in the sex industry felt heavily criticized by feminists who would ask them how they could possibly do what they were doing, instead of giving them support.

"All we do through blanket criticism," Borden continued, "is increase these women's victimization. They have to feel either that they are morally corrupt people or that they are non-responsible victims... What is so wrong with renting your body for two shifts a week if the alternative is a forty-hour-a-week job that you hate and makes you so burned out that all you can do is come home and watch TV at the end of the day? My point is that for men and women prostitution may be a valid choice given the options because I don't think the other options are that great. We have to begin to question the concept of work in general in this culture. As long as women can handle prostitution, society should give them the benefit of being able to make their own choices. And women ought not to have an automatic moral reaction against the women who do it."

The prostitution in *Working Girls* isn't that great an option, but for the women who can stomach the requirements of tricks such as "Fantasy Fred" – he likes to have his "date" pretend she's blind so he can cure her with "love" – it really doesn't appear to be much more "degrading" than accepting the sorts of jobs country singer Johnny Paycheck wanted his bosses to shove. The heroine of the film, Molly (Louise Smith), is a Yale graduate who can't figure out any other way to make $880 a day. When Dawn (Amanda Goodwin), the youngest hooker in the house, asks for help with a political science term paper on the subject of "Communist charisma," Molly is wittily pious: "I'm already renting my body, I don't want to sell my mind." But she's not joking when the "exotic," dark-haired Gina (Marusia Zach, an actress who collaborated with Borden on the screenplay under the name Sandra Kaye) asks why Molly won't take birth control pills: "I'm not going to screw up my hormones for two shifts a week." In her private life, Molly doesn't need the pills, as Gina remembers: "Oh, that's right, you have a girl friend, don't you?"

Molly does – she lives with a black woman – and she is bothered by her dishonesty; to justify her odd hours, she's told her lover that she is a caterer. Dawn has not levelled with her boy friend Jeff, either. "I've always been a whore, but never a groupie," she says proudly, and then adds primly, "I believe in fidelity. In the five years I've gone out with Jeff I haven't cheated on him once." Gina considered telling her man the truth because she thought that if he really loved her, he would accept her for what she was. "And then I thought, if he really loved me, how could he . . . ?"

The other inhabitants of the house include the old pro April (Janne Peters), sliding into self-defeat at forty-three; the neophyte Mary (Helen Nicholas), who does a "girl show" with Molly for a trick and afterward asks: "Do you think he knew I didn't like it?" which brings a devastating rejoinder from Molly: "Mary, he doesn't want to know"; and Lucy (Ellen McElduff), the madam, seen by the film as the real exploiter, as the girls' real enemy.

The johns do not have the dimension of the women, nor should they; as Borden has said, men who go to brothels to fulfil fantasies leave a large part of their personalities at home. They are nonetheless a varied lot, ranging from an intellectually pretentious construction boss to a rather sweet guy who sees Molly mainly to find out how to treat other women. In all cases, it is the women who are in control, a reflection of Borden's research. "I have completely lost my fear of men," Molly reveals, and Gina agrees: "You can handle any man as long as you know what his sexual trip is."

None of this is necessarily true of street prostitution, which Borden calls "another world." But in the world investigated by *Working Girls*, the limits and hazards are well-defined: each day is a ritualized matter of towels, condoms and post-coital *politesse*, followed by sisterly camaraderie when the women are alone. The entire film takes place during one day, primarily on one set; given its $300,000 budget, it is technically miraculous, marred only by an overblown performance from the madam. (Borden changed, and improved, the ending of the film subsequent to screenings at festivals in Cannes, Montreal and Toronto. She also elided one explicit sequence.) Too distanced to be called compassionate – the term can imply condescension – *Working Girls* is provocative, honest and disturbing. It's disturbing not because its subject is prostitution, but because, in the end, its subject is not prostitution, unless the word can be redefined to encompass all working people bereft of options.

May 15, 1987

❖

River's Edge

Directed by Tim Hunter
Written by Neal Jimenez
Starring Keanu Reeves and Ione Skye

Down by the river on a bridge, a child. Boy or girl? Hard to tell. A boy. Wearing a single earring and a scowl, he drops a doll into the water. Hearing a howl, he turns with a start from the grey foam swallowing the doll and sees this: down by the river on the bank, a body. Female. Nude. The howl, earsplitting but strangely without pain, comes from a fat boy, high school age. The child gets on a bike and pedals away, excited but strangely unafraid. The fat boy, excited but strangely unfazed, goes to school. He tells his friends he's killed a girl. He tells them the victim is one of their classmates. His friends don't believe him. The fat boy takes them down by the river. They believe him. Unsettled but strangely unmoved, they go about their business. They do not call the cops.

The opening of *River's Edge*, a corrosive study of peer pressure and moral degeneration that faintly recalls *Lord of the Flies*, sets the queasy tone for what proves to be one of the blackest, funniest, most disturbing and annoyingly lingering American films of this or any other year; the annoyance occasioned by the film's tendency to linger is not because *River's Edge* is not good, it's because it's too good. Not since director Tim Hunter helmed another teen film, *Over the Edge*, eight years ago (*River's Edge* is an update of the previous movie), has the heavy metal adolescent emptiness of high-school-cum-shopping-mall life in North America been so thoroughly explored. Thoroughness is only part of the achievement: *River's Edge* differs from the majority of films on the subject – from the majority of films, period – by never telling the audience how to factor from the virtually surreal sociological data a comfortable equation to make sense of nonsense. The mess is left in your lap.

Written four years ago by Neal Jimenez, then a film student chronologically close to his characters (he was twenty), and based on a 1981 case in Milpitas, Calif., the script is an original amalgam of melodrama, absurdist comedy and postmodernist affectlessness – it's bopper *film noir*. In its presentation of parents as narcissistic antique hippies, there are parallels to *Over the Edge*'s Me Generation dope-smoking folks, but these authority figures even more outlandishly lack responsibility. The nominal hero, Matt (Keanu Reeves), is faced with a parent who gets stressed out and declares, "I'm going to give up all this mother bullshit." There's only one good thing to be said about Mom: she's not too proud to share her dynamite dope with the kids.

The teacher at the local high school is in a different kind of daze; he's a relic of the sixties, lost in a nostalgic fog, who lectures his pupils on times that "mattered" and upbraids them for feeling nothing about the death of their classmate even as he clearly feels no strong emotion for anything under thirty and after Woodstock. He's become a thing he once hated, an anti-youth bigot.

The despised youths of *River's Edge* are not the rebelliously angry adolescents of *Rebel Without a Cause* or a host of other teen "classics." These teens are so blanked out by dope, booze, illiteracy and hopelessness they are terrified not only of ambition but of any emotion. (Hence, the anesthesia of dope. Advises one of the boys: "I just say we get the Russians stoned. Might mellow 'em out a touch.") Their "leader" – he's a nominal leader in the way that Matt is a nominal hero – is Layne (Crispin Glover), whose ethics have been inculcated exclusively by television and the movies. Confronted with the murder of one friend by another, he opts unhesitatingly to support John Samson (Daniel Roebuck), the clearly psychotic killer of Jamie, the body down by the river, because Layne has learned from television and the movies that loyalty is an admirable trait. "Jamie's dead, dammit," he argues, "there's nothing we can do to save her. I happened to like Jamie. But John's still alive. Don't you see that?"

Many of his friends are uncomfortable with the stance, but they initially make no waves; they continue to get high, visit their dope dealer, Feck (Dennis Hopper), and discuss the murder with a deadpan, abstract bloodlessness reminiscent of post-doctoral symposia on the use of aquatic imagery in *The Iliad*. But Matt, whose little brother, Tim (Joshua Miller), is revealed to be the bad seedling doll-murderer of the movie's opening – he was "killing" his sister's toy – is unable to live with his discomfiture and takes action; in one of Jimenez' many ironies, this moral act, the movie's first, is treated by the police as a crime.

The lone adult in *River's Edge* who does feel a connection to the kids is Feck, the drug dealer – but he, too, is a murderer. Whereas John Samson killed to capture "control," Feck murdered for romance. "I killed a girl once. No accident. Put a gun to the back of her head and blew her brains out the front. I was in love." Lecturing John Samson on the "morality" of murder – it can be fine, Feck maintains, if you care for the victim – the dealer is appalled to find that Samson did not care for his girl friend and thus terminates their we-have-so-much-in-common relationship in a vignette that is a perverse parody of John Steinbeck: Of Mice and Meanness.

With the exception of Crispin Glover, an actor whose avian mannerisms lift him into the heaven invented by Thespis for performers who overact with sincerity, the *River's Edge* cast is extraordinarily adept. Years ago, director Hunter cast then-unknown actors Vincent Spano and Matt Dillon in *Over the Edge*; it's likely that his two discoveries here, Keanu Reeves and the gorgeous Ione Skye, daughter of Donovan, may evolve into stars of a similar magnitude. (The cast's expertise works against the film's gloomy vision: these kids must be all right, at least off screen.)

With its horror movie music, tracking shots that echo *Halloween*, and hilariously witless wit ("I cried when that guy in *Brian's Song* died, you'd think I could cry for someone we hung around with"), *River's Edge* is both a send-up of, and an answer to, much of what passes for teen entertainment. Although primarily despairing, it does in the end toss a matchstick of hope to its drowning children: the intelligently ambiguous conclusion may not qualify as buoyant, but on this barren river's edge, a passing twig can easily be mistaken for a life-saving log.

June 5, 1987

Full Metal Jacket

Directed by Stanley Kubrick
Written by Stanley Kubrick, Michael Herr and Gustav Hasford
Starring Matthew Modine, Adam Baldwin, Kevyn Major Howard,
Dorian Harewood and Arliss Howard

"This is Vietnam, the movie," a Marine sardonically tells a camera crew toward the end of *Full Metal Jacket*. Modesty is not something you expect from a Marine but in this case, the jarhead is displaying too little arrogance instead of too much. Had he said, "This is war, the movie," he would have been right on the money. Against the greatest stylistic odds – how do you stage violence without glamorizing it? – and against all commercial good sense – do you really want another tour of Vietnam, especially with a guide who refuses to give you the tingly romantic sequences that make even movies about unjust wars a dirty pleasure? – director Stanley Kubrick has come forth with what may be the best war movie ever made.

Strong words. *Full Metal Jacket* is strong stuff. But so, for all their dissimilarities, were *Apocalypse Now*, *The Deer Hunter* and *Platoon*. What makes *Full Metal Jacket*, written by Kubrick, Vietnam journalist Michael Herr (*Dispatches*) and novelist Gustav Hasford (his book, *The Short Timers*, gives the film its skeleton), different is Kubrick's artistry and control, and his almost perverse, but philosophically progressive, refusal to impart to chaos a coherent narrative contour. *Apocalypse* exulted in the opera of war, *Deer Hunter* turned it into Olympic myth, and *Platoon*, for all its eye-wrenching verisimilitude, in the end reduced it to the melodrama of "good" soldiers versus "bad." There is no opera in *Full Metal Jacket*, no myth, no good soldiers – and no bad ones.

Kubrick's point is that there is no morality in war; there are kindnesses and cruelties, to be sure, but because war itself is a moral mockery, they exist in an ethical vacuum. The most astounding aspect of the film is its avoidance, even while implicitly drawing a moral, of an explicit statement. *Full Metal Jacket* is violent, caustic, ironic and cold, an amoral object formed from a camera gliding majestically across slow-motion carnage (this is the picture Sam Peckinpah must have dreamed of making) while refusing to blink an eye or shed a tear. The only other work of war art with this kind of muted, magisterial austerity is Bertolt Brecht's episodic chronicle of the Thirty Years War, *Mother Courage*, but instead of focusing on the mother who will do anything to survive, Kubrick trains his relentless lens on her elder son, who will also do anything to survive. And who will die.

The first forty-five minutes are confined, with the kinetic claustrophobia that gave Kubrick's *The Shining* its kick (remember those corridors?), to Parris Island, S.C. (everything in the movie was re-created in England), where virginal Marine recruits are being deflowered by their drill instructor, Gunnery Sgt. Hartman (Lee Ermey). The opening images are of the symbolic shearing of the soldiers' locks; the defoliation of their spirits follows as everything drops from them save the bright gleam of their lust to kill. Sgt. Hartman orchestrates the dehumanization with endless insults that escalate into an aria of obscenity (one of the few printable examples: "You're so ugly you could be a modern art masterpiece") that sings a single primal melody: "Your rifle is only a tool. It is a hard heart that kills."

One of his murderous time bombs, a fat kid nicknamed Gomer Pyle (Vincent D'Onofrio), goes off too soon in a vignette that, for all its vibrating evil, kisses off what happens to him and his victim as no more than bad luck, a Marine occupational hazard. When Sgt. Hartman invokes Texas sniper Charles Whitman and assassin Lee Harvey Oswald, both ex-Marines, as individual examples of "what one motivated Marine and his rifle can do," he's not joking. You don't blame the machine if it malfunctions, you don't even blame the mechanic; you merely junk the machine and replace it, which, from the standpoint of manpower administration, is what war is all about. Kubrick's tone here reverts for the first time in years to the inky satire of *Dr. Strangelove*; the sequence feels the way a laugh from a death mask must sound.

The remainder of the movie, set in Hue during the Tet offensive, reconnoitres more familiar terrain. The recruits, Joker (Matthew Modine), Animal Mother (Adam Baldwin), Rafterman (Kevyn Major Howard), Eightball (Dorian Harewood) – he's a black who talks of "putting a nigger behind the trigger" – Cowboy (Arliss Howard) and Crazy Earl (Kieron Jecchins), move through an already blasted urban landscape and waste it. Crazy Earl sums it up: "After we rotate back to the world, we're gonna miss not havin' anybody worth shootin' at." He's the pessimist. The optimist, Lieut. Lockhart (John Terry), puts it this way: "Inside every gook there is an American tryin' to get out."

When he released *The Shining*, from the novel by Stephen King, Kubrick took a lot of heat from critics who accused him of denying people the pleasure they expect of a horror film; those same critics are likely to accuse him this time of wrecking war movies. Well, *Full Metal Jacket* is about war movies, but it is not of them. In *The Shining*, Kubrick tried, with mixed success, to expose and analyze the inner-spring of the horror genre, something David Lynch accomplished with *Blue Velvet*. With *Full Metal Jacket*, he wins the war. The picture does indeed deny the pleasure associated with celebrating masculine bravery in a good cause, *à la* John Wayne, and it also denies the plea-sure associated with lamenting the waste of masculine bravery in a bad cause, *à la Platoon*. *The Shining's* camera prowled the halls – the movement of the movie was penetrating. Here, the major motion is lateral, as though the camera is recording for future generations a frieze. Or a comic book. The director keeps his distance, always.

Full Metal Jacket (the title refers to a type of bullet, copper-jacketed to achieve a truer aim, an apt symbol for the men made by the Marines) will perhaps strike some veterans as unsympathetic toward the soldier's plight, and to a degree, it is, but not because Kubrick is bereft of compassion. That he refuses to move empathetically into the world he records is indicative of his intellectual fastidiousness, and probably of his off-screen morality. The lesson he has learned from so many war movies, both pro- and anti-, is that to move in too close is to move in for the kill.

June 26, 1987

❖

The Devil in the Flesh

Directed by Marco Bellocchio
Starring Federico Pitzalis, Maruschka Detmers,
   Riccardo de Torrebruna, Alberto di Stasio

In discussing his decision to modernize Raymond Radiguet's 1923 novel *The Devil in the Flesh* (the first film version, directed by Claude

Autant-Lara, was released in 1947), Italian auteur Marco Bellocchio (*Fists in the Pocket*) has said, "Originally we intended to do a faithful adaptation of the book, but as we worked on the screenplay, we quickly realized it would be more interesting to set it in modern-day Italy. In my film, Pulcini (one of the characters) passes from political extremism to complete bourgeois conformity, accepting all its values, order, law and religion. This, for me, is an illustration of the dramatic reality of Italy today." That, for Bellocchio, is a tragedy.

Yet nowhere in the shimmering tone of *Devil in the Flesh* is doom to be found – this is a sun-dappled, erotic and extremely formal film. Radiguet's anarchic novel was about a French schoolboy's affair with a woman whose husband was serving his country in the First World War. Bellocchio has complicated the plot, and the meanings to be derived from it, immensely. Now, an eighteen-year-old student, Andrea (Federico Pitzalis), develops a passion for a gorgeous young woman, Giula (Maruschka Detmers), who plans to marry an ex-terrorist, Giacomo Pulcini (Riccardo de Torrebruna), as soon as he gets out of prison; Pulcini is being pardoned for his earlier activities because he has become an informer and has embraced "complete bourgeois conformity."

Amid much else, the movie analyzes the possibility – the necessity – of combining passion and order. (Classical anarchism is not, of course, a philosophy of chaos, despite its reputation as such.) Pulcini represents airless order; the half-mad Giula, who at the opening of the film feels a bond with a deranged black woman threatening suicide from a rooftop, is unbridled instinct. Between those two impossible alternatives, a world of superego vying with a world of id, Bellocchio proposes a third option in the person of Andrea, the son of a psychiatrist (Alberto di Stasio) whose practice is devoted to encouraging his patients to adjust to a status quo Bellocchio finds repulsive. The son, consciously rejecting the father, practises sexual anarchy but skirts self-destruction – he takes examinations from instructors he does not respect while informing them that he is playing a game whose serious-ness he understands but does not condone. He terrorizes them on their own turf, but he is not a terrorist: he pushes the system as far as it can go without damaging himself.

The examinations focus on a passage from *Antigone* and it is here that Bellocchio emotionally reveals the film's *raison d'être*. He argues firmly on behalf of Antigone's decision to defy her father Creon's order that she not bury the body of her brother, just as Andrea has defied his father's order to stop seeing Giula, who happens to be one of his father's patients; the father is himself attracted to Giula but wrongly believes her to be "completely insane."

"Andrea has this rare quality which allows him to combine love with lucidity as to courage and responsibility," Bellocchio has explained. "The boy has the courage to revolt against his psychiatrist father. I am not against the family. I am against the principle which says that a son must accept his father's laws."

Devil in the Flesh, which has all the emboldened clarity of its hero, puts its principles into practice by pushing against the authoritarian bounds of conventional filmmaking. The pacing is unpredictable; paradoxes are paramount (Giula's father was killed by a group of terrorists similar to those she admires); the score by Carlo Crivelli is lyrical yet intrusive; the images call unabashed romantic attention to themselves (Bellocchio's camera openly swoons over the bodies of his two leads); and most of all there is the brief sequence that has made the film famous, an explicit act of fellatio performed in close-up by Giula on Andrea as he tells her the story of Lenin's return to St. Petersburg from Switzerland in 1917. Cleared without cuts to the astonishment of Christendom by the Ontario Film and Video Review Board, the sequence is tender, curiously unshocking and cannily subversive, which is precisely how Bellocchio is asking that passion be perceived.

To underline his intentions, the director has dedicated *Devil in the Flesh* to Massimo Fagioli, an Italian psychoanalyst who has been stripped of his Freudian credentials because he promotes – and practises – a form of analysis that attempts to remove from traditional therapy its Judeo-Christian underpinning (like Jung, Fagioli sees much of Freudian theory as "sin" renamed) and to add to it a progressive political dimension. *Devil in the Flesh* is not in the final analysis about the devil in the flesh at all; it's about a host of demons trying to invade and thereby control the flesh. To Bellocchio, their names are legion: church, state, the family, the military, the psychiatric establishment, terrorist cells; any institution, in other words, that claims indisputable authority over the individual.

June 26, 1987

Jaws: The Revenge

Directed by Joseph Sargent
Written by Michael de Guzman
Starring Michael Caine, Lorraine Gary and Lance Guest

"The first time's the best for everything. After that, you know too much and nothing's ever quite the same."

No joke. The speaker is Hoagie (Michael Caine), a charter pilot based in the Bahamas in *Jaws: The Revenge,* and although he's talking about tourism and not moving pictures, his sentiments fit *The Revenge* as tightly as the latex stretched across the mechanical shark's fins. *Déjà vu*'s too kind a term to describe what happens in the latest chapter in the lives of the characters created so long ago in print by Peter Benchley and brought to life – and, eventually, to death – on screen by Steven Spielberg.

This time, the writer is Michael de Guzman, the director is Joseph Sargent, and the premise is that the shark has it mystically in for the Brodys of Amity. The Brody bunch, you will remember, was led by Roy Scheider, until the great white shark came to visit. Munch munch. By now, the beast has munched his way through any number of Brodys in three instalments, but as the fourth begins, the Brody family –

what's left of it – is still living in Amity and is still going into the water. Off the top, another Brody gets it and Mother Brody (Lorraine Gary) announces, "I don't want anyone in the family near the water." This is found by the surviving Brodys to be unreasonable, which may indicate that the shark has it in for the Brodys because he has been charged by some higher power with ridding the coastline of the terminally stupid.

To get away from her grief, Mother Brody joins a surviving son, Michael (Lance Guest), in the Bahamas, where he is employed as a marine biologist; he spends his days diving. "You're all I have left, I don't want you working in the water!" Mother Brody repeats, but Michael dismisses this as evidence that Mother has yet to come to grips with her grief over the death of the other Brody. Meanwhile, Mother meets the pilot Hoagie and they strike up a somewhat sodden romance. During one of their trysts she confesses that she is certain that the shark that's eaten so many in her family will, like Jesus, come again.

She's right. Although great white sharks are not supposed to like warm water, the thing appears in no time. Munch munch. Now totally unhinged, Mother reacts to the danger by jumping in a boat and, free of weapons of any kind, going straight after the undersea hot dog – even after years of special effects refinement, the mechanical marauder continues to look like a great-toothed knackwurst. Why would she do such a thing? "I had to do it," she declares. "There was nothing else to do." What about heading for high ground?

July 22, 1987

❖

Un Zoo la nuit (Night Zoo)

Written and directed by Jean-Claude Lauzon
Starring Gilles Maheu and Roger Le Bel

"Life is crazy, not organized along proper dramatic lines." – *Jean-Claude Lauzon*

Un Zoo la nuit (*Night Zoo*), Quebec writer and director Jean-Claude Lauzon's emotionally, thematically and technically kaleidoscopic film is an adroit balancing act performed on a wire suspended just above the gutter. It is probably the most assured, sophisticated first film ever produced in this country. It is certainly the most amoral.

Because Lauzon learned the basics of Montreal's criminal underclass by participating in it in his teens, and because the movie is not so much about that class as it is an unapologetic expression of its less than tender sensibilities, albeit with a dazzling high-tech sheen, *Zoo* is destined to provoke and even to shock bourgeois audiences from first frame to last. If Lauzon never loses his balance, and he doesn't, he never permits viewers to gain theirs: the plotting is elliptical, the wit is dry enough to qualify as parched, drug-dealing and abuse are accepted with a shrug, murder is implicitly condoned, sex and perversion are seen as identical.

The film opens in an empty apartment. An answering machine records a cryptic message about a gift. Cut to a prison. The "gift," a bodybuilder, is delivered to the cell of Marcel (Gilles Maheu), the hero. The "gift" rapes the hero. Released subsequently to the streets of Montreal, streets shot with a photogenic smoky expressionism that recalls the opera of Bernardo Bertolucci (*Last Tango in Paris*) more than the grime of Martin Scorsese (*Mean Streets*), Marcel is a man with a mission: to save his life, or maybe only his money, he is going to have to send the two crooked cops a "gift" bigger than the one they sent him.

Zoo tells two stories. The first is a remorselessly violent account, brutally yet beautifully made, of the terrorization of Marcel by the crooked cops (Lorne Brass, Germain Houde) and of Marcel's inevitable terrorization of them. The movie's moral universe can be inferred from the fact that the cops think the hero has burned them to the tune of $200,000 on an enormous cocaine deal – and they are right. Although depicted as evil incarnate – Lauzon swears they are not caricatures – the cops do have a sense of humour. One of them graciously tells Marcel, "We will even let you pay in Canadian dollars."

Marcel's girl friend (Lynne Adams), a punk prostitute, is meanwhile pulled into the misadventure, first by Marcel, who does a rooftop Last Tango in Montreal number on her – he virtually rapes her – and then by the cops, who abuse her in a terrifying scene many people will find impossible to watch. For the men in this world, women either do not exist or are objects to be toyed with, then smashed; they are caged beasts exploited by caged heat. The whore has one telling line: "When a guy comes here," she explains to Marcel in relation to her work in a grotty peep show, "at least I know what he wants. With you, I never know."

"My father and my sisters were walking basket cases . . . Then one day, looking at my father naked on his deathbed in an unheated slum room, I saw we had the same eyes and I said to myself, 'Is that what life comes down to?' My father never talked to me. I make him talk in this film."

One of the criticisms levelled against *Zoo* at the Cannes Film Festival, where it was nonetheless accorded a standing ovation when it opened the prestigious Director's Fortnight series, was that the second story, movingly detailing Marcel's growing empathy with and respect for his father (Roger Le Bel), was tangential to the urban thriller opening; *Zoo*, it was said disparagingly, was two movies in one.

It is. But what zoo showcases a single species? What life does not have two or more stories to tell? What person does not have at least two personalities? Marcel's grisly crusade, psychopathic in its lack of conventional morality and guilt (one of the disturbing but perhaps indisputable statements made by the movie is that conventional morality is irrelevant to much of what the world has become and that guilt is a self-destructive luxury), is sharply contrasted with Marcel's equally fervent affection for what's left of his family. And therein lies the true subversiveness of *Zoo*: the accepted North American wisdom that morality is founded in the family – unless, of course, you're talking Italian families in gangster movies – is rejected. There is plenty wrong with Marcel's morality from society's standpoint, but there is nothing wrong with his relationship to his father. And, more subversive still, as Marcel comes to appreciate his father's sweetness, his father sweetly embraces his son's outlaw ethic.

The two stories are integrated until the last half hour; that's when Lauzon winds up the thriller and focuses exclusively on the father. At that juncture, the title, which referred initially to Montreal, assumes a literal meaning – Marcel and his father go hunting in a zoo at night. The shift from one story to another marks *Zoo* as a post-modernist mainstream narrative in the tradition (already, there is a tradition) of *Paris, Texas* and *Full Metal Jacket*, and it's curious that critics in Cannes who never discussed or even noticed *Zoo*'s subject matter (and its refusal to ask questions about, let alone to judge, what matters to its subjects) were sent into fits of critique-pique over the film's narrative temerity: it tampers, they observed in horror, with the rules of storytelling.

"Curious" is maybe too timorous a term for an age in which what is said and shown is subordinate, in the esthetic canon of movie reviewing, to the structure in which it is displayed. This is not to argue that because *Zoo* is amoral, it is immoral: its sociological value is, precisely, that Lauzon has daringly not distanced himself from his people and their milieu. His eyes are not wide with terror, even if ours are. But to witness the violence, the sexism, the homophobia, the exploitation – the collapse of society – that this movie unblinkingly offers up, and then to complain that the film should have been simpler and more streamlined as entertainment (*Diva*, which romanticizes similar material, has been regularly invoked as an example of how it should have been done) – well, that's a specimen from the Zoo le cinema that's every bit as scary as any beast in *Zoo la nuit.*

September 16, 1987

Fatal Attraction

Directed by Adrian Lyne
Written by James Dearden
Starring Michael Douglas, Glenn Close and Anne Archer

Someone to Watch Over Me

Directed by Ridley Scott
Written by Howard Franklin
Starring Tom Berenger, Mimi Rogers and Lorraine Bracco

Is this synchronicity or serendipity, or what? British filmmakers Adrian Lyne (*Foxes, Nine and a Half Weeks, Flashdance*) and Ridley Scott (*Alien, Legend, Blade Runner*) have always had a lot in common, but this is ridiculous: *Fatal Attraction,* from the former, and *Someone to Watch Over Me,* from the latter, are close enough in style, tone, plot and "production values" (that means money) to be identical twins, albeit identical twins reared apart. Has anyone ever seen Adrian Lyne and Ridley Scott in the same place at the same time?

Both films are sexy romances set in New York, both revolve around the perils of adultery (the message is that fornication kills), and both climax with thrillerisms craftily engineered to leave audiences munching their seats in suspense. One of the differences is that *Fatal Attraction* evolves toward the cheaply manipulative and silly, while *Someone to Watch Over Me* retains at least a modicum of respect for the plausible, if not for the probable.

But before the trio of differences, eight similarities:

1. Scottlyne began its career as a director of chic commercials for British television.

2. Scottlyne was "discovered" and supported by David Puttnam, ex-head of Columbia Pictures.

3. Scottlyne has a sometimes fatal attraction (*Flashdance, Legend*) to style over substance.

4. Scottlyne is addicted to smoke and fuzz (*Foxes, Alien*) as a visual strategy.

5. Scottlyne often views relationships as mechanistic and sadistic (*Nine and a Half Weeks, Blade Runner*).

6. Scottlyne likes ominous music that tends to sound like an impacted subway train.

7. Scottlyne likes hand-held, jerky camera movements.

8. Scottlyne likes sudden close-ups of knives, oranges and navels. (A knife plunging into a navel orange is the ultimate Scottlyne close-up.)

The differences:

1. In *Fatal Attraction*, one of the women (Glenn Close) is crazy as a bedbug and the other (Anne Archer) is nice as pie. In *Someone to Watch Over Me*, one of the women (Mimi Rogers), a witness to a murder, is wealthy and cultivated, and the other woman (Lorraine Bracco), the wife of the cop assigned to watch over the wealthy woman, is lower middle-class and crude, but both are, in their own spheres, admirable. This means that *Someone to Watch Over Me* is a more interesting movie.

2. In *Fatal Attraction*, the man (Michael Douglas) who has the affair with the bedbug is a self-serving, moderately insensitive yuppie. In *Someone to Watch Over Me*, the cop (Tom Berenger) who has the affair with the wealthy women is a self-sacrificing, extraordinarily sensitive tough guy. This means that *Someone to Watch Over Me* is a much more interesting movie.

3. In *Fatal Attraction*, Michael Douglas (*Romancing the Stone, The China Syndrome*) demonstrates yet again that as an actor, he makes a

good producer – he has the charisma of chilled consommé. In *Some-one to Watch Over Me*, Tom Berenger (*Platoon*, *The Big Chill*) demon-strates yet again that as an actor, he makes a sizzling movie star – he has the charisma of chili con carne. This means that in *Fatal Attrac-tion*, the heart beats wildly with terror, while in *Someone to Watch Over Me*, it beats wildly with terror and romance; and that means that Scott and Lyne, by coming closer together than ever before, have moved, paradoxically, farther apart.

October 9, 1987

Matewan

Written and directed by John Sayles
Starring Chris Cooper, Will Oldham and Mary McDonnell

When union organizer Joe Kenehen (Chris Cooper), a member of the Wobblies "back when it meant sumthin'," arrives in Matewan, W. Va., in 1920, he is required to pass a test. Fearful that Joe may be working *sub rosa* for the "company store" – the Stone Mountain Coal Co., which controls the town and the people in it – the locals put it to him. "Who wrote *The Iron Heel*?" they ask. "Jack London," Joe answers. And: "Where is Joe Hill buried?" Joe's right again: "All over the world, they scattered his ashes." Because Joe passes with flying colours (red and pink predominate), he's permitted to set about trying to liberate Matewan from the clutches of a despotic institution slightly more feu-dal than the Catholic Church under the Borgias – at least the popes allowed as how things would get better for the dead.

Loosely based by writer-director John Sayles on his own novel, *Union Dues*, *Matewan* is enlivened with a history untaught by U.S. schoolmarms, a history kept alive in folk songs, back issues of *Mother*

Jones and the misty memories of aging radicals. Sayles' labour of love, which concentrates on events leading to the Matewan Massacre, is a reminder that in the United States pluralism means more than an intimidating assortment of soda pop, and populism refers to something more than ball parks and Top Forty radio.

Unapologetically left-leaning (how do you dramatize the unionization of the coal mines of Appalachia and not side with the workers?), the picture is nonetheless alive to contradiction and irony. In an attempt to smash the union, Stone Mountain imports black scabs from Alabama and immigrant scabs from Italy. The good mountain folk of West Virginia react venomously against "all these niggers and dagos," but they are not alone in their racism: one of the blacks, mulling over the advisability of joining the union, wonders if membership will mean that "we're gonna have to work with those Eye-talian people?" The salt of the earth that peppers Matewan is all too willing to be rubbed into the nearest wound.

Only in the character of Joe Kenehen, a pacifist Communist, does Sayles (*Baby, It's You, The Brother From Another Planet*) flirt with hagiography, but a long speech in which Joe emotionally recalls his admiration for Mennonites imprisoned in Leavenworth for refusing to fight in the First World War – "Them fellas had never lifted a gun all their lives, but you couldn't find any braver in my book" – unearths the roots of his ideology cleanly and without sentimentality. *Matewan* is in any case wide enough in scope to contain one good man (even if the real world often is not). Between the bickering of the Italians and the blacks, and the atrocities committed by the company "enforcers," and the weakness for wild west violence that slumbers in the bones of the hill people, the human population of Matewan (town and movie) is Shakespearean in density and complexity. Sayles may be a leftist, but he's also a humanist and a realist. The nobility he finds in Matewan is nobility that is earned.

If Shakespearean tragedy is Sayles' structural model, his anthropological inspiration is the *Children of Crisis* series by psychiatrist Robert Coles, who devoted decades to investigating and recording the effects of oppression and social change on children (and through them, their parents) across the United States. Even as Sayles outlines the explosive political battles in Matewan, he takes a hard, unblinkered look at the psychological fall-out. The exotic narrator of the film, Danny (Will Oldham), a fourteen-year-old preacher, is the touchstone. Initially idealistic and somewhat self-righteous, Danny comes to understand that the high tide of history drowns the wary and unwary alike. The preternaturally mature boy preacher, who testifies promiscuously to both "hard-shelled" and "soft-shelled" Baptists (the latter, he explains, are "free-will folks"), is the most salient example of the extraordinary hillbilly verisimilitude of *Matewan*, one of the few films ever to be set in the Appalachians that accurately captures the folkways and speech patterns ("I wouldn't pee on him if his heart was on fire," says the police chief) of a people customarily relegated to moronic local colour in Hollywood films.

Matewan ends predictably, as it must, with the Matewan Massacre, but Sayles has unpredictably staged the debacle not as a *Bonnie and Clyde tour de force* calculated to get the audience esthetically high on the strange beauty of death, but as an awkward comedy of terrors designed to shock onlookers with the slapstick reality of violence. (The town of Matewan is located in the West Virginia county of Mingo, the same county that gave the world the legend of the feudin' Hatfields and McCoys.) Sayles' achievement in *Matewan* is anomalous in political filmmaking: he celebrates laudable ends without attempting to whitewash less than laudable means.

October 9, 1987

❖

The Glass Menagerie

Directed by Paul Newman
Written by Tennessee Williams
Starring Joanne Woodward, Karen Allen, James Naughton and John Malkovich

"I was fired for writing a poem on the lid of a shoe-box." – *Tennessee Williams,* *"Portrait of a Girl in Glass"*

Tennessee Williams' early and all but forgotten short story, "Portrait of a Girl in Glass," completed in 1943 but not published until 1948, is in essence a plot outline for one of the greatest American plays ever written, *The Glass Menagerie,* a domestic memoir that is stiflingly mundane in detail but airily lyrical in execution – it is, indeed, a poem on the lid of a shoe-box. The theme, clearly elucidated in director Paul Newman's appropriately stifling yet airy adaptation of the play, is stated in an even earlier work, the 1940 playlet entitled *The Long Good-Bye*: "You're saying good-bye all the time, every minute you live. Because that's what life is, just a long, long good-bye – to one thing after another."

In *The Glass Menagerie,* Williams bids goodbye to people – to his manipulative Southern belle mother, Amanda (Joanne Woodward); to his manipulated frail sister, Laura (Karen Allen); to Laura's reluctant Gentleman Caller, Jim (James Naughton); and to Tom (John Malkovich), an angrier, more intolerant version of himself. And he bids goodbye to places – to the provincialism of his home town, St. Louis, Mo.; to the drudgery of his work at a warehouse; and to the drama of his furtive homosexual encounters (never stated but unmistakably implied). He bids goodbye, but he leaves nothing behind – "Oh, Laura, Laura," Tom cries, "I tried to leave you behind me, but I am more faithful than I intended to be!"

Newman's production, photographed both fluidly and claustrophobically by Michael Ballhaus in the faded yellows of old photograph albums, thankfully treats the text as sacred while the actors treat the characters as people. Woodward's Amanda is unexpectedly solid and even a little bawdy: she is attractive enough to suggest that although Amanda may be deluded, her account of a romantic past that encompassed seventeen gentleman callers is no invention. Amanda is often characterized as a near-lunatic; that Woodward sees her as basically sane – "I'm just bewitched by life," in Amanda's words – renders her disregard of the needs of her children all the more frightening.

"Honey," Amanda tells Laura, "I have to put courage in you for living." Karen Allen's Laura transcends the unexpected – she's a revelation. Because Allen is also more earthbound than actresses normally assigned the role, her delicacy is less physical than spiritual; because she is pretty, her belief that she is plain is particularly poignant. This is one of the few Lauras to embody Williams' description of his sister in "Portrait of a Girl in Glass": "I don't believe that my sister was actually foolish. I think the petals of her mind had simply closed through fear, and it's no telling how much they had closed upon in the way of secret wisdom."

James Naughton's Jim, a full-bodied performance of a sketchily written role, opens that secret wisdom in a long scene alone with Laura. The Gentleman Caller has been invited to a family dinner in hope (the hope is Amanda's) that he will think Laura comely and therefore a suitable candidate for betrothal. He does and he does not. He does not see her as a wife – he is otherwise engaged – but he does permit himself a momentary flirtation. Bypassing Laura's pathological shyness, his gentle male intrusiveness (he may be gentle merely because he has nothing to lose) locates under her fluttering, childish ways a woman desperate to emerge from a girl. He touches Laura's capacity for love and then hastily withdraws his hand, his fingertips singed by the heat of her desire, his own heart touched by the ache of hers.

Tom, a portrait of the artist as a young man, watches it all and will remember it all – forever. John Malkovich's performances on film are invariably distinctive and invariably mannered, but in this instance, distinction and mannerism meld; it is reasonable to assume that this strange boy, feline in sensuality and poetic in anger, will actually become Tennessee Williams. To get out of his suffocating house, Tom tells his mother he is going to the movies. Other short stories by Williams, especially "The Mysteries of the Joy Rio" and "Hard Candy," reveal the subterfuge (Tom went to the movies; he did not necessarily watch films), but Malkovich is the first actor in a major production to play that subtext, to treat Tom as a (homo)sexual being with a life outside his family's flat. (In discussions with Newman, Malkovich even argued that Tom was attracted to the Gentleman Caller.) Previous Toms were bound not for the Broadway stage but for the football field. This Tom is bound for a peculiarly nostalgic, bittersweet glory – the crystalline bars of his melancholy menagerie will refract phantom memories into rainbowed light all the rest of his clouded days.

November 4, 1987

❖

Wall Street

Directed by Oliver Stone
Written by Oliver Stone and Stanley Weiser
Starring Charlie Sheen, Michael Douglas and Daryl Hannah

Writer-director Oliver Stone, the creator of *Platoon*, has left Vietnam behind, but he hasn't left the battlefield. In *Wall Street*, his nervy, frenzied look at insider trading on the stock market, he presents company takeovers as parables of moral warfare – the engagements are carried out on financial front lines where the uniforms are suits by Armani, the trenches are expensive French restaurants, and the weapons are computer printouts.

Like Caryl Churchill's theatrical satire *Serious Money*, *Wall Street* does not assume knowledge of the intricate workings of the stock market nor does it presume to clarify those workings for the uninitiated. Instead, Stone's script makes towering mountains out of mysterious minutiae, confident that although we may not be able to classify the rocks, we will be able to map the terrain. The gambit is successful: if *Wall Street* does not reveal the nuts and bolts of the Wall Street machine, it does unveil the psychology of the men who operate it. And are operated by it.

The plot goes back to Genesis. Adam is Bud Fox (Charlie Sheen), a young institutional stockbroker; wealth is the apple; the snake is Gordon Gekko (Michael Douglas), a composite of a half-dozen financiers, including Donald Trump and Ivan Boesky; and Eve is an interior designer (Daryl Hannah), an ambitious woman who wants "to do for furniture what Laura Ashley did for fabrics." The eventual expulsion of innocent Bud Fox from his expense-account Eden is a foregone conclusion.

By way of editing timed to approximate the feeding frenzy of a shark and lines that punch the solar plexus ("Lunch," snarls Gekko, "is for wimps;" and: "That's the thing you gotta remember about WASPS, they love animals, they can't stand people"; and: "Greed is good"), Stone paves Wall Street in blood – his critique of the exploits of the élite highway robbers who raid rather than produce is convincing. Less convincing is the dewy Hannah as a tough New Yorker. Martin Sheen as Bud Fox's stalwart working-class Dad is another embarrassment – the role is simply too saintly, though he does have one nice speech ("Money's something you need in case you don't die tomorrow"). In addition, there are occasional spasms of the pulpy prose that mars even Stone's best work – in this case, a frightened Fox looks out at the Manhattan skyline and wonders aloud, "Who am I?" (The answer is, the product of a screenwriter who doesn't always know when to shut up.)

But Douglas's portrayal of Gordon Gekko is an oily triumph and as the kid Gekko thinks he has found in Fox ("Poor, smart and hungry; no feelings"), Charlie Sheen evolves persuasively from gung ho capitalist child to wily adolescent corporate raider to morally appalled adult. Early on, Fox is queried as to what became of one of his dates and he replies, "She asked the wrong question: 'What are you thinking?'" This is an acidulous movie about a boy who learns not to resent that question, a boy with a short lease on a street where bodies live in pampered paradise penthouses while the minds wallow in hellishly unethical gutters.

December 11, 1987

The Dead

Directed by John Huston
Written by Tony Huston (from a short story by James Joyce)
Starring Cathleen Delany, Helena Carroll, Ingrid Craigie,
    Anjelica Huston and Donal McCann

"It was always a great affair, the Misses Morkan's annual dance. Everybody who knew them came to it, members of the family, old friends of the family, the members of Julia's choir, any of Kate's pupils that were grown up enough and even some of Mary Jane's pupils too. Never once had it fallen flat. It had gone off in splendid style as long as anyone could remember . . ."

In the James Joyce novella, *The Dead*, which concludes the collection of short stories entitled *Dubliners*, the Misses Morkan – Aunt Julia (Cathleen Delany), Aunt Kate (Helena Carroll) and niece Mary Jane (Ingrid Craigie) – preside over the annual dance at their Dublin home on the Feast of Epiphany, January 6, 1904. The events are unspectacular, domestic, even mundane. The two elderly women and their younger sidekick serve a dinner of roast goose to more than a dozen people; Mary Jane entertains at the piano; Aunt Julia sings "Arrayed for the Bridal"; a guest recites a poem about loss, "Broken Vows"; another guest, an Irish tenor, performs "The Lass of Aughrim" – and Gretta Conroy (Anjelica Huston), wife of Gabriel Conroy (Donal McCann), nephew to the aunts, is deeply moved.

Later, at the hotel room the Conroys have retained for the night – the Dublin weather is frightful with snow – Gretta explains to her husband that "The Lass of Aughrim" was the favourite song of one Michael Furey, who died years ago at the age of seventeen. "I think," she cries, "he died for me." Gretta falls asleep. Her husband peers from the window of the hotel into the snow and experiences a triple epiphany: he sees that he is not as important to his wife as he had believed; he sees that the past lives on in the present; and he sees that in some ineffable way, the living and the dead inhabit the same tenuous, transparent cosmos. Snow continues to fall, blanketing the world of the living in the silence of the dead.

One year ago, on the set of *The Dead* in an industrial park in Valencia, Calif., where the interiors were shot, the ailing John Huston, directing his scrupulous adaptation of the Joyce novella, said, "We all are in the act of becoming the past," and added, "In *The Dead*, there is a sense of the wholeness of life with death." It was already evident from his son Tony Huston's reverent script – the chatter accompanying the arrival of the guests has been invented and the thematically congruent poem "Broken Vows" has been interpolated, but the words are otherwise virtual carbons of Joyce – that *The Dead* would be, in the director's words, "a motion picture like no other." It is more than that: it is a masterpiece, John Huston's finest film, and one of the finest in the history of movies.

But at a brief seventy-six minutes, it is a subtle, almost miniaturized masterpiece. What makes it unique is not only its musical dialogue and structure, and the equalling lilting yet naturalistic performances of the Irish actors who form the large and surprisingly comic cast, but the attitude with which Huston views the material. Joyce scholars have long debated the meaning of Gabriel's insights: does he see how alone and isolated each person is (the existential interpretation) or does he experience a transcendent oneness with the universe (the spiritual interpretation)? Written when Joyce was a cranky twenty-six, the novella is open to either extrapolation, but the movie, directed by a beneficent Huston at the age of eighty, is not. (Huston died of complications resulting from emphysema on August 28, 1987, at eighty-one.) One of the hallmarks of "acceptance," the final stage reached by some (but by no means all) terminal patients, is a rejection of the trivial and an unaffected embrace of the natural order; the denial of death is replaced by a personalized philosophical awareness that lives should end in oblivion. *The Dead* is the only movie I have ever seen, excluding sections of Jean Renoir's uneven swan song, *The Little Theatre of Jean Renoir*, that feels as if it had been made from the stage of acceptance. Huston, who broke rules throughout his prolific creative life (*The Dead* was his forty-first film), productively went to his grave constructing the most appropriate of eulogies: *The Dead* stands as the epitaph of a man who cheated death slightly by understanding it fully. Huston's all-encompassing understanding is merely hinted at in Joyce's story; in the movie, it is realized with strangely comforting force and finality.

But *The Dead* is primarily about the living – as Gabriel says in his after-dinner speech extolling the virtues of "the three graces," the Misses Morkan, "Our work is among the living." Huston's avuncular affection for the Irish (Joyce was far more ambivalent) is given free expression in the characterizations of:

• two drunks, the undignified Freddy Malins (Donal Donnelly), who slurs in the bathroom, "I've never been able to relieve myself in the presence of another, otherwise I'd have enjoyed the army," and the dignified Mr. Browne (Dan O'Herlihy), who tells the cadaverous Aunt Julie that her quavering rendition of "Arrayed for the Bridal" showcases her voice at its best;

• Aunt Julia, who responds to the flattery with, "Thirty years ago I hadn't a bad voice as voices go," and Aunt Kate, who upbraids the Holy Pontiff for ejecting from the choir women who "have slaved all their lives" in favour of "little whipper-snappers of boys";

• Freddy Malins' mother, Mrs. Malins (Marie Kean), who gossips, "I heard that Verdi's morals were dubious, very dubious indeed," and complains, "Turkey to me tastes like chicken soaked in water then wrung out";

• and Gretta and Gabriel Conroy, who exemplify the disturbing power of shadows cast by shades. As the tenor trills "The Lass of Aughrim" in the novella, Gabriel comes upon his wife listening "in the gloom of the hall": "There was grace and mystery in her attitude as if she were a symbol of something. He asked himself what is a woman standing on the stairs in the shadow, listening to distant music, a symbol of. If he were a painter he would paint her in that attitude . . . *Distant Music* he would call the picture if he were a painter."

Huston and his cinematographer, Fred Murphy (*The State of Things, The Trip to Bountiful, Hoosiers, Five Corners*), are painters, and the sequence in which Gretta pauses on the stairs, framed in a stained glass window like a mannerist Madonna, to listen to the strains of that song about disintegration, is hushed and beautiful and unbearably melancholy. "Generous tears filled Gabriel's eyes," Joyce writes. Generous tears must have filled Huston's eyes, because they fill the eyes of the viewer; they drip from the cheeks like Joyce's snowflakes, "falling faintly through the universe and faintly falling, like the descent of their last end, upon all the living and the dead."

February 5, 1988

The Manchurian Candidate

Directed by John Frankenheimer
Written by George Axelrod
Starring Frank Sinatra, Laurence Harvey, Janet Leigh and Angela Lansbury

The Manchurian Candidate is a mystery movie that became a bona fide mystery on its own: the hyper-realist paranoid thriller with baroquely satirical overtones was released in 1962, but was later pulled from the theatres by one of its stars and owners, Frank Sinatra, in the wake of the assassination of John F. Kennedy. Sinatra felt there were uncomfortable parallels between novelist Richard Condon's recondite plot, which involved an ingenious Communist scheme to brainwash a U.S. citizen with the goal of conditioning him into becoming an assassin, and the events surrounding Kennedy's demise

– remember Lee Harvey Oswald's little sojourn in the Soviet Union? There were other, more disturbing similarities, but now that Sinatra has allowed the picture to resurface, they must remain a mystery or they will destroy the mystery for audiences discovering this wonderfully berserk movie for the first time.

It can be reported that there are "coincidences" that elicit gasps, but even people with no recollection of the minutiae of the Kennedy assassination will watch with their mouths open. Long before it was shelved, thereby automatically earning it legendary status, *The Manchurian Candidate* had attracted extraordinarily laudatory reviews; the movie to which it was most frequently compared was *Citizen Kane*, which it does indeed resemble in its bizarre mixture of sophisticated wit, epic political paranoia, outrageous psychological vulgarity and exhibitionistic technical energy. Like *Citizen Kane*, *The Manchurian Candidate* turns American pop into American art.

(Re)viewed a quarter of a century after it was made, it can be seen clearly as a creature of its time – Joseph McCarthy and the Cold War are its true subjects – but it is as wildly entertaining as the only other movies it brings to mind, John Huston's *Prizzi's Honor* and William Richert's *Winter Kills*, two political black comedies also inspired by Richard Condon novels. And it is as politically slippery as glasnost; leftists may find it reactionary, while right-wingers are bound to suspect they are being mocked. (Here and there, it is reactionary; here and there, they are being mocked.) Mostly, George Axelrod's script reflects unerringly the political confusion and schizophrenia of the decline of Camelot at the end of the New Frontier: it's got a humanist head and a black heart.

Shot by Lionel Lindon in gleaming black and white, the saga begins in Korea. Several soldiers, including Bennett Marco (Sinatra) and Raymond Shaw (Laurence Harvey), are captured by the North Koreans. Rescued and returned stateside, the lugubrious and snotty Shaw, the step-son of conservative U.S. Sen. John Iselin (James Gregory), goes to work for a liberal political journalist and pines for a lost love, Jocie Jordan (Leslie Parrish), the daughter of another senator, Thomas Jordan (John McGiver), who is also a liberal. In *The*

Manchurian Candidate, liberalism means approving of the American Civil Liberties Union; to Shaw's dowager mother (Angela Lansbury), that means harbouring Communist sympathies. (In some areas of the United States, where such beliefs persist, *The Manchurian Candidate* is no period piece.)

Meanwhile, Marco and his veteran buddies are tormented by a strange dream in which one of their number commits murder in front of an audience consisting variously of Russians, Chinese and elderly lady gardeners interested in hydrangeas; the dream is central to the movie's mystery and, like everything else in *The Manchurian Candidate*, it is choreographed by director John Frankenheimer with an oddly stately pizazz. In its blend of almost pompous seriousness, impertinent humour and splashiness for its own sake, the style of this thriller about political conventions actually resembles them – it sees the future of the United States as a cheerful conflict adjudicated by the outcome of a homicidal circus.

As the tormented and misanthropic Shaw – snapping off a recording, he snarls, "The Twelve Days of Christmas . . . one day of Christmas is loathsome enough" – the late Laurence Harvey reaches the majesty reserved to tragedy. Lansbury, whose character may have been prompted by *Generation of Vipers*, the Freudian monster-mommy book of pop psychology influential in the fifties, is seductive and repellent in equal portions (what a Lady Macbeth she would have made!). As her red-baiting hubby, a McCarthy dummy who whines, "I'd just be a lot happier if we could settle on how many Communists we know are in the Defense Department," Gregory is chillingly comic. Sinatra, invariably underrated as an actor, is seamlessly effective, but the thespian revelation of the film is Janet Leigh; on a train, she and Sinatra get to know each other in a scene that is one of the most gaudily surreal, yet inexplicably sensible, pick-ups ever written.

Gaudy, surreal, inexplicable, sensible: *The Manchurian Candidate* gets elected to cinematic immortality running on its own ticket on behalf of its own party. This is an oddball classic that leaves you weak with pleasure, a pleasure that lasts so long it has taken some commentators twenty-five years to realize that it begs the mightiest of the questions it raises. An evil Chinese Communist refers at one suspenseful juncture to those "uniquely American symptoms, guilt and fear." If guilt and fear are the uniquely American symptoms, what is the uniquely American disease?

March 11, 1988

❖

Bright Lights, Big City

Directed by James Bridges
Written by Jay McInerney
Starring Michael J. Fox and Kiefer Sutherland

You go in with trepidation. You've read *Bright Lights, Big City*, which boiled as a literary sensation about as long as a three-minute egg, so you know all about that. You know that it was a first novel by Jay McInerney, and that he is always being lumped with Tama Janowitz, who wrote *Slaves of New York*, and Bret Easton Ellis, who wrote *Less Than Zero*, in the pride of anti-literary literary lions, writers who are to writing what rock videos are to movies. You know that *BL, BC* got a lot of its fame because Jay McInerney worked in the department of factual verification at *The New Yorker* and told all; you knew when you read the book that he was being down and dirty about the high and mighty.

You go in with trepidation for a lot of reasons. You didn't much like the tone of the book, wherein the narrator, Our Hero, always referred to himself as "you," as in, "Here you are again. All messed up and no place to go." And you remember that the witticisms, like that one, were sub-Dorothy Parker, and that there was an awful lot of white, middle-class prejudice, as in, "Dracula Jews and zonked-out Africans" (that was about people on the New York subway) or "gnomes with black briefcases full of diamonds" (Our Hero's summation of Hasidim), or "his wife is no less formidable, being the one who wears the mustache in the family" (a Greek woman), or "his speech is Sunbelt Swish" (a gay Japanese co-worker).

Our Hero, you recall, had a busted-up marriage to a model and spent most of his time doing coke and getting sloshed and eventually fired. But then, just as you were ready to write the guy off as a total screw-up, there was the old one-two to the tear ducts: the guy was screwed up because his mother died. Since most people's mothers have died, or will die, it was easy for you to sympathize, but you still felt like you'd been, like, duped.

So by now you're wondering if you're going to see this movie at all, I mean, what are you, a glutton for punishment? But you think Michael J. Fox, Our Hero, is kind of cute, if you're into ten-year-olds, and you've been impressed with Kiefer Sutherland, and you know he's going to play Our Hero's best friend, sleazy Tad, whose "mission in life is to have more fun than anyone else in New York City," and you know Swoosie Kurtz is going to play the woman at *The New Yorker* who gives Our Hero a shoulder to sob on, and Oscar de la Renta is going to do the clothes, and anyway, you can't afford the plane fare to see the real bright lights in the real big city, and you figure that this might be the next best thing, even if you can't stand Our Hero.

And you know what? You're right. You're going to decide your time could have been better spent, but you're also going to figure this was not time wasted, either. Like Tad says in the book, "Taste is a matter of taste." First off, you notice that all the bigoted stuff in the book has been cut right out, snippety-snip. And you notice that even if Michael J. Fox does look like a child about to get molested when he gets into his undershorts, he is real good at being screwed up, and Kiefer Sutherland is even better, and Dianne Wiest really gets the tears going as the dying mother, and Swoosie Kurtz is really everything you hoped she'd be, and the director, James Bridges, really keeps the pretty colours coming at you.

273

And you notice something else. You remember that when they made *Less Than Zero* into a movie, they turned it into an anti-drug pitch, but they haven't done that here. You notice that *BL, BC* treats drugs as part of life, as an often destructive part of life, for sure, because they for sure are, but it doesn't overstate the case either, and try to make them look any less fun than they are, and if they weren't fun, for sure, they wouldn't be a problem, would they?

And you notice that as the movie goes on and the bright lights get dimmer for Our Hero as the city gets smaller, you're in the presence of a not-half-bad look at what can happen to bright kids who come to the city, any city, really, except maybe Tehran at the moment, convinced that it will solve their problems, and then wind up getting their bright lights punched out because they're carrying too much baggage from home, baggage that needs to be psychologically unpacked and put away. They're so weighed down by the past, they're not fast enough to duck in the present.

You hate the last image of the movie, which turns a symbol that's been used all the way through into a sledgehammer, but taken as a whole, it suddenly occurs to you that if the bright lights had been German and the city had been Berlin and the language had been foreign, a lot of people would be saying that this movie was an uncompromising portrait of the alienation of youth in urban centres and all that jazz, blah blah blah. So you figure, what the hell, go with it and enjoy it for what it is, which is C-plus, but A-minus for effort and B-plus for honesty, and since you gave the book a D-minus, you decide you're going to tell your friends to skip the book and see the movie. Then you're left with only one nagging question as you walk out of the theatre into the bright lights of whatever big city you happen to be in: how is Pepsi going to feel about Michael J. Fox doing so much coke?

April 1, 1988

The Moderns

Directed by Alan Rudolph
Written by Alan Rudolph and Jon Bradshaw
Starring Keith Carradine and Linda Fiorentino

"There was no plot in Paris in the twenties." – *Alan Rudolph*

For sixty years, people who were in Paris in the twenties have patronized people who were not: those were the days they thought would never end, they tell their friends.

In memoirs, they do not end. The days when Picasso painted Gertrude Stein, and Gertrude Stein pained Alice B. Toklas, and Alice B. Toklas affronted Ernest Hemingway, and Ernest Hemingway affronted everyone – those days have gone on for decades. In the eighties, they have become a mini-publishing industry and a major motivating myth of the modern art of the post-modern era: Scintillating Salons; or Eden on the Seine; or The Last Time I Saw Paris Was The Last Time I Saw Art.

Pardon Alan Rudolph while he demurs. *The Moderns*, his dreamy invention of Paris in the twenties, doesn't buy the myth, it demolishes it with off-centre aphorisms ("Everybody hates repeating gossip, but what else is there to do with it?"), primary colours, black-and-white stock footage, and a galaxy of stellar performances.

Propelled along at a leisurely lope by Mark Isham's blueish jazz, Rudolph presents a 1926 Paris (shot in Montreal) in which the innovations in modern art are already over, and commerce, in the form of venal dealers and greedy collectors and uncritical critics, is fixing to devour the leavings. Even that sacrosanct mistress of the shock of the new, Gertrude Stein (Elsa Raven) herself, is wilting in the warm winds of fashion. "American painters are twenty-six years old this year," she announces to American painter Nick Hart (Keith Carradine), who is thirty-three, the age Christ was crucified. Nick Hart, a modernist Christ, can be resurrected only if he leaves his holy Parisian city and moves to the next centre of everything: Hollywood, U.S.A. "I'm tired of these pictures," grouses Oiseau (Wallace Shawn), the Paris gossip columnist for the *Chicago Tribune*, "I wanna go where the pictures move."

The two extremes in Rudolph's delectable moralist fairytale are represented by Hart and Stone – Nick Hart, the painter who creates for love, and Bertram Stone (John Lone), the collector who acquires for status. Hart may or may not be good, but he does burn with the desire to produce, career be damned. Stone, "a rubber baron" (prophylactics), wants to purchase respectability; foiled, he subjects a particularly bosomy nude by Modigliani to a mastectomy and declares that art is given value by the hard cash he shells out for it. (All dealers deny it; all dealers know it's true.)

Between Hart and Stone, the *moderne* rats race: Rachel Stone (Linda Fiorentino), once married to Hart, now under the Stone; Libby Valentin (Genevieve Bujold), a Canadian art dealer who speaks her own patois and judges art and people by her own amoral standards; Nathalie de Ville (Geraldine Chaplin), a manipulative dilettante who wears two deceptive black tears painted under each eye and is beginning to wrinkle like Isak Dinesen; the gossip Oiseau, whose reported suicide triggers from Hemingway (Kevin J. O'Connor) the admission that "It makes me feel like a coward"; and Hemingway, who is admonished by Stein, "Remember Hemingway, the sun also sets."

The famous names are not the *raison d'être* of *The Moderns*, which is neither history nor gossip column, but a lush debunking of commercialized culture. That's why surreal backdrops are occasionally recruited and why, in one memorable sequence, the camera pans from the fashions of Paris in 1926 to a group of Parisian punks in the same pose.

And that's why Rudolph has tossed into *The Moderns* matrimonial melodrama (Hart's attempt to dislodge Rachel from the Stone); esthetic critiques ("Art is only an impression . . . an infection . . . a rumour"); sociology ("Drink and permanent attachments have been the undoing of almost all our friends"); and good jokes (declaring

Paris to be "uncivilized," the art dealer orders a taxi to drive her to Cannes) and bad ("You ought to work on that," the columnist advises Hemingway after Hemingway dubs Paris "a portable banquet"). The result is a heady, pungent potpourri.

One of Rudolph's most astute realizations is that for Americans, nothing happens where Americans are not. At the end of *The Moderns*, Hollywood having been dubbed the city of the future (though Hart fears "it'll be more fun to watch the movies than to make them"), the expatriates leave, bidding Paris adieu with nostalgic fanfare. For the Yankee moderns, their absence is the indisputable signal that there's no there there. For Alan Rudolph, their hubris is the very definition of modernism: there's no there anywhere.

July 22, 1988

The Last Temptation of Christ

Directed by Martin Scorsese
Written by Paul Schrader (from the novel by Nikos Kazantzakis)
Starring Willem Dafoe, Harvey Keitel and Barbara Hershey

These are things that *The Last Temptation of Christ* is not: disrespectful, irreverent, blasphemous, anti-religious.

This is what *The Last Temptation of Christ*, directed by Martin Scorsese (*Taxi Driver*) from a Paul Schrader (*Mishima*) script inspired by Nikos Kazantzakis' classic novel, is: a serious, intense, two-hour and forty-minute, wide-ranging exploration of what Kazantzakis saw as the conflict played out in the soul – in all souls – between spirit and flesh. Scorsese and Schrader have made a courageous film that people of all religions or no religion should be able to watch with identical fascination.

But it is important to stress that this is not the shimmering, haloed Christ of Sunday school art, though it is to a large extent the Christ of the Gospels and of great religious art. But which Gospels? In his novel, Kazantzakis drew freely from all accounts of Christ to create a composite portrait of a contradictory man at first afraid of accepting his intuition that he might be God. Christ's evolution regarding his fate in the novel is essentially from unbeliever to revolutionary to pacifist to – finally, in the single stunning stroke that is a departure from any account of his life – an understanding of the power of myth to provide comfort to human beings. (I am here using myth in the sense used by psychologists – a myth is a story that is so true to human nature that its facts are irrelevant.) The novel leaves Christ's actual divinity open to interpretation and the film follows suit.

What neither leaves open to interpretation is that Christ's struggle to reconcile himself to his salvation is hypnotizing to us because it is a mirror of our struggle. For Martin Scorsese, one of the world's most talented directors, that struggle has historically resulted in his best work: *Mean Streets, Taxi Driver* (also written with Paul Schrader), *Raging Bull.* But until now in Scorsese films, his heroes were men who struggled for salvation without knowing what salvation was or what, or whom, they had to embrace or avoid to reach it. More than any other Scorsese hero, Christ does know, which is why although *The Last Temptation of Christ* shares with Scorsese's other major movies a violent, hallucinatory texture, it never feels like Jerusalem Taxi Driver.

(In the tradition of movies about Christ, it has three influences: the gritty verisimilitude of Pier Paolo Pasolini's *The Gospel According to St. Matthew,* the see-sawing complexity of Luis Bunuel's *Simon of the Desert,* and the sudden eruptions of satiric humour that marked Norman Jewison's *Jesus Christ Superstar.*)

Christ (a charismatic but not supernatural Willem Dafoe) is introduced as a carpenter, of course, but as a carpenter who is making crosses for the Romans and is obsessed by visions of his own crucifixion. His friend Judas (Harvey Keitel), a Zealot, chides him with, "You're a Jew killing Jews, you're a coward. How will you ever pay for your sins?" "With my life, Judas," Jesus replies. "I don't have anything else."

But he does have a past. In a scene that is in the novel but not in the movie, he played footsie – literally, and that's as far as it went – with Mary Magdalene (Barbara Hershey); his lapse sent her on the road to whoredom. She enters the movie as a prostitute who hates him because he spurned her and hates God because He was the reason. "You're the same as all the others, only you can't admit it," she charges. "You're pitiful. I hate you." Jesus does not deny her anger. "I know the worst things I've done have been to you," he admits.

The traditional events of Christ's life (the miracles, the temptations, the sermons) are posed in *The Last Temptation of Christ* against a background, shot in Morocco, that is half-barbaric, half-civilized. There's no doubt as to why Jesus wants to clean these temples, with their moneychangers, their offal and their moral filth. When the High Priest argues that the temples are being protected by the moneychangers – because of them, no Roman money is spent within – Christ screams, "God is not an Israelite." Around him society is in disarray if not decay, which leads him to sympathize with the Zealots. At his most revolutionary, he calls for the adoption of the sword and momentarily removes his own beating heart to demonstrate his sincerity, and then squeezes it in his hand to validate his rage. These and similar miraculous events (the raising of Lazarus, for example) are free of the swooning angelic choirs slurped on trivial, vulgar religious epics such as *King of Kings* or *The Greatest Story Ever Told*. Working with Michael Ballhaus' dusty, zooming camera, and Peter Gabriel's music, indebted to Africa and the near East, Scorsese builds a swirling cinematic house of marvels in which all magic is possible.

The only levity Scorsese permits himself is his parody of the cameo casting of the Biblical dramas of yore (he has Harry Dean Stanton as St. Paul, Andre Gregory as John the Baptist, David Bowie as Pilate) and a style of humour that is a product of the movie's vernacular language. "That's what I love about you, Peter," Judas cracks, "you're as steady and solid as a rock. No one can change your mind.

What good are you?" And when Judas wonders why Jesus changes his positions so often – first he's a man of war, then a prince of peace – Jesus shrugs, "God only talks to me a little bit at a time. He only tells me what I need to know."

The hysteria that *The Last Temptation of Christ* has engendered among fundamentalist Christian groups is not only misplaced but myopic. The Bible, equivocal about so much, is unequivocal that Christ lived as a man, after all, and with one exception, the doubts and fears and torments he experiences in the movie are a matter of biblical record. The exception is the "last temptation" that gives the movie its name, a heartrending interlude during which Jesus is shown what might have been, had he rejected his assignment (to save the world, if you will, or to martyr himself unnecessarily, if you won't). It begins when an undefined emissary approaches him, prior to his death on the cross, and tells him that God has decided that His son has suffered enough.

This "last temptation" is perhaps the reason the novel has been studied closely and respected mightily: it contains within it a parable of the human yearning to find an inhuman paradise. Those who are religious believe that the yearning is dangerous because paradise is available only after death. Those who are not religious, but are spiritual, believe it is dangerous because the desire for unending happiness can lead only to woe – to selfishness, oppression and self-delusion. *The Last Temptation of Christ* questions the very nature of the quest for salvation and concludes that, for the religious, the answer is to follow God; for the secular, it is to follow your heart. Given the obstacles he faced, Scorsese's own last temptation must have been to chuck the entire idea of making a movie of this depth and dangerousness. That he persevered indicates he has incorporated fully his hero's difficult conviction that the good thing is not often the easy thing.

August 10, 1988

❖

Dear America: Letters Home From Vietnam

Directed by Bill Couturie

On screen, the story of Vietnam has been told in the framework of historical documentary (*Hearts and Minds, Mills of the Gods*), domestic drama (*Coming Home*), opera (*Apocalypse Now*), post-modern minimalism (*Full Metal Jacket*), buddy westerns (*The Boys in Company C, Hamburger Hill*), red-neck propaganda (*Hanoi Hilton*) and macho myth (*The Deer Hunter*), not to mention comedy (*Good Morning, Vietnam*) and melodramatic tragedy (*Platoon*).

Short of disguising the context – cf. the forthcoming ultra-violent U.S. potboiler *The Beast*, which transforms Russians into Americans, Mujahideen into Viet Cong and Afghanistan into Vietnam – there doesn't seem to be much left to be said, or to be seen, about the war the United States lost. But *Dear America: Letters Home From Vietnam* for the first time tells the story of the war in the words of the men who actually waged it, along with the pictures and home movies they took while they were actually doing it. The information the film imparts is thus primarily of an emotional nature.

Director Bill Couturie's hope that "people come away from *Dear America* with the sense that they've finally seen Vietnam from underneath the soldier's helmet" has been fulfilled and his contention that "*Dear America* is Vietnam as you've never seen it before – the joy, the love, the camaraderie, as well as the heartache," is justified. The letters, culled from a book of the same title, are read by an A-list of U.S. actors, including Tom Berenger, Willem Dafoe, Robert De Niro, Kevin and Matt Dillon, Michael J. Fox (how did a Canadian get in there?), Sean Penn, Howard Rollins, Jr., Martin Sheen, Kathleen Turner and Robin Williams.

For the most part, the strategy is successful although it is initially discomforting to hear Williams, De Niro and Fox, with their recognizable voices, rattle on about Vietnam experiences while pretending to be the eighteen-year-old grunts we see on the screen in awkward, touching and sometimes frightening home movies. (*Dear America* also utilizes news broadcasts and stills – the entire range of available visual archival material.) But the discomfort is momentary and the film's biggest risk – a climactic performance by Ellen Burstyn reading from the letters Eleanor Wimbish composed to her dead son William Stocks – pays off in catharsis.

The letters come home chronologically; at the top of the war, the missives are optimistic and patriotic. "I've never seen such bravery and guts before, and I'm stunned by it," writes First Lieutenant James M. Simmen. "You shoulda seen my men fight. They were going after wounded men no one else would go after. You shoulda seen my brave men. It would give you goose pimples." But Corporal Kevin Macaulay, while retaining his patriotism, is losing his optimism. "Dear Mom and Dad, I guess by now you're worried sick over my safety. I am unhurt and have not been touched. I think with all the death and destruction I have seen in the past week I have aged greatly. I feel like an old man now. I am scared by it, but not scared enough to quit. I am a Marine and hope some day to be a good one. Please pray for us all here at Khe Sahn."

As the music of the period (from Elvis Presley's "Blue Christmas" to Bob Dylan's "A Hard Rain's Gonna Fall") heats up and the war itself gets hotter, the letters become angrier, sadder and more depressed. "Dear Madeline, I tell you truthfully I doubt I'll come out of this alive. In my original squad, I'm the only one left unharmed. In my platoon there's only 13 of us. It seems every day another young guy 18 or 19 years old like myself is killed in action. See ya, if it's God's will. I have to make it out of Vietnam though, 'cause I'm lucky. I hope. Ha ha. Love, Ray." Private Raymond Griffiths was killed on the 4th of July, 1966.

The waste of the past, a waste that will continue into the future with the shattered lives of so many Vietnam veterans, is appropriately underlined in the present: the movie concludes with Bruce Springsteen's rendition of "Born in the U.S.A." and Eleanor Wimbish's words to her son, words she deposits at the Vietnam War Memorial in Washington, D.C.:

"Dear Bill:

"Today is Feb. 13, 1984. I came to this black wall again to see and touch your name, William R. Stocks, and as I do I wonder if anyone ever stops to realize that next to your name, on this black wall, is your mother's heart, a heart broken 15 years ago when you lost your life in Vietnam.

"They tell me the letters I write to you and leave here at this memorial are waking others up to the fact that there is still much pain left, after all these years, from the Vietnam War.

"But this I know. I would rather have had you for 21 years, and all the pain that goes with losing you, than never to have had you at all.

"Mom."

September 13, 1988

Bird

Directed by Clint Eastwood
Written by Joel Oliansky
Starring Forest Whitaker and Diane Venora

He was, as every jazz fan knows, a bird with a pair of broken wings: Charlie Parker, nicknamed Bird, was the most influential jazzman since Louis Armstrong, but he died an alcoholic and drug addict at the age of thirty-four in 1955. Dr. Robert Freymann, the attending physician, assumed he was looking at the body of a man in his sixties.

That scene is in director Clint Eastwood's indigo film biography, *Bird*, but Parker's personal tragedies never overwhelm Eastwood's love of the saxophone player's art. Unlike, say, *Lady Sings the Blues*, which reduced Billie Holiday to heroin soap opera (and to the squeak of Diana Ross's vocal . . . uh . . . instrument), Eastwood puts everything in perspective: if anything overwhelms his movie, it is Parker's music. Time and again, the plot comes to a halt to permit *Bird* to soar the only way he knew how, on stage. Eastwood has also solved the perpetual problem facing biographers of musicians (do you use their music or do you fake it?) with ingenuity: music director Lennie Niehaus cleaned up Bird's original tapes and then adorned his solos with new arrangements and new players. The approach is appropriate because Bird's music was far more progressive – more "modern" – than the work of the majority of his colleagues.

At two hours and forty-three minutes, Eastwood's *Bird* is a hypnotic, darkly photographed, loosely constructed marvel that avoids every cliché of the self-destructive-celebrity biography, a particularly remarkable achievement in that Parker played out every cliché of the self-destructive-celebrity life. To escape a relentless downward spiral, Eastwood and screenwriter Joel Oliansky have fractured chronology much the way Parker fractured melody – there are flashbacks, flashforwards, and flashbacks within flashforwards. "It's a complicated film in some ways," Eastwood accurately warned earlier this year. "Audiences are going to have to pay attention or they might get lost in it. That's OK. I think there's room for these kinds of movies, and if they're not going to pay attention, they shouldn't come. Maybe we should put a disclaimer on it: Paying Attention Required."

But paying attention is rewarded. The recreations of the New York jazz scene of the forties and fifties are loving in their detail and hallucinatory in their power. As Parker, Forest Whitaker holds the camera with a towering performance that misses only one aspect of the musician's personality, his legendary sexual charisma. ("He was so charismatic," Eastwood has said, "that even when he wasn't being a good boy, people tolerated him." Whitaker's Parker does not inspire that level of indulgence.)

The women in Parker's life have been reduced to one, Chan Parker, who is given a riff by Diane Venora that is as supple and sultry as a Parker solo. Venora also clarifies the mystery of Chan's relationship to Parker: why would a sane woman put up with an almost insane man? Venora's interpretation: for a woman possessed by jazz body and soul, only the most brilliant jazzman on earth was suitable, his personal problems be damned.

Although those personal problems did damn him, Eastwood refuses to simplify the connection, if any, between Parker's self-destructiveness and his music. "I don't think anyone ever solves the mystery of someone like Parker," the director argued at the Cannes Film Festival. "It dates back to van Gogh and other self-destructive artists – no one knows why." *In The Lives of John Lennon*, Albert Goldman writes, "Withdrawal from heroin is no worse than a bad case of the flu, but junkies are notoriously incapable of suffering, which is one of the reasons why they become junkies in the first place." That explanation neatly fits Eastwood's *Bird*, but it begs the central question: why are junkies notoriously incapable of suffering? Eastwood doesn't pretend to have the answer, nor does his movie. *Bird* merely laments the fact that because Charlie Parker's pain threshold was so low, his fans were robbed of a lifetime of pleasure.

October 14, 1988

Rain Man

Directed by Barry Levinson
Written by Ronald Bass and Barry Morrow
Starring Tom Cruise and Dustin Hoffman

From the startlingly beautiful first shot – hanging precariously from the cables of a crane, a cherry-red Lamborghini flies across the top of the screen – *Rain Man* is a big, bright pleasure machine. But it's also a double-barrelled Hollywood howitzer: by combining two unbeatably commercial genres (the road movie and the buddy movie) with two unquestionably talented movie stars (the cerebral Dustin Hoffman, the sexy Tom Cruise), it has stockpiled all the ammunition it needs to mow down competition and blast holes in criticism.

There's more. Because Hoffman is cast against type as an "autistic savant" named Raymond Babbitt, a neurologically impaired embarrassment who has been institutionalized most of his life, and because Cruise is Raymond's bitter brother, Charlie, a greedy entrepreneur who will learn valuable lessons in charity from Raymond's maddening affliction, *Rain Man* is also the season's comedy with "heart." It's the Christmas picture that cares, the UNICEF epic, and that must explain why no one seems to notice, or to care, that from minute to minute, the story itself is second-hand hokum.

Credit for the nearly impenetrable disguise should be shared. As the furiously insensitive and unapologetically self-centred Charlie Babbitt, Cruise surpasses his superb performances in *The Color of Money* and *Risky Business*. As the "autistic savant" Raymond, who can multiply 312 by 183 without thinking but doesn't know how much change he should receive if he spends fifty cents on the dollar, Hoffman painstakingly brings to half-life a man whose limited emotions have a surprising capacity for summoning limitless emotions in those he meets.

Meanwhile, director Barry Levinson (*Diner*; *The Natural*; *Good Morning, Vietnam*) and Australian cinematographer John Seale (*Careful, He Might Hear You*; *Witness*; *Gorillas in the Mist*) never miss finding a new angle on everything from urban Cincinnati, where Charlie virtually kidnaps Raymond from a plush private institution for the mentally impaired, to the fields of the U.S. Midwest, where the brothers put in time because Raymond bleatingly refuses to fly, to sun-slaked Los Angeles, where they face the music in the form of a custody hearing.

At the outset, Charlie callously kidnaps his brother because their father has bequeathed the family's entire fortune, $3-million, to an administrator at the hospital that has taken care of Raymond, without Charlie's knowledge, for decades. Until the hated father expires, Charlie has no idea that he has a brother, although he does have dim memories of a "rain man" who sang to him when he was a frightened infant.

In the six days it takes the duo to cross the country (reprising *Dominick and Eugene*, *Things Change*, *Midnight Run*, *Of Mice and Men*, and innumerable road movies), Charlie alters the reactions of a lifetime and learns to love. Raymond, by diagnostic definition incapable of change, nonetheless learns to dance, crack jokes and kiss girls. The unbelievably swift enlightenment on both sides is greeted with delight by an audience entranced. Only after the Hollywood hypnotism wears off is it apparent that *Rain Man*, fundamentally an artsy sentimentalization of "The Odd Couple," is somewhat less than the sum of its perfect parts.

December 19, 1988

Dangerous Liaisons

Directed by Stephen Frears
Written by Christopher Hampton
Starring John Malkovich and Glenn Close

Until an unwarranted moralistic fillip at the end, *Dangerous Liaisons*, adapted by Christopher Hampton from his own hit play, *Les Liaisons Dangereuses*, is a decadent celebration of wanton cruelty. Naughty enough to qualify as dangerously wicked and stylishly sophisticated in some eyes, the farce spends nearly two voyeuristic hours panting over the antics of psychopathic fornicators, then lets the audience off the hook for relishing the ruthlessness by putting the evil-doers on the hook. When Cecil B. DeMille used to do this, it was called hypocrisy; when auteurs of the calibre of Hampton and Frears (*My Beautiful Laundrette*) do it, it's called art.

Frears has said that the 1782 novel from which Hampton derived his play, and in turn his screenplay, was "really revolutionary," even though the author, Choderlos de Laclos, was "bourgeois." What the novel is or isn't is a moot point: the only thing "really revolutionary" about the movie, set in the France of the 1780s but played by U.S. actors, is its undisguised delight in silky snakiness.

The coolest serpent – he actually hisses – is the Vicomte de Valmont (John Malkovich), who is enlisted by an ex-lover, the cold-hearted Marquise de Merteuil (Glenn Close), to destroy an enemy of the Marquise's by seducing a fifteen-year-old girl. All of that takes place, and more: the film is an extended panorama of passionless coupling, perfumed bitchery and powdered plotting. The comments made by the actors about the movie are funnier than anything in it. Malkovich thinks there's a little Valmont in each of us (speak for yourself, bud), and Glenn Close comes up with a faux feminist theory to mitigate the Marquise's manipulativeness: "She's very modern – a highly intelligent woman born in the wrong century. She really had no outlets for her brilliance except for manipulation." Sure, and if Marie Antoinette had been born in a different century, she wouldn't have been Imelda Marcos.

Peter Greenaway, in *The Draughtsman's Contract*, and Stanley Kubrick, in *Barry Lyndon*, have both made this movie, but from a moral – or at least a distanced – perspective. Frears jumps right in and asks us to greet with glee Malkovich's "erotic" Casanova act. It doesn't work: no matter how many times the script instructs us that Valmont is "conspicuously charming," Malkovich is not charming, conspicuously or otherwise; had Kevin Kline or Mandy Patinkin been cast in the role, the script would have had an even chance of telling the truth. The other leading performers (in addition to Close: Michelle Pfeiffer, Swoosie Kurtz, Keanu Reeves, Mildred Natwick, Uma Thurman) are out of their stylistic depth in a piece that was crafted for the Royal Shakespeare Company's actors, of whom it has often been said, they could make the reading of the telephone directory interesting. The challenge posed by *Les Liaisons Dangereuses* must have been comparable.

December 22, 1988

❖

84 Charlie MoPic

Written and directed by Patrick Duncan
Starring Richard Brooks and Nicolas Cascone

"If men went to war for women, and for unborn generations, then she was going to find out what they went through. Sam[antha] didn't think the women or the unborn babies had any say in it. If it were up to women, there wouldn't be any war. No, that was a naive thought. When women got power, they were just like men. She thought of Indira Gandhi and Margaret Thatcher. She wouldn't want to meet those women out in the swamp at night.

"What would make people want to kill? If the U.S.A. sent her to a foreign country, with a rifle and a heavy backpack, could she root around in the jungle, sleep in the mud, and shoot at strangers? How did the army get boys to do that? Why was there war?" – *Bobbie Ann Mason*, In Country

Patrick Duncan's astoundingly visceral re-creation of the banal, boring, sadistic and compassionate activities of a squad of six men on patrol in Vietnam may be the purest study of the effects of war on personality since *The Trojan Women*: its greatness is belied by the simplicity of its approach.

The motion-picture operator of the title, "MoPic" (Byron Thames), is assigned to an undistinguished reconnaissance unit in the central highlands of Vietnam in 1969. The unit is led by a stunningly competent black man, "OD" (Richard Brooks), and includes a scatalogical, wise-cracking radio operator, "Easy" (Nicolas Cascone), who quips, "What's the problem with war? Too violent"; a South Carolina "Cracker," who thinks, "The army's the only real equal-opportunity employer I ever saw"; a hunky near-psychotic, "Hammer" (Christopher Burgard), who says, "We're the sanest killers the army's got, mercenaries kill for money, sadists kill for fun, paratroopers kill for both"; a social-climbing officer, "LT" (Jonathan Emerson), who declares, "The advancement potential is enormous . . . wars don't come along very often, it's the chance of a lifetime for a career officer"; and "Pretty

Boy" (Jason Tomlins), who advises, "During monsoon, dry socks are better than sex."

MoPic's job is to follow the company on its patrols and to record on film for the benefit of incoming troops – the even younger bodies soon to bulge the green body bags soon to come – the strategies the guys have learned to cope with the jungle, the enemy and themselves. (Separating those three things is not always easy.) MoPic's flick, a teaching machine for killers, is to be called Lessons Learned. Lessons are learned aplenty, but they are not the sorts of lessons the army is apt to want to teach to raw recruits. Like Stanley Kubrick's *Full Metal Jacket*, *84 Charlie MoPic* presents a lot of killing without romanticizing a second of it.

There are thematic connections between *Full Metal Jacket*, *Apocalypse Now* and *84 Charlie MoPic*, but writer-director Duncan, himself a Vietnam veteran, eschews any temptation to turn the Vietnam experience into cinematic myth or epic: he's out to answer Samantha's deceptively ingenuous questions.

"The problem with war movies is that they become movies about war, and not the warrior fighting it," Duncan has said. "I don't want to work out any good versus evil symbolism in my film. My goal is to show the audience what happened to the young men in the Vietnam conflict, not on a soul-searching level, but what physically happened to them. I wanted to make the most intimate war film that could possibly be made."

He has. The conceit is that every frame of footage is shot by MoPic's camera as possible fodder for his propaganda documentary. As guys crouch in hiding while the enemy marches by, we hear their sharp, terrified breathing. During an ambush, the endangered MoPic is unceremoniously handed a weapon while we hear his sharp, terrified breathing. And during the climax, the fate of the camera – the fate of the very movie we've been watching with sharp, terrified breathing – is thrown symbolically into the air. *84 Charlie MoPic* gets so close to the face of fear that its lens is smeared by tears.

In addition to forgoing large statements (though Duncan does make the largest statement of all: war is the destroyer), *84 Charlie*

MoPic avoids the clichés of the Vietnam film genre. No opera (*Apocalypse Now*). No bestselling soundtrack (*Good Morning, Vietnam*). (There are only two tunes, in fact, "Susan on the West Coast Waiting" and "Catch the Wind," both by Donovan, and there is no background music whatever.) No scenery – bloody (*Hamburger Hill*), majestic (*The Deer Hunter*) or panoramic (*The Killing Fields*). And no straining for compositional glory – time and again, Vietnam has been dubbed a dirty little war, but *84 Charlie MoPic* is the first Vietnam picture in which the war feels both dirty (filthy, really) and little (tiny, actually).

It's also the first Vietnam film that gets under the complicated carapaces of what Duncan refers to as warriors – ordinary U.S. working-class kids in extraordinary situations. The white racist Cracker, for example, has developed a loving relationship with the tough black man OD. MoPic would like to know if their love will survive southern prejudices back home. "We don't ask questions like that out here," the Cracker snaps. "That's a real world question. Why don't you ask me that back in South Carolina?"

In common with the somewhat pathological Hammer, who keeps a lizard named Fido as a pet, Cracker is in Vietnam partly because he was taught by his daddy that virtue is a good job well done, regardless of what that job might be. (Cracker's daddy once made something beautiful for a rich woman out of black oak then painted it "whiter 'n milk" when she ordered him to; painting that beautiful black wood white nearly broke his heart, but he did it.) "People like me just go from day to day tryin' to get food on the table," Cracker explains. "You're supposed to do your job the best you can, you like it or not." Facing possible death, the lean and mean Hammer looks into the camera. "I want to tell my dad that I did a good job," he whispers, holding down a sob so big it feels like a fist buried in the throat.

84 Charlie MoPic is a masterpiece about boys literally dying for approval.

May 5, 1989

❖

Jesus of Montreal

Written and directed by Denys Arcand
Starring Lothaire Bluteau and Catherine Wilkening

"The twenty-first century will be mystical, or it will not be." – *André Malraux*

Jesus of Montreal is sinful, but not because it's blasphemous, anti-religious or even anti-Christian: it's sinful because it's so much fun. In an institutional religious context, sin customarily requires confession and expiation. Although Quebec writer-director Denys Arcand (*The Decline and Fall of the American Empire*) is no longer a practising Catholic, he is Christian on a deep level that has nothing to do with superficial debates over the divinity of Jesus Christ. He does indeed exact payment for the pleasures he provides in the first hour of *Jesus of Montreal*: in the second hour, pleasure is replaced by profundity. The final tally: Pleasure 2, Expiation 0. It turns out that profundity is its own kind of pleasure. And its own metaphysical reward – for *Jesus of Montreal*, the meaning of life is nothing more and nothing less than the search for the meaning of life.

In modern Montreal, a young actor, Daniel (Lothaire Bluteau), is hired to impersonate Jesus Christ in a Passion Play staged by a local church. "The text," a priest (Gilles Pelletier) explains, "is a bit dated" – he asks Daniel to find fellow actors interested in collaborating with him on an updated script that the troupe will then perform on a mountain in the summer. Daniel tracks down the colleagues who will become his disciples in unlikely places (dubbing porno movies, for example) and inspires them with a fervour that is religious. The company enthusiastically sets out in search of the historical Jesus.

The Jesus they resurrect is the Jesus of the Gospels, not the Jesus of the cathedrals, and the priest is therefore horrified by what he sees as the "liberties" that have been taken with the tale. Daniel soon discovers that arguing historical validity with this cleric is useless, and appealing to Biblical authority – Daniel maintains that most of what is being presented in his updated Passion Play can be found in the Bible

– only infuriates the priest further. "The Bible can be made to say anything," the priest shouts. "I know, from experience."

The structural strategy of the technically perfect *Jesus of Montreal* is simple in definition, complex in execution. As Daniel and his troupe become enmeshed in the events of Christ's life, the spirit of Christ takes over the troupe – the actors find themselves replicating, in a contemporary context, the Stations of the Cross. The ingenious Arcand has even invented an acceptably scientific stand-in for the resurrection; the intellectual joy occasioned by the picture grows out of the intricate manner in which the filmmaker has modernized the 2,000-year-old story while remaining true to its spirit.

The spiritual joy engendered by the picture – by the end, *Jesus of Montreal* is an ode to self-sacrificial joy – has nothing to do with its abundant cleverness. Arcand had originally planned to employ Malraux's contention that "the twenty-first century will be mystical or it will not be" as the movie's epigraph. "Naturally, art is the salvation, at least for some of us," he has elaborated. "Each person has his own spirituality, whether it's art or esotericism, or the extra-terrestrials. We haven't yet recovered, in the Western world, from the disappearance of religion. We haven't recovered from the shock of Hegel. There are no longer solutions applicable to everyone. We ask ourselves, and we will continue to ask for a long time, the same old questions: Who are we, where do we come from, where do we going? Therefore we are trying, as does Jesus/Daniel, to find a kind of code of ethics, a moral doctrine, in the middle of endless contradictions."

The solution found by Daniel, an authentic Jesus Christ Superstar, is by no means a solution applicable to everyone, but it serves to solidify what Arcand has accurately characterized as "a movie of ripping contrasts, from madcap comedy to absurd drama reflecting life around us – shattering, trivial, contradictory." For Arcand, "life around us" consists of "supermarket displays presenting the most unlikely collections: novels by Dostoevski competing for space with eau de toilette, Bibles, pornographic videos, the collected works of Shakespeare, photographs of the earth taken from the moon, astrological forecasts and posters of actors and Jesus . . ." Arcand's movie is its own supermarket – the display is every bit as eclectic and surreal as the one he describes – but at the checkout counter, it is the supermarket that pays the customer. This movie sends the shopper home with a secularized but nonetheless sacred sense of life: it fills the eyes with rapture, the mind with energy and the heart with love.

September 13, 1989

Distant Voices, Still Lives

Written and directed by Terence Davies
Starring Freda Dowie and Pete Postlethwaite

"'England's not a bad country,' says Liz, as they get in the car, to drive toward Pallanza [in Italy].

"'No,' says Alix. 'No.' The lake glitters, the mountains soar, the coloured sails catch the evening sun, and the shadows of the Lombard poplars are long. 'No,' says Alix, 'England's not a bad country. It's just a mean, cold, ugly, divided, tired, clapped-out, post-imperial, post-industrial slag heap covered in polystyrene hamburger cartons. It's not a bad country at all. I love it.'" – *Margaret Drabble*, A Natural Curiosity

"Later I understood: a good memory is about one-third cure and two-thirds curse. . . . That boy's brain was a savings account with waste in it. . . . True facts had snagged and abscessed, their sharp ends in. His poor young head was a pincushion calendar. If they made my husband walk through one of these new aeroport X-ray machines checking for weaponry? why, just his memory would set it off." – *Allan Gurganus*, Oldest Living Confederate Widow Tells All

The advertisements for *Distant Voices, Still Lives*, an idiosyncratic masterpiece and one of the few films in history that gloriously earns the appellation "Proustian," announce that "In memory, everything happens to music." Not every mind may be as musical as the memory of Terence Davies, the forty-five-year-old British writer and director of this severely autobiographical feature, but movie audiences can be thankful that Davies, until now unknown outside the film-festival circuit, looks back melodically on the echoing voices and still-born lives of the people he has known – his memory is indeed a weapon, but his music blunts the blows.

The narrative logic of *Distant Voices*, which concentrates on a working-class wedding and funeral in Liverpool, and of the companion piece *Still Lives*, which records another wedding several years later (it was in fact filmed two years after *Distant Voices*), follows the free-floating bob and bounce of unstructured recollection.

As *Distant Voices* opens to the strains of "I Get the Blues When It's Raining," Mother (Freda Dowie) is serving breakfast on the morning of the wedding of her elder daughter, Eileen (Angela Walsh). The bride-to-be laments the absence of the Father (Pete Postlethwaite), dead of cancer. Faster than you can say *Remembrance of Things Past*, each member of the assemblage – sister Maisie (Lorraine Ashbourne), brother Tony (Dean Williams), friend Monica (Debi Jones) – is returned to another place and time.

It transpires that Father was an abusive alcoholic who regularly wrecked Christmas and did everything else he could think of to wreck everything else. Davies is unkind in the extreme to his progenitor: one of the most powerful sequences in *Distant Voices* gives us Father beating Mother to a pulp while "Taking a Chance on Love" fills the theatre speakers.

"The family," Davies has said of the real-life model for his movie, "did not become happy until my father died."

Against a backdrop of dozens of songs ("backdrop" is probably the wrong term, in that the songs sometimes become the foreground, forcefully consigning the characters to the misty margins of memory), ranging from "My Yiddisher Momma" to "Love is a Many Splendored Thing," Davies reconstructs a brutal and brutalizing childhood alleviated only by communal sings in dismal pubs. Margaret Drabble may opine in *A Natural Curiosity* that the "new" England has become a horror show, but the "old" England of the forties in Davies' memoir is equally revolting. Yet, the experience of sitting through this movie is euphoric, so totally is Davies in command of his materials.

It's true that if you were to strip *Distant Voices, Still Lives* of the dark varnish of its images (the colour has been desaturated through a bleach by-pass printing process); and of the slippery surface of its liquid camera movements (the lens is memory's monocle); and of its elliptical, Proustian construction (the past folds in on itself like the petals of an evening primrose) – well, if you remove all of that, you are left with a sturdy but familiar armoire fashioned in the form of a casket for a pathological family. The "content" of *Distant Voices, Still Lives* is the stuff of psychoanalytic case history. But how many closets have been transformed by a genius carpenter into a monument to the malleability of the mind?

Knowing that Davies has said he invented virtually nothing in *Distant Voices, Still Lives*, it is fair to wonder if his family ever saw the prize-winning – to be quite literal about it – home movie. The answer is, yes. "Well, you know, the working class . . . Noel Coward, in *Brief Encounter*, didn't know the difference between compassion and condescension," Davies commented at the Cannes Film Festival. "The working class has rarely been written about honestly because working-class people have so rarely been writers. They didn't get the chance. Therefore, we were always seen as low comedy. I had to tell my actors – we are lumbered in England with this 'acting technique' – that I didn't want them to act working class, I wanted them to be. My family has seen *Distant Voices*. My mother, a great survivor, said, 'How could you remember all that?' My elder sister cried for two days because it opened so many wounds. But they were very proud of me, those two. The rest of them . . . when they came to visit my flat after the screening, they were more impressed with my bloody carpet and the like. 'Very nice bookshelves,' they said."

September 25, 1989

❖

Tom Jones

Directed by Tony Richardson
Written by John Osborne
Starring Albert Finney, Susannah York, Hugh Griffith and Dame Edith Evans

Inside Oscar, an encyclopedic history of the Academy Awards by Mason Wiley and Damien Bona, recalls 1963 this way: "If [Elizabeth] Taylor and [Richard] Burton titillated the public offscreen, *Tom Jones* excited it onscreen. British director Tony Richardson and playwright John Osborne, best known for 'angry young man' dramas like *The Entertainer* and *Look Back in Anger*, decided to have some fun, so they adapted an eighteenth-century novel by Henry Fielding into a rollicking bedroom farce. David Picker, an executive at United Artists, persuaded the powers-that-be to pick up the English picture for peanuts and advertise it with sexy posters for its U.S. release. The plot worked and the studio found itself with the highest-grossing foreign-made film ever distributed in America. It was so popular that a *New Yorker* cartoon depicted a patient wailing to his psychiatrist: 'Doctor, what's my problem? *Tom Jones* depressed me.'"

Nominated for ten Oscars, *Tom Jones* won four, including best picture and director (its star, twenty-seven-year-old Albert Finney, lost to Sidney Poitier for *Lilies of the Field*); with its wit, speed and bawdiness, it revolutionized screen comedy and influenced directors from Richard Lester to Francis Coppola; its success in the United States even produced a farcical political sideshow – in concert with many other lesser-known columnists, Hedda Hopper and Hazel Flynn called upon the country to protect itself from the redcoats. Flynn went so far as to whine, "The British have their own Oscar race. Why are they trying to run away with ours? It took them until after World War II to make even a few good pictures."

Like its hero, of whom Fielding wrote "he was born to be hanged," *Tom Jones* became a controversial, charming legend. But who would have thought that what seemed at the time, even to its admirers, to be an inconsequential if ingenious comedy, would be "restored" and would reopen in theatres some twenty years later, presented unapologetically as a classic? And who would have thought that the presentation would be correct? The fact is, *Tom Jones* is a classic, but the one question that should be easy to answer – Is it as good as we remember it? – goes begging. The new, restored *Tom Jones* is not the same film that won the Oscar in 1963. This one is seven minutes shorter.

Following a screening early last year, director Richardson decided that "although the audience laughed throughout the film, I couldn't help thinking that a few scenes played a little long." Richardson received permission to go back into the cutting room, along with sound engineer John Addison (the new print is in Dolby stereo), and proceeded to whack away. "The changes were necessary and helpful. The humour works as well today as it did in 1963 but audiences today are so much more sophisticated than they were twenty-six years ago. They like humour quick and punchy. I think the cuts substantially improve the film and enhance the actors' work."

Tom Jones *père* is certainly quick and punchy in memory; Tom Jones *fils* is quick and punchy in reality, and it is an absolute delight. True, as the wench Molly, Diane Cilento has been made up as a cross between Sophia Loren and Jackie Kennedy, rather than as a bawd out of Hogarth, and there are dated attitudes that have nothing to do with Henry Fielding and everything to do with the early sixties (this movie can be seen as a herald of the youth cult that would dominate Hollywood for more than a decade), but even the anachronistic aspects of *Tom Jones* are interesting. Most interesting of all: people actually thought its tame ribaldry (no nudity, blacked-out bedroom trysts, a famous eating scene that is raunchy but not revolting) on the edge of bad taste.

Neither performance nor screenwriting has dated a second. Finney – impossible to believe, watching this svelte and sexy creature, that he will become the bloated relic of *Under the Volcano* – holds the high jinks together with precisely the proper ratio of charm to scoundrel;

the magisterial Dame Edith Evans, as Miss Western, polishes her consonants into cascades of chrome (she erects a mountain range of inflection between the "c" and the "r" in the word "cruel" – you can see where Maggie Smith gets it); as the sweet and sensual Sophie Western, Susannah York is ethereally radiant yet paradoxically earthy; and Hugh Griffith's Squire Western, dismissed by Miss Western as "a purrrrfect goat" and a "countrrrrry stewwwwwwpot," lewdly incarnates the old rake's deterioration that will probably be the young rake Jones' fate.

But that's an extrapolation: Richardson's *Tom Jones* is scrubbed free of conventional morality and is in the end a celebration of the id. (The only people who pay for anything are the slow and stupid. "It is widely held that too much wine will dull a man's desire," the narrator intones. "Indeed it will, in a dull man.") Despite the British class system, the war with Scotland, sexually transmitted disease, and frightful personal and public hygiene, *Tom Jones* lives in a rococo paradise of outrageous invention. What of his exploitive infidelities? "Heroes," the narrator rationalizes, "are mortal, not divine. We are all as God made us and many of us are much worse." But this hero is, of course, both immortal and divine, largely because he casually supposes himself to be both: he is a precursor of what came to be called in the sixties a cool head and in the seventies a survivor. (In the eighties, he had a mortgage.) The narrator presciently sums up the lasting appeal of the myth of the libertine Tom, forever feckless, forever fortunate, forever young: "Heaven be thanked we live in an age where no man dies for love except upon the stage."

January 5, 1990

❖

Matador

Directed by Pedro Almodovar
Written by Pedro Almodovar and Jesus Ferrero
Starring Assumpta Serna and Nacho Martinez

The young Spanish director Pedro Almodovar, best known in North America for *Women on the Verge of a Nervous Breakdown*, sure knows how to begin a movie. *Law of Desire* opened with gay porn and *Matador*, which debuts belatedly in Canada today (it was shot in 1986, prior to *Law of Desire* and *Women on the Verge of a Nervous Breakdown*), kicks off with a horrific sequence in which a man masturbates to images of women being mutilated and murdered. And that is only the beginning – after the blood-red credits, a woman has sex with a man and skewers him in the back with a hat pin at the height of her excitement, as if that man were no more than a bull facing a matador at the so-called "moment of truth."

The "moment of truth," when a preordained death is witnessed and applauded by a cheering crowd, is central to the "art" of the bullring, and it's central to *Matador*, which subversively and none too subtly equates heterosexual attraction with fatality. (Almodovar is openly gay, but he is no heterophobe; homosexual passion was similarly depicted in *Law of Desire*.) The man masturbating prior to Matador's credits is Diego (Nacho Martinez), an ex-bullfighter who was gored, crippled, and now teaches bullfighting when he is not murdering women. The woman murdering the man is Maria (Assumpta Serna), a criminal lawyer who is now defending an innocent youth, Angel (Antonio Banderas), who has confessed to a couple of the murders his own attorney committed – it transpires that the virginal Angel is a telepath who has envisioned the killings accomplished by both Diego and Maria, and believes himself to be guilty of everything. Angel's mother is, not so coincidentally, a Catholic religious fanatic.

What in the name of all that is unholy is going on here? *Matador* is a healthy, satiric film about a culture's unhealthy, unfunny attitude toward sex and death – in Almodovar's eyes, repressing the former results in glamorizing the latter. Although the iconography is specifically Spanish and right out of *Carmen* – swirling capes, red roses and lips, swords that are phallic symbols and phalli that are swords – the movie takes its inspiration from Hollywood: Maria and Diego separately attend *Duel in the Sun* (1946) and pant with excitement as Jennifer Jones and Gregory Peck mortally wound each other and then crawl across the rocks to embrace.

So there's no doubt from the beginning as to how *Matador* will end. But *Matador* departs company from the famous sex-and-death movies to which it has been compared (Nagisa Oshima's *In the Realm of the Senses*, Bernardo Bertolucci's *Last Tango in Paris*) by actually analyzing the form itself. *Duel in the Sun, In the Realm of the Senses* and *Last Tango*, for all their operatic qualities, come on as "real" life. Not *Matador*. In addition to being about the wages of repressing "sin," this movie is also about art that pretends to be real. Almodovar argues that bullfights are reality that masquerades as "art" (the bull really dies), while movies such as *Last Tango in Paris* are art that masquerades as "reality" (Marlon Brando really lives). Like the equally postmodern and self-referential *Speaking Parts*, directed by Atom Egoyan, *Matador* refutes the naturalism of the past by presenting itself boldly and outrageously as a work of art. It superficially poses at being a little of everything, but it never really poses at being anything but a humorous series of artificially constructed questions (a great many) and answers (a few). The campy and melodramatic devices employed throughout (an eclipse occurs at the penultimate moment of truth; orgasm is signalled by lightning and a rainstorm; an attractive man confesses to a policewoman that he has attempted rape, to which the policewoman responds, "Some girls have all the luck") underline the exultant artificiality. Almodovar himself appears in the guise of an effeminate fashion-show director who declares that the real subject of his show is "Spain divided" ("Spain," he lisps, "is divided into the envious and the intolerant; I am both") and claims that "marriage is necessary, else there would be no wedding dresses."

One of *Matador*'s disquieting themes is a spin-off from that statement. At the end of *Last Tango in Paris*, *In the Realm of the Senses* and *Duel in the Sun*, the tragic deaths seem somehow "right" and audiences emerge having experienced catharsis. Why? Almodovar wants to know, and his answer is that culture, the Catholic Church, the media and who-knows-what-else – perhaps even human nature – have conspired to make death in general, and the death of passion in particular, into something that does indeed feel esthetically "right." ("They look so happy," quips a cop over an interlocked pair of *Matador* corpses.) Rather than pandering to that feeling, Almodovar asks us to notice its existence and ponder its meaning. But he's astonishingly honest regarding his own role as a gadfly social critic and enthusiastic esthetician. It's extremely easy to imagine the serious Almodovar behind the camera parroting the comic Almodovar in front of the camera: "Repressing sex and celebrating death are necessary," he might say, "else there would be no *Matador*."

January 26, 1990

Men Don't Leave

Directed by Paul Brickman
Written by Paul Brickman and Barbara Benedek
Starring Jessica Lange and Arliss Howard

Stella

Directed by John Erman
Written by Robert Getchell
Starring Bette Midler and Trini Alvarado

In her definitive 1974 book analyzing the treatment of women in movies, *From Reverence to Rape*, Molly Haskell began her chapter "The

Woman's Film" this way: "What more damning comment on the relations between men and women in America than the very notion of something called the 'woman's film'? . . . As a term of critical opprobrium, 'woman's film' carries the implication that women, and therefore women's emotional problems, are of minor significance. A film that focuses on male relationships is not pejoratively dubbed a 'man's film,' but a 'psychological drama.'"

The so-called woman's film reached its peak in the 1940s, when the men were away at war, though the ultimate example, *Stella Dallas*, with Barbara Stanwyck as the low-class blowzy broad who sacrifices her own happiness to shove her daughter into a higher social class, was made in 1937. (Based on a novel of the twenties by Olive Higgins Prouty, there had already been a silent version directed by Henry King with Belle Bennett as a supremely saintly Stella.)

At its best, the woman's film was notable for exploring emotions that were missing in male movies – in the woman's film, death tended to be painful rather than heroic and survivors suffered openly rather than remaining stoic. The stiff upper lip of the male film was counterbalanced by the quivering lower lip of the woman's film.

With the simultaneous release of *Men Don't Leave*, a re-make of *La Vie Continue* with Jessica Lange as a suffering widow, and *Stella*, a re-make of *Stella Dallas* with Bette Midler as a raucous altruist, the woman's film is back, which is good news and bad news. The good news is that *Men Don't Leave* (the only awful thing about it is the title) is an exceptionally honest and funny dramatization of the bereavement process – it's a sensitive comedy about mourning. The bad news is that *Stella* is an unintentionally hilarious mess, handily summed up by what Haskell sees as "the lowest level" of the woman's film – "[It] fills a masturbatory need, it is soft-core emotional porn for the frustrated housewife. The weepies are founded on a mock-Aristotelian and politically conservative esthetic whereby women spectators are moved, not by pity and fear but by self-pity and tears, to accept, rather than reject, their lot."

The original *Stella Dallas* certainly promoted conformity to the social and economic order, but the subversive wild card was the late

Barbara Stanwyck's astonishing performance, "what may at once be the most excruciating and exhilarating performance on film," as Haskell put it. Stanwyck's Stella was impossible to pigeonhole; she was maddeningly and marvellously real, even in the movie's most unreal sequences (standing outside in the snow watching her daughter get married, for example), and her saintliness was definitely on the sodden side, a Stella, to again quote Haskell, "who exceeds in stupidity and beauty and daring the temperate limitations of her literary model and all the generalizations about the second sex."

The Bette Midler Stella has none of Stanwyck's complexity – the Bette Midler Stella is vulgar but cuddly, a lewd Ewok. Because class ain't what it used to be (exposure to "Lifestyles of the Rich and Famous" and "Entertainment Tonight" would protect even the poorest, most naive viewer from committing the comic social gaffes made by the Midler Stella), there was probably no way to re-make *Stella Dallas* successfully, but surely the failure did not have to be of this magnitude. (What has happened to screenwriter Robert Getchell? The year Molly Haskell's book was published, he wrote *Alice Doesn't Live Here Anymore* for director Martin Scorsese.) There is some interesting acting, particularly from John Goodman as Stella's alcoholic buddy, and Marsha Mason, the woman who becomes stepmother to Stella's daughter. But the major supporting roles, the wealthy father and the love-child daughter, have been assigned to Stephen Collins and Trini Alvarado, respectively, and they're bland as *crème fraîche*. Although Midler isn't bland, her performance is less a characterization than a series of turns from her nightclub act (the bag lady, the lounge singer, even Sophie Tucker). Midler is one of the world's sweetest stars; that very likeability destroys any chance the movie has to transcend tearjerking.

Jessica Lange can be sweet and likeable (she was a yummy cream puff in *Tootsie*), but her scope as an actress is beginning to seem limitless. In *Men Don't Leave*, she is Beth, a middle-class mother suddenly widowed and left with a $63,000 debt and two boys, the hostile seventeen-year-old Chris (Chris O'Donnell) and the introverted nine-year-old Matt (Charlie Korsmo). Beth is wan and psychologically frail;

Lange is appropriately drab and listless – she doesn't ask approval for Beth, merely understanding. Beth does do her best for her boys, but her best is not enough: Matt turns into a thief, Chris into a snot. Meanwhile, Beth experiences a nervous breakdown. At first, she clutches irrationally at her children, then forgets their existence and takes to her bed. (Chris: "How long has she been resting?" Matt: "Four days.") Lange's melodic orchestration of Beth's regression, and of her eventual recovery, never strikes an irritating esthetic note, even when Beth is irritable beyond reason.

The difficulty experienced by a widow rearing children on her own is a classic foundation for a classic woman's film weepie, but *Men Don't Leave* is too accurate in psychology and too quirky in design to be patronized as a tearjerker. The script, by Barbara Benedek and Paul Brickman (directing his first film since *Risky Business*, which was his first film), economically Anglicizes its 1982 French model, *La Vie Continue* (*Life Goes On* is not an inspired title, but it's a lot better than *Men Don't Leave*), and for the most part avoids falling into the *Ordinary People* trap of glamorizing the milieu. (A hot air balloon ride is a mite grandiose, however, as is the Baltimore waterfront apartment occupied by Beth's boy friend, a composer.)

Men Don't Leave is peopled by people, not stereotypes. Beth goes to work for a caterer, Lisa (the phenomenal Kathy Bates, star of the Broadway play *'night, Mother*), who is bitter and bitchy, but recognizably real. (Beth is no prize – she applies for the job by informing Lisa, "I know food. I eat food.") Beth's seventeen-year-old takes up with a much older X-ray technician, Jody (Joan Cusak, nominated for an Oscar for *Working Girl*), who woos him by radiating his chest. And Beth's own boy friend, Charles (Arliss Howard, "Cowboy" in *Full Metal Jacket*), is unfazed when she develops a bloody nose in the clinch ("I've never had a real stigmata experience before," he laughs, "not while kissing"). The characters are so well-defined and the progression of the plot so unpredictable that a conventional ending feels out of the question – the movie must simply stop.

Unfortunately, there is a belated and unconvincing attempt to apply a *finis* to a story that doesn't have one (it's the *Alice Doesn't Live*

Here Anymore and *An Unmarried Woman deus ex machina*). The conclusion has led some reviewers to dismiss *Men Don't Leave* in a feminist fury – they claim that the movie's hidden theme is that women can't survive without men, ignoring the fact that Beth recovers when the man is not around. It's clear the "critical opprobrium" regarding the woman's film continues to exist, but it's decked out now in feminism. If a movie about a man whose wife died recounted his problems in raising his children and then provided him with a girl friend, would anyone think that the film was sexist or matronizing? Would anyone unearth a "hidden" theme to the effect that men can't survive without women? The double standard still exists. From reverence to rape and back to reverence again is a long journey, but it doesn't mean we've come a long way, baby.

February 2, 1990

❖

Lord of the Flies

Directed by Harry Hook
Written by Sara Schiff
Starring Balthazar Getty, Chris Furrh and Danuel Pipoly

When Sir William Golding's allegorical *Lord of the Flies* was published in 1954, and when Peter Brook's psychodramatic film version of it was released in 1963, perhaps it was still possible to be shocked by the notion that twelve- to fourteen-year-old English boys stranded on a desert island might shuck off "civilization" and revert to "savagery." Golding, surely the worst writer ever to win the Nobel Prize, confidently declared the transformation to be the result of "a defect in human nature."

But civilization ain't what it used to be, and neither is savagery. Thanks to the efforts of anthropologists, we understand "primitive" hunting cultures better than we once did – we know they're not as primitive as we thought – and thanks to the efforts of regimes around the world, we understand "advanced" industrialized cultures better than we once did – we know they're not as civilized as we assumed. Where does that leave *Lord of the Flies*, with its grand symbolism (each major character is stereotypically totemic – the Mystic, the Warrior, the Intellectual) and its hysteria about "human nature"? In terms of content it has dated irretrievably, a victim of modern anthropology, sociology and psychology; in terms of style and organization, it was never that good anyway. Rereading it now is sobering: It's so schematic it needs no Coles Notes. It is Coles Notes.

In his short story, "Martyrdom," published six years before *Lord of the Flies*, the late novelist Yukio Mishima had already claimed Golding territory with a flag that snubbed symbolism and hysteria. "He had begun to be bullied almost as soon as he appeared at the school," Mishima wrote of his protagonist, Watari, a boy the same age as the kids in *Lord of the Flies*. "He gave the impression of looking disapprovingly on the tendency, common to all boys, to worship toughness as a way of making up for their awareness of the vulnerability peculiar to their age. If anything, Watari sought to preserve the vulnerability. The young man who seeks to be himself is respected by his fellows; the boy who tries to do the same is persecuted by other boys, it being a boy's business to become something else just as soon as he can."

Peter Brook's memorable black and white film of *Lord of the Flies* was closer in spirit to Mishima's graceful simplicity and grasp of developmental psychology than to Golding's laboured complexity and élitist misapprehension of anthropology (symbols in any case tend to become people when made flesh by actors). The new, Americanized remake, less powerful than the original but honourable nonetheless, follows suit. Essentially, director Harry Hook (*The Kitchen Toto*) has made a horror movie about crazed Cub Scouts and an advertisement for the durability of Jockey shorts, with an occasional lyric image out of the pubertal paintings of Thomas Eakins thrown in. The music by Philippe Sarde is, sorry to say, a *Rite of Spring* rip-off; when the ratty boys break away from "civilization" to become a "tribe," it would have been more appropriate to have them fall into a rap trap.

But Hook's cast is admirably adept at getting across what little boys are made of. The once if not future leader, Ralph, the exemplar of civilization, is Balthazar Getty (it's a great joke that the actor happens to be the great-great-grandson of J. Paul Getty); the savage Jack, who apparently packed a book on Papua New Guinea prior to being stranded with his fellows (his makeup designs are pure *National Geographic*), is Chris Furrh (another joke: he's a Texan); Simon, the mystic saint, is Badgett Dale; and the born-to-be victimized Piggy, played by the best actor in the bunch, is Danuel Pipoly (the dirty-mouthed update of the script allows Piggy to be called Miss Piggy).

Does the Americanization matter? Strangely enough, considering the novel is widely held to be reflective of the British class system, the answer is no. As any teacher will tell you, every playground has a class system, which is the real subject of this *Lord of the Flies*: what boys do when boys will be boys, and what some boys will do when they decide to become men.

March 22, 1990

Pretty Woman

Directed by Garry Marshall
Written by J. F. Lawton
Starring Richard Gere and Julia Roberts

At minimum, there are three kinds of hooker movies: the realistic slice-of-seamy-life ones (*Working Girls*), the realistic but melodramatically plotted ones (*Klute*) and the unrealistic romantically flossy ones (everything from *Irma La Douce* to *The Owl and the Pussycat*). The special genius of *Pretty Woman*, which is great popular entertainment in the screwball comedy tradition, is to combine, at one time or another, all three forms under a Cinderella umbrella. The first line of the movie, which is also the last, covers it: "This is Hollywood!"

The Cinderella-Pygmalion hooker is Vivian Ward (Julia Roberts), whose world is a scuzzily realistic Hollywood Boulevard where the girls die of crack and can be bought for peanuts. Her Prince Charming-Henry Higgins is Edward Lewis (Richard Gere), whose world is a sumptuously realistic Beverly Hills where men die of heart attacks and can be bought for billions. She works the streets, he works the penthouses, but the work, as he comes to realize, is identical: "We both screw people for money."

J. F. Lawton's original script for *Pretty Woman* was entitled $3,000 (because Edward buys Vivian's services at that price for a week) and was, according to star Julia Roberts, a sombre account of the lives of the hooker and her john. Not the kind of movie to make money. So: hello, sitcom meister Garry Marshall (*The Flamingo Kid*), goodbye, verisimilitude – once Marshall entered, the thrust of *Pretty Woman* became to exit laughing. But enough of Lawton's research has been retained to give the dynamics between Vivian and Edward the clang of truth; although the positive has been accentuated, the negative has not been eliminated – and the in-between adds up to comic bliss.

On a trip to Los Angeles, the New-York-based Edward faces a hitch in a lucrative deal to buy a company he will then dismantle (Vivian's summation of Edward's job: "It's sort of like stealing cars and selling them for the parts"). For reasons that make no logical sense, Edward hires Vivian to accompany him to evening business meetings. He explains that he wants her at his "beck and call." "I would love to be your beck and call girl," she purrs, and lets him dress her up (on Rodeo Drive), take her to the opera (*La Traviata*) and introduce her to his friends (Vivian: "These people are your friends? Well no wonder you came looking for me"). She reciprocates – it's a good thing the puritanical Lucille Ball didn't live to see this – by doing something unprintable to him as they watch television reruns; they fall in love by watching Lucy.

Gere, fresh from the sour *Internal Affairs*, is all class and repressed sass as the wily and jaded Edward, who confesses, "Very few people surprise me." But Roberts, in her first starring role (her dying diabetic act in *Steel Magnolias* was nominated for a supporting Oscar), nearly steals *Pretty Woman* to sell it for the shiny parts: funny, sexy and moving, she's phenomenal. Her lanky Vivian, a Judy Holliday for the nineties, responds to Edward's assertion that people don't surprise him with, "Yeah, you're lucky, most of 'em shock the hell out of me."

The intelligence and wit of this glass-slipper heart-of-gold fantasy are shocking, too, but hell hath no part of the surprise. "The bad stuff is easier to believe, ever notice that?" Vivian asks. Yes ma'am, but sometimes, when Hollywood is at its best, the good stuff can be even easier.

March 23, 1990

❖

The Belly of an Architect

Written and directed by Peter Greenaway
Starring Brian Dennehy, Chloe Webb and Lambert Wilson

Shot in Rome in 1986 but only now being released in the wake of the commercial success of the controversial, scatological parable *The Cook, The Thief, His Wife & Her Lover*, *The Belly of an Architect* is unique in British director Peter Greenaway's pantheon: it is emotional and even moving.

Credit for the humanity that rises to the slick surface of the film – another of Greenaway's pessimistic, visually lush exercises in intellectualized game-playing – is due entirely to U.S. actor Brian Dennehy, a towering performer who transforms the character of Chicago architect Stourley Kracklite into a figure of tragic dimensions, a Lear-like fifty-four-year-old dying man raging against the human condition. In a long, drunken scene staged in front of the Pantheon, Dennehy achieves a level of screen acting – emotionally free yet technically controlled – that is as monumental as the building behind him.

During a visit to Toronto several years ago, Dennehy confided that until this film, he felt Greenaway treated actors "as he treats everything else, as geometry." Then he smiled and added: "I was, however, able to wrest control from him for a few minutes each day." Those minutes have resulted in a characterization that incarnates Zola's description of Schumann's Cello Concerto: "the voluptuousness of despair."

Kracklite has come to Rome with Louisa (Chloe Webb, of *Sid and Nancy*), his young wife, to oversee the installation at the Victor Emmanuel Building of an exhibition honouring the eighteenth-century French architect Etienne-Louis Boullée, about whom little is known. (The majority of his designs were never constructed; the actual designs for his unbuilt domed memorial to Sir Isaac Newton form the centrepiece of the exhibition.) Obsessed by Boullée, Kracklite permits his life and his person to fall apart: he loses control of his pregnant wife – she takes a twenty-eight-year-old lover, Italian architect Caspasian Speckler (French actor Lambert Wilson); victimized by politics he ignores at his peril, he loses control of his exhibition; and, thanks to a disorder based in his protruding belly, he loses control of his body.

Dennehy aside, *The Belly of an Architect* is essentially esthetic and philosophical business as usual for Greenaway, who has pedantically pointed out that the picture takes place over nine months, the term of a pregnancy: symbols proliferate, elaborate meals are consumed, vengeful infidelities are consummated or interrupted, classically styled music is used as an elegant counterpoint to inelegant pain, and puns are tossed off ("What is good for the goose is good for the philanderer") as juvenile respites from the angst and ennui that inform the film as a whole.

The unbusinesslike rage, power and compassion Dennehy embeds in Greenaway's tightly constructed geometry of demise are thoroughly unusual, however, and they provide the picture with the patina of greatness. Dennehy has commented that Greenaway, Woody

Allen and Stanley Kubrick have an identical view of reality as an existential joke – the punch line is death, of course – and he's right. But in this instance, the dramatization of the punch line transcends Greenaway's almost defensive intellectual rigour: Dennehy's personification of the "joke" of existence gives it the sting of the real thing.

July 20, 1990

❖

Arachnophobia

Directed by Frank Marshall
Written by Don Jakoby and Wesley Strick
Starring Jeff Daniels, Harley Jane Kozak and Julian Sands

An eight-part quiz with a couple of fangs and a lot of attitude:
1. Arachnophobia is:
   a) the fear of spiders.
   b) the fear of Steven Spielberg and any movie produced by his company.
   c) the fear of Steven Spielberg and any horror movie that is set in a cute country town and is produced by his company.
   d) the fear of Steven Spielberg and any horror movie that is set in a cute country town and tries to be funny and is produced by his company.
2. *Arachnophobia* is:
   a) a rip-off of *The Birds*, but not as scary.
   b) a rip-off of *Tremors*, but not as funny.
   c) a rip-off of *Gremlins*, but not as clever.
   d) a rip-off of *Poltergeist*, but not as gross.
3. Jeff Daniels is:
   a) the star of *Arachnophobia*.
   b) competent but not charismatic.

c) better in Woody Allen's *The Purple Rose of Cairo.*

d) fighting a losing battle.

4. Harley Jane Kozak is:

    a) the other star of *Arachnophobia* (Jeff Daniels' wife).

    b) a star of *When Harry Met Sally* (Billy Crystal's ex-wife).

    c) a star of *Parenthood* (Rick Moranis' wife).

    d) not a star at all.

5. John Goodman is:

    a) a starette of *Arachnophobia.*

    b) funnier than ever.

    c) hammier than ever.

    d) fatter than ever.

6. Frank Marshall is:

    a) the neophyte director of *Arachnophobia.*

    b) producer for Steven Spielberg of *Poltergeist.*

    c) producer for Touchstone Pictures of *Gremlins.*

    d) a producer who, as a director, steals from the films he has produced.

7. The worst thing about *Arachnophobia* is:

    a) it's long.

    b) it's derivative.

    c) it's dumb.

    d) it's farfetched.

8. The best thing about *Arachnophobia* is:

    a) pronouncing the title.

    b) reading the ad ("Eight legs, two fangs and an attitude").

    c) hearing the songs ("Don't Bug Me," by Jimmy Buffett; "Summer Wind," by Frank Sinatra; "I Left My Heart in San Francisco," by Tony Bennett; "Goin' Ahead," by Pat Metheny).

    d) knowing it will all be over.

ANSWERS: The answers to all of the above are all of the above.

July 21, 1990

❖

GoodFellas

Directed by Martin Scorsese
Written by Nicholas Pileggi and Martin Scorsese
Starring Robert De Niro, Ray Liotta and Joe Pesci

The good fellas in *GoodFellas* are bad boys to a man, and boys is the operative word – the gangsters in director Martin Scorsese's epic, which covers thirty years and runs some two hours (it whizzes by faster than a cartoon) are bullies on the lam. Scorsese has made plenty of movies about gangsters and assorted low-lifes (*Mean Streets, Taxi Driver, The Color of Money, Raging Bull*), but he's never before turned tough, emotionally demanding material into a comedy of duty-free macho manners. No so-called serious gangster film has ever been more fun, or less dangerous, or more intrinsically feminist, than *GoodFellas*. Even *I Married the Mob* was scarier.

Scorsese and Nicholas Pileggi have based their lushly decorated, panoramic picture on Pileggi's *Wiseguy*, a non-fiction account of the exploits of Henry Hill (Ray Liotta), a half-Sicilian, half-Irish crook who commenced his illegal activities at the age of fourteen in 1955. Thirty years later, married and presumably successful, he entered the Federal Witness Protection Program and ratted on his buddies. Hill's career began with construction rackets and evolved into hijackings, large-scale thefts (Hill's associate James Conway, played by Robert De Niro, masterminded a $6-million Lufthansa heist, until that time the largest cash robbery on U.S. record), extortion, arson, drug-smuggling and murder. Henry Hill may have lost friends, but he sure knew how to influence people.

His life in crime is presented festively, energetically, with a smile at the corner of the screen. In *The Godfather*, Francis Coppola inflated gangsterism into an operatic metaphor for the state of capitalism; in *I Married the Mob*, Jonathan Demme saw it as a corner-store metaphor for the soullessness of working-class kitsch; but in *GoodFellas*, Scorsese is mute as to the meaning of gangsterism, and there is no obvious effort to make these characters either sympathetic, or symbolic of anything but themselves. Instead, he concentrates his artistry on film-making, on visual textures, startling montage and aural time travel. The music is brilliantly employed as a blaring Brechtian commentary – the credits list forty-three popular songs (you hear every one of them), including "Rags to Riches," "Hearts of Stone," "Sincerely," "Stardust," "Roses Are Red," "Leader of the Pack," "Atlantis," "Beyond the Sea," "The Boulevard of Broken Dreams," "Frosty the Snow Man," "Unchained Melody," "Danny Boy," "Sunshine of Your Love," "Jump into the Fire," "Memo From Turner," "What Is Life" and Sid Vicious' immortal version of "My Way." I've listed so many of the tunes because they are the key to Scorsese's attitude toward the fellas, and they indicate the progress of the plot.

The Brectianisms don't stop with the music. Throughout *Good-Fellas*, Scorsese is at great pains to remind us that we are watching a movie – there are freeze frames, over- and underhead angles, expressionist lighting (a funeral scene is scarlet), and at least one moment during which a character addresses us directly. The Brecht who posted signs in theatres warning viewers not to "stare so romantically" would have approved.

Scorsese has also directed his actors with Brechtian restraint. Ray Liotta, the intimidating gangster in *Something Wild*, is surprisingly low-key as Henry Hill, a man whose motives remain inscrutable to himself. His abused wife, Karen Hill (Lorraine Bracco), could have become the heroine of the piece, but Scorsese is no sentimentalist and understands all too well why this couple is together. (When Hill is imprisoned, she goes into the cocaine trade.) The other gangsters run the grungy gamut from the foul-tempered Tommy DeVito (Joe Pesci), who shoots a kid in the foot because it takes the kid too long to bring him a drink, to De Niro's James Conway, a man with the metabolism of a lizard, to the avuncular Paulie (Paul Sorvino), a man you wouldn't want as a relative.

Brecht always claimed that his plays were comedies – he thought that even his tragedies were comedies and he further claimed that it was up to the audience to find his themes. (That was ironic, of course, in that he tended toward the didactic.) *GoodFellas* does precisely what Brecht said he was doing: it gives us some splendiferous pieces, but it leaves it to us to fit them into a thematically coherent puzzle. The effort is pure pleasure.

September 21, 1990

❖

The Silence of the Lambs

Directed by Jonathan Demme
Written by Ted Tally
Starring Jodie Foster, Anthony Hopkins and Scott Glenn

Happy heart day. To celebrate it, you might consider taking in Hollywood's bloody Valentine, *The Silence of the Lambs*, a psychological thriller about a female FBI trainee, Clarice Sparling (Jodie Foster), and her relationship with an imprisoned psychopathic serial killer, Hannibal "The Cannibal" Lecter (Anthony Hopkins), who has been known to chow down on the hearts and other succulent parts of his victims. Dr. Lecter (he's a shrink) is one cool dude – during a medical exam, he grabbed a nurse and rather dramatically got into her face. "His pulse never went above eighty," trainee Sparling is told, "even when he swallowed her tongue."

Why would Hollywood release *The Silence of the Lambs* on Valentine's Day? "Because," Jonathan Demme, its brilliant director, has maintained with tongue not entirely in cheek, "the movie is a love story." It is: the ambivalent interaction between Lecter and Sparling, who needs Dr. Lecter's help to find another serial killer still at large, perversely covers most of the romantic bases, with the exception of sex. The idea here, reproduced from Thomas Harris' novel of the same name, is that Dr. Lecter loves Sparling's spunk and is excited by her wounded psychological profile (Lecter sniffs pain like most people sniff flowers). Sparling meanwhile learns to love Lecter's intelligence and, through what amounts to shock therapy, is able eventually to confront the dark side of herself.

Heretofore cast as a defiant and frequently sluttish victim – it began with the nearly pre-teen hooker in *Taxi Driver* and was capped by the Oscar for *The Accused* – Foster is flawless in a role that is a welcome departure from all that gyrating suffering; trainee Sparling may be vulnerable, but she is no victim. As for Anthony Hopkins' hissing psychopath, Dr. Lecter – well, he's chilling sick fun (Hopkins is a master actor), but the character is a theatrical conceit; the sense of decimated humanity that Kathy Bates brought to her serial killer and "number one fan" in *Misery* is missing in Lecter's pyrotechnical action.

The Thomas Harris novel, *The Silence of the Lambs*, is an inferior sequel to *Red Dragon*, in which Lecter also figured. *Red Dragon* became the Michael Mann movie, *Manhunter*, to which Demme's *The Silence of the Lambs* is infinitely superior. But *Lambs* is finally a failure, a failure that is a function of its success: it's too good. The magic of Kathy Bates aside, director Rob Reiner had no pretensions to high art in *Misery*, but Demme (director of *Something Wild*, *Stop Making Sense*, *Melvin and Howard*, *Married to the Mob*) certainly does, and the material – juicy pulp – is squeezed dry under the pressure. Screenwriter Ted Tally's adaptation removes key subplots (the personality of a kidnap victim, the problems of Sparling's superior, played by Scott Glenn) and exaggerates others (Anthony Heald's psychiatrist is a villain out of a silent movie) while rendering the evocative symbolism of the title crass as the bellow of a buffalo.

The plot thus becomes annoyingly straightforward and predictable, which is bizarre in a Jonathan Demme film – until now, he has been most notable for the carefully detailed peripheries of his pictures. The ending is especially annoying. In a movie that means to be artful esthetically and realistic psychologically, the fates of assorted characters smack of cliffhanging more suitable to the *Halloween* and *Nightmare on Elm Street* cycles. *The Silence of the Lambs* is an uneasy beaker brimming with crude oil and spring water. Demme can't decide if he's after the Jason of *Medea* or the Jason of *Friday the Thirteenth.*

February 14, 1991

Jungle Fever

Written and directed by Spike Lee
Starring Wesley Snipes and Annabella Sciorra

Film Critic going in, you may guess there's no getting out: As Stevie Wonder sings, the credits fly feverishly by in the form of street signs, some of which indicate the actual geographical locations (Harlem, Bensonhurst), while others expose the real psychological locales, urban jungles at tribal war. In working-class Italian-American Bensonhurst, there is a sign that warns "No Niggers"; a Harlem freeway exit proudly proclaims the place to be "A Guinea Free Zone."

Dedicated to Yusef Hawkins, a black teenager killed by a gang of Italian kids from Bensonhurst, Spike Lee's *Jungle Fever* opens with examples of epithets that explicitly define and implicitly condone racial bigotry. However, this magnificent miscegenation movie – one of the most complex, painfully funny films ever made in the United States on the subject of race relations – can in no way be construed as support for the abysmally polarized status quo. *Jungle Fever* is out to change things, in whatever way art can change things, but it's not about to minimize the massive, inbred nature of that which requires alteration.

In fact, the second hour of the picture, which mercilessly analyzes the equally racist reactions of Bensonhurst and Harlem to the love affair between black architect Flipper Purify (Wesley Snipes) and his Italian-American secretary, Angie Tucci (Annabella Sciorra), is an elegantly choreographed descent into twin Dante-esque hells circumscribed by colour. Jungle fever, indeed: Lee's vision of interracial relations makes Darwin look like Disney.

Structurally, *Jungle Fever* gives us a his-and-hers story. Flipper Purify is a happily married buppie, loving husband to Drew Purify (Lonette McKee), a white-featured black woman with skin the colour of *café-au-lait*, and loving father to little Ming (Veronica Timbers). Flipper works at a white architectural firm owned by partners Jerry (Tim Robbins) and Lesley (Brad Dourif), a couple of parasites unfortunately presented with the same satirical stereotyping Lee deployed on the Jewish clubowners in *Mo' Better Blues*.

The self-empowered Flipper is a success despite, not because of, his background. His father is a defrocked but nonetheless fundamentalist minister, The Good Reverend Doctor Purify (Ossie Davis), who believes he was tossed out of his church because the Devil got control of his parishioners ("The Devil," Flipper argues, "had little if anything to do with it"). His mother, Lucinda Purify (Ruby Dee), is a compassionate but nonetheless senile toady who supports her children, not always intelligently, behind their father's rigid back. Flipper's elder brother, Gator (Samuel L. Jackson, winner of best supporting actor at the Cannes Film Festival), is a flamboyant lost cause, a crackhead who confesses of the family's colour television set, "I smoked it."

Angie Tucci is an unmarried, working-class Italian woman, the less-than-content caretaker of a violent, racist father (Frank Vincent) and two similarly violent, racist brothers (David Dundara, Michael Imperioli). Until Angie goes to work for, and falls in love with, Flipper, the only grace note in her graceless life is sounded by her boy friend, Paulie Carbone (John Turturro), a bookish variety-store operator who has what may be impossible dreams of educating himself beyond the dead-end bigotry of Bensonhurst. The problem in the relationship is that the extremely attractive and lively Angie feels no passion for the homely and boringly decent Paulie.

As *Jungle Fever* blooms and temperatures rise, Lee gives each of his major characters an aria in which they reveal, or attempt to conceal, their deepest feelings. Paulie's father, Lou Carbone, pungently played by that multi-ethnic ham, Anthony Quinn, has a lacerating few minutes in which he remembers that although his wife wouldn't speak to him for years (he beat her, was unfaithful to her), she washed his back every day of her life and otherwise fulfilled her "wifely duties" – "That," he recalls with psychotic nostalgia, "was a fucking marriage!"

Flipper's wife has her aria, too, a simmering summation of what it was like to grow up "high yellow" – as the memories bubble to the surface, her remembrance of things more present than past becomes a hot howl of blistering rage. Supplementing the solos are duets, trios, quartets and, in one memorable instance, a choral arrangement for a group of black women bemoaning the unfaithfulness of black men. Like Robert Altman's masterpiece, *Nashville*, Lee's *Jungle Fever* listens to the (overlapping) voices of people whose life-songs, if heard at all, are invariably switched off.

In common with the films of Rainer Werner Fassbinder, whose cameraman, Michael Ballhaus, has obviously influenced Lee's brilliant Ernest Dickerson (Lee and Dickerson, unapologetic film freaks, went to school together), there are no solutions in *Jungle Fever*, and no happy endings, easy or otherwise. *Do the Right Thing* was the title of an earlier Lee film; in this one, doing anything is as dangerous as doing nothing. To the darkly claustrophobic, ingrained pessimism of his theme, Lee brings a joyously acquired galaxy of cinematic smarts. Individual scenes evoke not only Altman at zenith, but also the more operatic of the Italian directors (Luchino Visconti, Bernardo Bertolucci) and the most operatic of the Italian-Americans (Martin Scorsese). The barometric use of music – Stevie Wonder for a crack mansion; Frank Sinatra for Angie's Italian hell-house; Mahalia Jackson for Flipper's unholy home – is schematic, but remarkably effective at measuring cultural pressure.

For all his talent, Lee's past pictures, especially *Mo' Better Blues*, *She's Gotta Have It* and *School Daze*, have queasily combined the schematic with the sexist. *Jungle Fever* does not, in part because, as Angie Tucci, the luminous Annabella Sciorra refutes the script's suggestion that Angie became involved with a black man because she was curious about the size of his penis. According to reports from the set, Lee and the actress argued bitterly over this contention – Lee continues to maintain that *Jungle Fever* is about "the myths" races have of each other – and Sciorra recently refused to be interviewed by *Vanity Fair* for an article on Lee. In the movie, however, Flipper makes the charge and Angie says, "Do you think that was it?" The look on her face leaves no doubt that, from her point of view, Flipper's desire to dismiss her love for him as phallic curiosity is at best crude machismo, at worst calculated dishonesty. Without saying another word, she gets the last one. Lee may feel that his movie thus lost an artistic battle to a woman. If so, he should know that in losing the battle, *Jungle Fever* won the war.

June 7, 1991

❖

Black Robe

Directed by Bruce Beresford
Written by Brian Moore
Starring Lothaire Bluteau, Aden Young and August Schellenberg

Black Robe, a visually extravagant Canada/Australia co-production, is exhilaratingly shocking, an intelligent priests-and-Indians costume drama that frequently provokes uncomfortable thoughts and inter-mittently incites unpleasant emotions. But how could an honest, historically sound film recounting French Catholicism's spiritual colonialization of the native peoples of Quebec do otherwise? Perhaps because the movie's commercial prospects are problematic at best, there is one historical departure – the actors playing the French char-acters in screenwriter Brian Moore's adaptation of his own 1985 novel speak English. Contemporary French-Canadians may be thankful for small favours.

Father Laforgue (*Jesus of Montreal* star Lothaire Bluteau), an asce-tic zealot who looks like an El Greco saint and who sincerely believes he has been sent to New France (seventeenth-century Quebec) to save the heretofore doomed souls of "savages," undertakes a journey from Samuel de Champlain's fort to Ihonatiria, a minuscule Jesuit mission. Joining him are a young, naive carpenter, Daniel (Aden Young), and a group of Algonquins led by a wise but not clichéd chief, Chomina (August Schellenberg), who is accompanied by his gorgeous daughter, Annuka (Sandrine Holt). She is a cliché – Princess Tiger Lily. Did no native chieftains ever sire less than beauteous women? Did all Indian princesses fall in love with white guys? (That trollop Pocahontas has a lot to answer for.) Daniel and Annuka do fall in love, of course, but Australian director Bruce Beresford (*Driving Miss Daisy*) fortunately emphasizes the unusual cultural clash in their relationship rather than the banal hormonal congruity.

Dances With Wolves is inevitably evoked. Although there are similarities, in a reasonably progressive world, they would be common to any cinematic exploration of North American aboriginal history. In both pictures, Indians are presented with sensitivity, sympathy and some ethnographic accuracy, and in both they speak their own languages (subtitled in English) when it would be logical for them to do so. However, *Black Robe*, virtually completed before *Dances With Wolves* was released, is as complex in its narrative and as even-handed in its psychology as Kevin Costner's Oscar-winning epic was simple and, occasionally, simplistic. Australian director Fred Schepisi's masterpiece, *The Chant of Jimmie Blacksmith*, is the film to which Beresford's work bears primary comparison, not *Dances With Wolves*.

This is not in any event a good-Indian-guys versus bad-white-guys Western (or Eastern). While examining cultures in ugly collision, *Black Robe* recognizes that general values on all sides are expressed by specific individuals on each side. Some of those individuals, white and Indian, are prettier (less dogmatic, more compassionate) than others. The life-affirming native religions in the film certainly come across as preferable to the life-denying Christianity of the period, but that's not special liberal pleading, it's humanistically informed reporting; the tone is journalistic rather than moralistic. The man in the "black robe," the psychologically fascinating Father Laforgue, is not a man in a black hat. A true believer tortured by his need to pass out tickets to heaven, he experiences a profound if incomplete conversion to a less rigid world-view.

Meanwhile, the "savage" tribes (Algonquin, Huron, Iroquois) are clearly differentiated in terms of customs: Some engage in gratuitous cruelty, others do not. (Beresford's staging of various forms of inter-tribal torture is always graphic, never gratuitous.) It's important to recall in this context, as the film implicitly does, that so-called pan-Indianism (pan-nativity?) was a consequence of the European con-quest of the continent. During the time in which *Black Robe* is set, tribes sharing or disputing the same territories often had little in com-mon. The Hopi, Navajo and Pueblo Indians of the southwest, for example, were more distinct from each other culturally and linguisti-cally than today's French are from today's Germans.

That the natives in *Black Robe* speak their own languages while the French converse in English is supremely ironic. The decision to require even French-Canadian actors to deliver their lines in the dom-inant tongue of the continent was no doubt based on strictly commer-cial considerations (were the dialogue to be entirely in French and the native languages, *Black Robe* would be ghettoized as a "foreign-language film" and would automatically reach a smaller audience), but there is an unintentional symmetry here.

Black Robe is about the successful appropriation of native lands and the attempted appropriation of native souls – it's about cultural genocide, a satanic "missionary" act that includes obliterating lan-guage. French, English and Spanish colonializers all played holier-than-thou devil to the indigenous inhabitants (who were no angels) of North America; two members of the unholy trinity have since been bedevilled by the third. Dog-eat-dog, indeed: French-Canadians and Hispanic-Americans now know how it must have felt to have been the tastiest puppy in the pound.

Produced in Canada by Robert Lantos, *Black Robe* is a technical achievement of the highest order. The Australian cinematographer Peter James, who worked previously with Beresford on *Driving Miss Daisy*, sees the Quebec winter wilderness with a gelid pictorial precision that elicits gasps and raises goose bumps; not since *The Grey Fox* has any Canadian landscape been so well served. Given that landscape, the characters could easily have become tiny figures in it, but the actors – including but not limited to Bluteau, Young, Holt, Schellenberg, Tantoo Cardinal and Billy Two Rivers – are excellent. *Black Robe* wraps a hideous period of history in a frosty ebony shroud. Who would have thought that viewing a gussied-up corpse would be cause for cinematic celebration?

September 5, 1991

Barton Fink

Directed by Joel Coen
Written by Ethan and Joel Coen
Starring John Turturro, John Goodman and Judy Davis

Jack Lipnick (Michael Lerner), the head of Capitol Studios, is advising neophyte screenwriter Barton Fink (John Turturro) on how to revise a script the mogul thinks will be unacceptable to audiences in 1941. "They don't want to see a guy wrestling with his soul. Well, maybe a little bit, for the critics." Lipnick, a porcine, vulgar combination of the least attractive aspects of Harry Cohn, Jack Warner and Samuel Goldwyn, is sure he knows what "they" want and it sure as hell is not to think. Lipnick would hate *Barton Fink*.

The phrase "sure as hell" is not used loosely in this context. As expertly crafted by brothers Joel and Ethan Coen (*Blood Simple, Raising Arizona, Miller's Crossing*), *Barton Fink* is a Faustian satire in which Hollywood is seen as the Hades to which good writers are sent to go bad. Contrary to Lipnick, the Coens assume audiences want nothing more than to see a man wrestling with his soul. So far, the brothers have been correct – *Barton Fink* gobbled up three awards (best picture, director, actor), an unprecedented feat, at last spring's Cannes Film Festival, and it is doing well in its initial release in the United States. Score one for the smart guys.

This hip morality tale is by no means perfect – it's not the masterpiece *Miller's Crossing* was – but it is stylish, intelligent, witty and more than slightly creepy. The film opens on the night of leftist playwright Fink's first Broadway triumph. A complicated, self-absorbed artist who looks like George S. Kaufman but writes like Clifford Odets, Fink is devoted to his own integrity and to the common man, in that order. When he is offered a job in Hollywood, an old friend, Garland Stanford (David Warrilow), persuades him to take the money. "The common man," Stanford points out, "will still be here when you get back."

In Hollywood, Fink/Faust meets Lipnick and is assigned to work on a wrestling picture for Wallace Beery (there was such a movie, *Flesh*, which was directed by John Ford and released in 1932). He also meets the legendary, legendarily alcoholic Southern novelist W. P. Mayhew (John Mahoney), a genius whose self-destruction has been so thorough his scripts and novels are being written by his secretary, Audrey Taylor (Judy Davis). The Mayhew lush is, of course, based on William Faulkner, who did in fact work on *Flesh*. (No one has suggested that his secretary wrote *The Sound and the Fury*, however.) And finally, at his purgatorial digs, the Hotel Earle ("A Day or a Lifetime"), Fink meets another tenant, life insurance salesman Charlie Meadows (John Goodman), a common man who may be the death-dealing devil in hail-fellow-well-met disguise.

Outfitted with a panoply of surrealistic technical trickery and a mystery that has an irritatingly ambiguous non-solution, *Barton Fink* is nonetheless a remarkable movie, thanks largely to the writing of the (anti-)hero and to John Turturro's astonishing delineation of him.

Turturro's Fink prides himself on his powers of observation but is so busy congratulating himself on his perceptiveness he actually sees little and hears less. Asked what he does for a living, he piously responds, "I'm not sure any more. I guess I try to make a difference."

(That and a dime will buy you a bean sprout.) Watching Fink agonize over the wrestling movie, Audrey Taylor tells him tactfully to mellow out – "It's really just a formula. You don't have to type your soul into it." But Fink, who's Hamlet with the ego of Richard III, does. This man is so terrified of losing his soul he ironically winds up giving it away.

Although the film belongs to Turturro (it was written for him), he generously leases it to Davis, Goodman, Mahoney and Lerner. All play their second fiddles flawlessly (particularly Lerner, who has had a lot of practice – he has impersonated both Harry Cohn and Jack Warner in other movies). As always in the films written and directed by the Coen brothers, there are innumerable self-conscious cultural references and cinematic in-jokes (the California sea-coast, for example, is a direct copy of the view from Judy Garland's house in *A Star Is Born*), but the cute stuff is not essential to understanding the underlying issue or to enjoying the movie's energetic treatment of it. The conflict – artistic purity versus commercial corruption – is as old as evil and as up-to-date as tomorrow's "Entertainment Tonight."

September 13, 1991

The Fisher King

Directed by Terry Gilliam
Written by Richard LaGravenese
Starring Robin Williams, Jeff Bridges, Amanda Plummer and Mercedes Ruehl

When *The Fisher King* was named most popular film at Toronto's Festival of Festivals, director Terry Gilliam, long considered an *enfant terrible* because he refused to compromise his "vision" in surrealistic movies such as *Brazil* and *The Adventures of Baron Munchausen*, responded to the honour with a faxed statement: "Thank you for justifying my decision to sell out."

Is *The Fisher King* – in which Robin Williams plays Parry, formerly a professor of medieval history and currently a New York City street person on a seemingly psychotic quest for the Holy Grail – a sell out? Certainly not: It's a literate, visually attractive romantic comedy about the difficulty, and necessity, of healing the pains of the past. It's a tenderly optimistic yet unsentimental tall tale, a "Hollywood film" in the best sense of the term – it's a fantasy that makes you feel good without leaving you coated in glucose. If this is what Gilliam means by selling out, selling out should happen a lot more often.

Richard LaGravenese's script, inspired by the legend of the Fisher King – he was the guardian of the Holy Grail, the cup used by Christ at the Last Supper and later the vessel in which drops of divine blood were collected during the Crucifixion – is the first Terry Gilliam film that the Monty Python alum has not himself written. But the script gives every evidence of having been worked on not only by Gilliam, but by his exceedingly luminous cast – Robin Williams' manic character, Parry, often sounds like a manic character invented by Robin Williams, while erstwhile radio talk show host Jack Lucas brings to mind characters played in the past by Jeff Bridges. Jack Lucas is, of course, played by Jeff Bridges.

As *The Fisher King* opens, Jack Lucas is the hottest, meanest mouth on New York's airwaves. But he puts his foot into it, firmly and perhaps permanently, by telling a listener that yuppies are "evil" people who "don't feel love – they only negotiate love moments." The listener takes the condemnation to heart and walks into a yuppie nightclub with a gun; he kills a good portion of the clientele and himself. Three years pass. Jack Lucas is now a disconsolate alcoholic working in a video store; the only joy in his life, until he meets Parry, is his girl friend, Anne (Tony award-winning actress Mercedes Ruehl), a long-suffering co-dependent he treats abominably.

Parry, a spritzing sprite who lost his wife some years earlier, is as wounded as Jack, but Parry has his cuckoo quest for the Holy Grail to energize him. He tries to recruit Jack to the cause – "There has to be a Grail! What were the Crusades? A Pope publicity stunt?" – but Jack is dubious. Not even Parry's revelation of the location of the Grail convinces him. Jack merely rolls his eyes and says disbelievingly, "Some billionaire has got the Holy Grail in his library on Fifth Avenue?" Nonetheless, Jack does ask Anne, a Catholic, if she has heard of the existence of the sacred object. "Yeah," she responds, "it's, like, Jesus' juice glass."

The quest affords Gilliam the opportunity of showcasing four exemplary stars – the fourth and sometimes funniest member of the team is Amanda Plummer as a klutzy introvert who Parry thinks is perfection personified. Bridges has for twenty years been one of the United States' most dependable cinematic actors and his performance here is up to his usual lofty standard; Jack's pain and pleasure are communicated with understated economy. Williams' comparatively gaudy role has been closely tailored to his roomy talents – his Parry is a softer, teddy-bear variation of Trudy, Lily Tomlin's cosmically connected bag lady. And Ruehl's Italianate Anne is sultry, salty, and full of absolutely no nonsense.

The quartet is abetted by a roster of hugely supportive players, including singer Tom Waits as a panhandling bum who declares, "I'm what you call kind of a moral traffic light," and Tony Award-winning actor (for *Grand Hotel*) Michael Jeter, who belts out a hilarious parody of the climactic musical number from *Gypsy* – it's entitled "Rose's Turn" – in the gender-bending drag (hose, garter belt, moustache) of the sort once favoured by The Cockettes.

At one point in this blithe picture, a character is criticized for reading "trashy romance novels," a comment that sends Parry into high dudgeon. "Don't say that!" he snaps. "There's nothing trashy about romance!" Well, there's nothing trashy about this romance, Terry Gilliam's so-called "sell out" movie. The only "selling out" of which Gilliam may be guilty is embedded in his stance of faux sophistication. To pretend that *The Fisher King* is a "sell out" is a form of selling out – it's like pretending that the Grail isn't Holy.

September 20, 1991

❖

The Falls

Written and Directed by Kevin McMahon

In *Lila, An Inquiry into Morals*, the new book by Robert M. Pirsig (*Zen and the Art of Motorcycle Maintenance*), an American in a bar in upstate New York declares of Canadians, "There are two kinds. The one kind disapproves of this country for all the junk they find here, and the other kind loves this country for all the junk they find here." Those two kinds of Canadians, along with all kinds of Americans and a sampling of other nationalities, come together every day in Canada's most surrealistically American city, Niagara Falls, Ont., one of the authentic unnatural wonders of the world. The schism between the town – kitsch capital of Canada, if not of North America – and the reason for the town's existence – an authentic natural wonder of the world – is the subject of writer-director Kevin McMahon's evocative, visually beautiful documentary *The Falls*.

McMahon and his primary collaborators (photographer Douglas Koch, musician Kurt Swinghammer) have structured *The Falls* as nothing less than a historical inquiry into morals. The investigation begins with Natives, who had no fear of the falls, and continues with the Europeans who arrived in the seventeenth century, and who saw the falls as evil. Why? Not only because their culture, based on The Fall, was figuratively and literally afraid of falling ("Think of Icarus, or Humpty-Dumpty"), but because they saw unusual natural phenomena as evidence that the world had "collapsed under the weight of our sins."

So, as Kurt Vonnegut Jr. used to say, it goes. "Each generation," the narrator of *The Falls* argues, "sees a new world, but it's all in the framing." The film offers a primer on the beliefs, or "framing," of the eighteenth and nineteenth centuries, from the Age of Enlightenment to the Industrial Revolution, and on up to the post-modern present, all while sticking scrupulously to the falls as metaphor. It's an ingenious strategy, and for the most part it works. However, there is an occasional portentousness in the narration Kevin McMahon has written for his sister, Rita McMahon, to read – when she intones the word "profaning," it echoes electronically – that is more appropriate to a high-school lecture hall than to a feature-film theatre. For a while, I thought the narrative pomp might be a parody of the traditional National Film Board of Canada "voice of God" style; then I thought not – it's a circumstantial extension, not a send-up. And *The Falls* was produced with NFB participation.

But that's pretty much a quibble over a supremely pretty movie. If it is indeed "all in the framing," this film has it all. Composed predominantly of languid tracking shots of the sort directors Peter Greenaway and Jean-Pierre Lefebvre have spent their careers perfecting, *The Falls* communicates the grandeur of the tumbling tonnes of water by bathing the eyeballs in soaking, wide-screen splendour; the shots of the falls illuminated at night are at once gaudy and overwhelming, exact cinematic replicas of Canadian artist David Thauberger's famous paintings of the same site. ("A place," as he once put it, "famous for being famous.")

On land, *The Falls* even treats the kitsch of the Freaks of Nature Museum and similar tourist haunts of Niagara Falls, Ont., with fairness. Sure, the traps are emblematic of the horrors of commercialization, but, like Las Vegas, they are lively and cheerfully colourful in their decadence, a bevy of tacky but still game strippers. (They're fun to watch, but you wouldn't want to live with one.) Some of the tourists are held up to ridicule, *à la* the "villains" in the documentary *Roger & Me*, but there is nothing else to do with the visitor who scrutinizes side-by-side wax facsimiles of Abraham Lincoln and Martin Luther King and announces that the latter "must have been the servant" of the former.

Residents are not held up to ridicule. One, the last of a family of daredevils, has lived next to death so long (a father and two brothers were taken by the falls) he has developed an utterly resigned relationship to it: He reveals that it bothers him not a bit to guide people who have cancer up to "the whirlpool," the part of the falls where suicide is easy.

And the movie has true horrors to expose: The chemical dumps on the American side are far more damaging than the cultural dumps on the Canadian shores. A mother speaks movingly of the plight of her daughter and other cancer-ridden children reared in the Love Canal area, while ecology experts show us birds and fish that surpass in mutated hideousness anything in the comparatively tame Freaks of Nature Museum.

"It's all in the framing" – eventually, the film intermarries the naturally sacred and the unnaturally profane with breathtaking dexterity. An innocuous water slide, for instance, suggests technologically induced pollution; happy tourists in yellow slickers walk through a tunnel to an observation deck, appearing unearthly and ominous, like aliens from a science-fiction film or mad medical technicians on their way to perform sadistic experiments; and the sterile hydroelectric installations recall both the dystopian nightmare city of *Metropolis* and the high-tech space station utopia of *2001: A Space Odyssey*. "It's all in the framing" – *The Falls* has brilliantly framed Niagara Falls as the picture of a civilization.

November 8, 1991

Korczak

Directed by Andrzej Wajda
Written by Agnieszka Holland
Starring Wojtek Pszoniak and Ewa Dalkowska

His real name was Henryk Goldszmit, but he is remembered by history as Dr. Janusz Korczak, a *nom de plume* he adopted from a nineteenth-century novel. He was born in Warsaw in 1878 or 1879 to a middle-class Jewish family, and from the time he was a child dreamed of being a doctor to children. He embarked on his study of medicine at Warsaw University in 1899 and his dream came true: he became the world's first official pediatrician – the "Karl Marx of children," as he put it.

He was famous and influential – he even had a radio show for kids – and he virtually invented, in the operation of his orphanage, the concept of children's rights. His 1929 book, *The Right of the Child to Respect*, revolutionized child psychology; the brilliant Swiss psychotherapist Alice Miller (*Drama of the Gifted Child*) is but one of Dr. Korczak's disciples.

This is not the period of Dr. Korczak's life covered in detail by Polish director Andrzej Wajda's unusual, unsentimental biography, *Korczak*, which harks back to the relatively simple films (*Kanal, Ashes and Diamonds*) with which Wajda began his distinguished career in the late fifties. (That career is over, at least for the time being. Elected to the Polish Senate, Wajda, sixty-five, has retired from cinema to devote his energies to politics.) Instead, Wajda (pronounced Vi-Dah) concentrates on the last two years of Dr. Korczak's life, from October, 1940, when the Nazis sealed off the Jewish ghetto in Warsaw, to August, 1942, when the doctor, having no choice, led the two hundred orphans under his care into the gas chambers at Treblinka. "Reformers come to a bad end," Dr. Korczak wrote in one of his many broadsides. "Only after their death do people see that they were right and erect monuments in their memory." The monument erected by Wajda and scriptwriter Agnieszka Holland (writer-director of *Angry Harvest* and *Europa Europa*) shows us that Dr. Korczak was "right" but not that he was a saint; as embodied by Polish actor Wojtek Pszoniak, who here resembles Donald Pleasence, he is a protean pedagogue.

In interviews, Pszoniak has explained the man he plays as well as anyone. "I gently got into Korczak's world. After a few months, I saw not one Korczak, but two: one in the adult world, a demanding, difficult man, and the other, completely different, the Korczak of children, understanding and loving with a love I would call metaphysical. Not a maternal love. Not a paternal love. [Korczak was a childless bachelor.] A love of its own kind. He obviously identified with children. In each child he found himself. He thought that sacrifice was an improper word. He meant to take care of children. Since he could not save them, he wanted to be with them when they most needed him. He wanted to protect them from fear and terror, defend their dignity."

In this episodic, remarkably balanced dramatization – there is a chilling scene involving rapacious Jews who are co-operating with and making money from the Nazis – the last thing Dr. Korczak cares about is his dignity (which of course means that he retains it). "And your dignity?" someone asks when Dr. Korczak pleads with the Nazis on behalf of his orphans. "I have no dignity," he replies, "I have two hundred children." Those children, "good" and "bad," are realistically individuated in the film; they are exemplars of Dr. Korczak's contention that "there are no children – there are people."

Wajda and his cinematographer, Robby Muller (*Paris, Texas*; *Wings of Desire*; *Down by Law*), have shot *Korczak* in a grainy, intentionally artless black and white that makes the integration of actual Nazi footage of the ghetto possible. Wajda never exploits that footage: he first depicts the Nazis making their repellent yet historically invaluable movies and only then reveals what their cameras are recording. The purity of the technique is matched by the content. Offered a Swiss passport as a means of escape, Dr. Korczak refuses, declaring that no true father would abandon his children to save himself. His logic is incontrovertible and accessible; there is nothing mysterious or exalted about his integrity. The greatest achievement of this great film about a great man is that for all of Dr. Korczak's undeniable heroism, he remains a flawed, mortal man. *Korczak* renders the heroic human.

November 22, 1991

❖

Basic Instinct

Directed by Paul Verhoeven
Written by Joe Eszterhas
Starring Michael Douglas and Sharon Stone

Everybody connected with *Basic Instinct* should be spanked and put to bed without supper, but on the basis of the evidence at hand in this sado-masochistic disaster, they might enjoy it. After all, *Basic Instinct* is a perverse, lame-brained thriller that is pornographic, misogynist and homophobic. If that makes it sound appealing, I should also add that it's silly, boring and intellectually insulting.

It's already famous, of course, for two reasons. One: Joe Eszterhas was paid a record $3-million for the script, making him the most expensive something on the Hollywood block. Two: Gay groups throughout the United States have launched protests against the film, vicious protests whose only precedent was the outcry against *Cruising* (1980). (*Basic Instinct* is basically a remake of *Cruising* crossed with *Fatal Attraction*.) The gay objection is that the movie features three female characters, all murderous and all bisexual, and that their homicidal activities are explicitly related to their sexual orientation. The gay groups are correct: *Basic Instinct* presents lesbians as spidery – but sexy – man-haters and murderers.

Filmgoers familiar with the *oeuvre* of Dutch director Paul Verhoeven will recognize the phobias. *Total Recall*, that phallocentric celebration with Arnie [Schwarzenegger] plugging a woman in the forehead and saying, "Consider this a divorce," was his movie, and so was the art-house hit *The Fourth Man*, which began with a sequence in which a female spider killed and consumed her mate. It was widely assumed back then, before Verhoeven went to Hollywood, that *The Fourth Man*, released in North America in 1984, was satirical, but I remember standing with the director in the lobby of a Toronto theatre when *The Fourth Man* received its Canadian première courtesy of the Festival of Festivals – he was furious that the audience was laughing. Later, when he realized the film was a hit for whatever reason, he started telling interviewers that Toronto audiences were the first to understand that he had made a comedy. How do you define Opportunist?

The audience at a preview screening of *Basic Instinct* certainly laughed – at the film, not with it. The plot – a hard-drinking detective (Michael Douglas) tries to trap a suspected killer (Sharon Stone) he may understand all too well – is that rare thing, obvious and obtuse at the same time. The acting is abysmal; the music, by Jerry Goldsmith, bangs your head repeatedly against a wall of synthesized noise; and Verhoeven's direction consists primarily of jerking the camera from taut female breast (Stone) to sagging male bum (Douglas). (There's no way, in describing this movie, to avoid making it sound cheaply entertaining, but it's not.)

As the suspected killer, Stone does a Theresa Russell routine – she's simultaneously sultry and vacant – but she comes off better than anyone else in the picture because her character, a mythic monster mined from a male id, is not meant to be real. (If she is meant to resemble a terrestrial female, Joe Eszterhas is really weird.) As for Douglas – he seems to think he's doing a deluxe, X-rated reprise of *The Streets of San Francisco* (he is) and proceeds accordingly. He and George Dzundza, the actor who plays his equally hard-drinking part-ner, are the only people the script accepts as human beings.

The basic instinct motivating *Basic Instinct* is that the anyone who is not a middle-aged, middle-class, white heterosexual male alcoholic is bisexual female scum. The company that financed this film, Carolco, has fallen upon hard financial times. There is a God. And She ain't pleased.

March 20, 1992

❖

Unforgiven

Directed by Clint Eastwood
Written by David Webb Peoples
Starring Clint Eastwood, Gene Hackman and Morgan Freeman

For eleven years, William Munny (Clint Eastwood), infamous as a demonic hired killer, has been a domestic angel. When *Unforgiven* opens, the psychopath once feared throughout the West is no more – he is a poor but happy pig farmer, father to two beloved children, husband to an adored wife. Although the plains of Kansas are bleak and amenities are nonexistent – the story takes place in the 1880s – Munny has found peace; he has even provisionally pardoned himself for his murderous past. But then his wife dies and his hogs acquire a deadly fever; his family faces starvation.

Enter a shifty-eyed, runty boy full of rage, The Schofield Kid (Jaimz Woolvett). The Kid rides up to Munny's ramshackle farm – it's so impoverished, it makes Dorothy Gale's homestead look like the Emerald City – with a proposition. In the town of Big Whiskey, The Kid explains, two cowboys have viciously disfigured a brothel-based prostitute (Anna Thomson). The town's possibly corrupt sheriff, Little Bill Daggett (Gene Hackman), has let the sadists off with a slap on the wrist – a fine of six horses – and the prostitute's colleagues are infuriated. Hence, the women, led by the madam, Strawberry Alice (Frances Fisher), are offering a handsome reward, $500 a corpse, to anyone who will kill the cowboys. The hot-headed Kid claims to have experience as a cold-blooded killer, but it's pretty clear he needs someone with Munny's icy expertise to bring off the caper; it's also pretty clear The Kid worships Munny as a dark deity, a role model from hell.

Unforgiven, shot mostly in Alberta (and largely at night, and in the rain) is Clint Eastwood's thirty-sixth starring role, his tenth Western, and the sixteenth film he has directed. It is arguably his finest achievement; it is certainly his apex as an actor. The character of William Munny, a compendium of every gunslinger and cop Eastwood has played, from *Rawhide*'s Rowdy Yates to Dirty Harry Callahan to The Man With No Name, can be seen superficially as Clint's Greatest Hits.

But Munny transcends his precedents to become a truly tragic figure, a country-western combination of Lear and Richard III. Gaunt, grim, guilt-ridden – but still deadly, with a psychotic streak no less deep because it has run silent for years – Munny is a memorable sinner/saint, a character so complex his actions are difficult to condone or condemn. Eastwood treats Munny as a good therapist treats a troubled client, with objectivity and understanding, and without sentimentality or moral judgment.

Each character in David Webb Peoples' dense, unexpectedly stately, non-violent script (the inevitable gore is employed sparingly) is treated with that same, somewhat distanced clarity. These people, some of whom could have jumped from the pages of Cormac McCarthy's primal 1985 Western novel *Blood Meridian*, are existential strangers in a stark metaphorical land, an elemental West in which the traditional black hat/white hat frontier myth is exposed as a simplistic farce.

When Munny agrees to join The Kid, he does so with a proviso – a third person, Munny's old partner, Ned Logan (Morgan Freeman), also domesticated, must be added to the odyssey. Freeman's Logan, Hackman's sheriff and Woolvett's Kid initially appear to be rather transparent clichés, but as *Unforgiven* tightens its unforgiving screws, all three evolve in ways that are unpredictable yet logical. (The drama in this movie is predicated entirely on psychology.)

Two secondary characters, a snaky outlaw, English Bob (Richard Harris), and his mewling biographer, W. W. Beauchamp (Saul Rubinek), are more or less what they seem – comic relief, albeit of a gruesome variety – and that does come as a relief, because this brave, uncompromising movie desperately needs its rare interludes of levity.

Clint Eastwood is now sixty-two years old; there has never been a career to compare to his. Once reviled, and justifiably, as an actor with the warmth of a girder and the depth of a rain drop, he nonetheless became for years the world's most popular performer. Having acquired power, he exploited it to create artful but essentially non-commercial movies – *Honkytonk Man*; *White Hunter, Black Heart*; *Bird*. *Unforgiven* is about a man who cannot escape his past. Eastwood has. Who would have thought that the cheroot-smoking, poncho-wearing star of all those surreal spaghetti westerns would turn into one of Hollywood's most daring filmmakers?

August 7, 1992

❖

Visions of Light

Directed by Arnold Glassman, Todd McCarthy and Stuart Samuels

That a documentary entitled *Visions of Light: The Art of Cinematography* is papered with pictures of beautiful places and unforgettable people is predictable. That it fulfills its mandate to impart a wealth of information tracing the evolution of the cinematographic art is to be expected. But that it engages viewers on so many levels – the intellectual, the emotional, the historical, the personal – is surprising. Never less than respectably "educational," *Visions of Light* is frequently more than that: It viscerally reminds those of us to whom movies are important (or once were important) why we became entranced by the cinema in the first place. A movie about movies, *Visions of Light* is also a movie about memory.

In the months since its première last spring at the Cannes Film Festival, I've watched *Visions of Light* several times with varied audiences, some cinematically sophisticated and others naive. In every venue, the response has been identical: As the images of the past parade past, viewers become joyfully hypnotized. A standard ninety minutes in length, *Visions of Light* nonetheless unreels so rapidly in the mind that bewildered patrons sometimes look at each other as the lights come up and parrot Peggy Lee: "Is that all there is?" The principle of the wind-chill factor has taught us the simple phenomenological fact that it's not what a thing is, it's how it feels. This movie feels like a flutter-by, probably because all of the times and a majority of the people in it have fluttered by.

Although it does not and cannot encompass all there is – there are significant omissions – *Visions of Light* is reasonably comprehensive, extending back to the birth of the medium and up to the day before yesterday. If lots of great movies are left out, so many are included that the experience is euphorically disorienting. Paying attention to the images, to the interviews with the cameramen (there are only two women), and to the personal memories invoked by the combination, is to come perilously but pleasantly close to a perceptual pile-up. Perhaps only popular music has the nostalgic retrieval power of these sequences.

The overall organization is chronological, with digressions – as Allen Daviau (*E.T.*), arguably the most articulate of the interviewees, puts it, "In the beginning, there was a man with a camera." The man with a camera in the beginning was Billy Bitzer, D. W. Griffith's collaborator on *The Birth of a Nation* (1915) and *Intolerance* (1916); not until Gregg Toland shot *Citizen Kane* in 1941 for Orson Welles was there a comparable superstar behind the lens. Toland was inspired by the stark chiaroscuro of German expressionism. "The Germans in the twenties," John Bailey (*Ordinary People*) explains, "were really the cutting edge."

Unfortunately, we see little of that edge – one of the failings of *Visions of Light* is that it is profoundly Amero-centric. (It's a production of the American Film Institute.) Non-Americans do appear, but they speak primarily of the films they have made in the United States. The clip accompanying Sweden's Sven Nykvist is *The Unbearable Lightness of Being*, for example, rather than one of his Ingmar Bergman movies (for black and white: *The Seventh Seal*; for colour: *Cries and Whispers*). Similarly, Germany's Michael Ballhaus is quizzed on Martin Scorsese, for whom he photographed *The Last Temptation of Christ* and *GoodFellas*, rather than on the seventeen innovative films he shot magically under impossible conditions for Rainer Werner Fassbinder. The French New Wave gets no more than a dribble of attention. Oddly, given that *Visions* was co-produced with NKH/Japan

Broadcasting, there are no films from Akiro Kurosawa – nor from any Asian auteur, though cameraman James Wong Howe's U.S. career is carefully explored. The single European picture discussed in detail is *The Conformist*, a perfect movie shot by Vittorio Storaro in 1969 for Bernardo Bertolucci.

The three directors of *Visions* – Arnold Glassman, Todd McCarthy, Stuart Samuels – give short shrift to their own country in one particular: the western. There are a couple of clips (one is from John Ford's *She Wore a Yellow Ribbon*, which won Winton C. Hoch an Oscar in 1949), but they are so brief they qualify as subliminal. There is no supporting commentary whatever on the genre, a genre as visually influential, world-wide, as film noir, and far more influential than the "New York school" of the fifties, which receives an inordinate amount of analysis.

By nature selective, historical surveys invite this sort of carping. Happily, the virtues of commission dwarf the sins of omission. We are treated to a riveting sequence from a 1931 Joan Crawford vehicle, *Possessed*, in which the actress stands on the platform by a slow-moving train peering at the lives framed in the windows. Conrad Hall reveals that a legendary composition of Robert Blake from *In Cold Blood* in 1967 – portraying a soon-to-be-executed murderer, Blake stands by a rainy window, causing tear-like tracks to be reflected on his face – "was purely a visual accident. The visuals were crying for him." There are more than 100 of these visual epiphanies, accidental or otherwise.

The matter-of-fact modesty evinced by Hall ("I feel particularly involved in helping to make mistakes acceptable") seems to be characteristic of cinematographers, with one rule-proving exception, Gordon Willis, who was the director of photography on *Annie Hall* and *Manhattan* for Woody Allen and *The Godfather* trilogy for Francis Ford Coppola. (He has reason to be egomaniacal.) "Gordon, the Prince of Darkness," Hall laughs approvingly. "He has made an art of underexposure." Willis concedes that he may have "gone too far" on occasion – a chocolate-coloured *Godfather* scene between Al Pacino and Morgana King corroborates his confession – but he adds, "I think Rembrandt went too far a couple of times."

340

Some years ago, Adele Freedman published *Painter of Light*, a study of the artist Gershon Iskowitz. These "painters of light" do intermittently, despite the obvious silliness of Willis' Rembrandt comparison, deserve to be known as artists of the first-rank; the late Nestor Almendros' palette on *Days of Heaven* (whatever happened to its director, Terrence Malick?) is equivalent in power and thematically germane beauty to anything in a gallery.

Unlike the art of painters, the art of cinematographers, as they point out, is communal. The reaction of the audience to this art is communal, too – you need only attend a theatre where *Visions of Light* is being screened to feel the acknowledgment of shared experience. There is now a sadness inherent in that experience, the sadness of knowing that video and other culturally fragmenting technologies are poised to destroy the already severely diminished splendour of sitting in a dark room with strangers marvelling in unison at images in motion. Pauline Kael once wrote that to see a great movie on television is "a crime, the victim of which is yourself." The video revolution has paradoxically given us a new shared experience: We are all victims.

April 23, 1993

Arnold Schwarzenegger

To: the editors of *The New Yorker*.
From: your far-flung French correspondent.
Re: possible article for "Talk of the Town."
Subject: Arnold Schwarzenegger.

We happened the other day to be in the south of France on the Cote d'Azur, where the strawberries are in season and the Cannes Film Festival is in progress. We briefly toured the sites of La Croisette, the main Cannes drag, and indeed found it to be a drag – since it was the weekend, the *rue* was rife with tourists hoping to catch a glimpse of a major motion picture star, preferably American. The star-spotting fever was exacerbated by the presence of a statue, four storeys in height, of Arnold Schwarzenegger holding a gun approximately the size of the state of Maryland. A promotional device for a film called *Last Action Hero*, the statue was floating on a barge in the Mediterranean. The barge was anchored so as to be visible, day and night, to the entire village of Cannes. If vulgarity can be said to have an apotheosis, the statue of Arnold is destined for divinity.

We decided to look up the statue's model. To do so, we found it necessary to hire a car to drive us to the Hotel du Cap, which is in Cap d'Antibes, which is several kilometres from Cannes in the direction of Italy. The Hotel du Cap, which is as beautiful as it is expensive (cash only, please), was a fitting location for Arnold, who is also as beautiful as he is expensive. He is, we heard one journalist remark, "the biggest thing to come out of Austria since Hitler." We decided not to point out the obvious to the journalist: The difference between Hitler and Arnold is that whereas Hitler failed to conquer the world, Arnold has succeeded. Although he came to Cannes without a movie – only a few minutes of *Last Action Hero* were screened – he was interviewed by fifty-four publications and eighty-two television stations.

We found Arnold, clad in a *Last Action Hero* T-shirt and simple shorts, on the marble terrace of the Hotel du Cap. Behind him, the sea was azure, as advertised. The sun slanting on his famous face was strong; even nature was co-operating with Arnold by giving him his own spotlight. He was the Sun King.

Despite his radiance, not to mention his size – legs like redwoods, biceps like basketballs – we rapidly realized that Arnold is unpretentious; he is certainly not humble, but he has not lost a common touch. He said he does not "run around with bodyguards all over town." We had the impression that for Arnold, being a star is a job. We would be willing to bet he does not take his work home with him.

About his work, he was candid: He did not pretend to be an artist. It might be nice, he agreed, to play a character life-size rather than larger-than-life; however, it will not happen. "I would most likely not play this kind of a role because I don't think people would accept me," he said, smiling. "I don't think the public would want to see me as a drug dealer."

In *Last Action Hero*, the public will see Arnold as a good guy, a policeman who announces, "I don't want to take lives, I want to protect lives." Arnold has taken many lives on screen in the past, but in *Last Action Hero*, the violence is minimal. "He is," he said, referring to his character, "much more of a human being. We tried to make the movie much more acceptable for the whole family. Since I have a family, I ask myself what I want to show my kids. The need for entertainment is quite different from one decade to another."

We asked Arnold what he meant by that. "Mood," he said. "There has been a whole shift in mood. People are much more into the mood of helping each other. You have to see that and go with that." Arnold added that he could see the same mood shift in politics, world-wide. (Bosnia is presumably bucking the trend, or is perhaps not yet aware of it.)

What happens in the world is important to Arnold because he is a global phenomenon; he chooses a script, he explained, only if "people all over the world will get the jokes and will get the story and it will mean something to them rather than just in the United States or Europe or Japan. I'm supplying people with what they want to see. That's my responsibility in show business, to entertain people all over the world."

We left Arnold on the terrace and drove back to Cannes, our mood shifted and much improved; it was comforting to know that Arnold is taking his responsibility seriously.

May 17, 1993

❖

Jurassic Park

Directed by Steven Spielberg
Written by Michael Crichton and David Koepp
Starring Sam Neill, Laura Dern and Jeff Goldblum

Some day, historians will look back on all this with amazement: How, they will ask, could so many have become so excited over so little? *Jurassic Park*, Steven Spielberg's relentlessly kinetic visualization of Michael Crichton's sci-factoid thriller about a dinosaur theme park, is perfectly passable kiddie escapism. It has a thrill or two, and a chill or three, but it has no poetry, little sense of wonder, no resonant subtext (Jungian or otherwise), no art. Bereft of tears and light on laughter, it's an amusement park ride and a junk food dinner, all in one – momentarily diverting yet ultimately meaningless, it fills you up with nothing. When it's over, it's gone. Extinct.

But the bountiful beasties are beautiful: The six varieties on show (Tyrannosaurus rex, Velociraptor, Brachiosaurus, Triceratops, Gallimimus, Dilophosaurus) move realistically and emote effectively. There is one breathtaking sequence, the charge of a herd of harmless but huge critters fleeing a meat eater. The saurians are divided, just like people in adventure movies – just like the people in this adventure movie – into good and bad. Good: the big-eyed herbivores (though E.T. is cuter). Bad: the towering carnivores (though RuPaul is scarier).

They are brought back from extinction by scientists, good and bad, who manipulate saurian DNA preserved in the stomachs of 65 million-year-old mosquitoes trapped in amber. Instead of using this knowledge for scientific/humanitarian purposes (whatever they might be), the evil scientists and an unscrupulous developer, John Hammond (Richard Attenborough), create Jurassic Park, the sole purpose of which is to make money by giving folks an expensively-produced experience. (Post-modern paradox: *Jurassic Park* is Jurassic Park).

Apparently never having seen a monster movie in their lives, two of the good scientists, paleontologist Dr. Alan Grant (Sam Neill) and paleobotanist Dr. Ellie Sattler (Laura Dern), are dangerously lax on the dangers of Playing God. But their kookie mathematician friend Ian Malcolm (Jeff Goldblum) knows a plot when he sees it. In one of his few coherent speeches (he tends to chatter manically), he warns, "Dinosaurs had their shot and nature selected them for extinction."

The actors in *Jurassic Park* accomplish their psychologically simple, physically demanding tasks competently. Neill's Grant is serious and quizzical, Dern's Sattler is perky and independent, Attenborough's Hammond is pompous and irresponsible, and Goldblum's Malcolm is eccentric and comic (he's been giving this performance for rather too many years). The chief villain, a computer expert, is played by the amusing, ever more rotund Wayne Knight.

The adults are supplemented by two children, of course, a boy (Joseph Mazzello) and a girl (Ariana Richards), of course, and they are precocious and adorable and lizard-literate, of course, and we know that no matter how grim the going gets, they will triumph, because this is a Steven Spielberg movie and Steven Spielberg does not kill children.

That's *Jurassic Park*'s biggest deficit – a systematic avoidance of structural novelty. Its melodramatic devices were old when dinosaurs were young. We've been exposed to the narrative and technical tricks repeatedly in other Spielberg hits, especially *Jaws, Close Encounters of the Third Kind, E.T., Raiders of the Lost Ark* and the *Indiana Jones* series. The rapid editing, the dramatic backlighting, the assaultive sound effects (Dolby Migraine in selected theatres), the pounding John Williams score, the comic book storytelling, the shift from one exotic locale to another – well, it's easy to see why Spielberg's producer, Kathleen Kennedy, has said, "It was one of those projects that was so obviously a Spielberg film."

Like its predecessors, *Jurassic Park* will make millions. It's already impossible to escape the promotional tie-ins (there's actually a display in the movie), some of which are more bizarre than any creature

345

known to fossilization. At McDonald's, for example, the fries now come in a paper dinosaur head: T. rex appears to be puking potatoes.

Some day, scientists will pick through the fossilized remains of Hollywood. They will find *Jurassic Park*. They will screen it. They will use it to reconstruct life eons ago, when directors and producers roamed, if not ruled, the earth. Citing the film as evidence, the scientists will release their conclusion: Movies died out because they got too big for their pea-sized brains. The scientists will have a name for the extinct species: Cinesaurus.

June 11, 1993

Biography

Jay Scott was born Jeffrey Scott Beaven in Lincoln, Nebraska, in 1949, and at young age moved with his Seventh Day Adventist family to Albuquerque, New Mexico. His mother, Muriel, a high school teacher, was an enthusiastic collector of Native art and artifacts, a passion she passed on to her son. He attended the local high school, where he won several writing awards and performed with the drama society. Later, he studied art history at New College in Sarasota, Florida, and tried unsuccessfully to become an actor. While at New College he met his future wife, Mary, and they married in 1968.

To avoid being drafted to fight in the Vietnam War, in 1969 Jay and his wife moved to Toronto, where he worked at the *Daily Commercial News*, a construction-trades paper. When they learned he was ineligible for the draft, they moved back to New Mexico, where he enrolled at the University of New Mexico to study psychology and acting. He wrote reviews of plays for the student newspaper, and for one summer he was a reporter at the *Albuquerque Journal*. One semester short of earning his degree, he quit school and became a full-time journalist, covering the police beat. In true Hechtian tradition, he reported fires, car accidents, local crime, and City Hall. For the twelve-part series of articles he wrote on the treatment of the mentally ill he was awarded the American Bar Association's Silver Gavel.

In the early 1970s, Jay headed north to work under the name of Scott Beaven for the Calgary *Albertan*, where he wrote arts reviews and won his first National Newspaper Award. In 1977 he was hired by the *Globe and Mail* and became Jay Scott. At the *Globe* he wrote the popular FYI column, feature articles, and later became the paper's full-time movie reviewer, winning two further National Newspaper Awards. He also wrote food reviews for the *Globe*, art criticism for various art journals and books, feature articles for the *Village Voice* and *Première* magazine, and book reviews for *Chatelaine*. He started his television career with appearances on CBC's "The Journal" and later had his own show, "Jay Scott's Film International," on TVOntario. During this time, Jay divorced and began a long-term relationship with Gene Corboy, who died of AIDS in 1989.

Jay Scott's first book, *Midnight Madness*, a collection of his movie reviews, was published in 1985, and his second, *Changing Woman: The Life and Art of Helen Hardin*, in 1989. He also contributed introductions to the books *The Prints of Christopher Pratt 1958-1991*; *John Nieto*; and *Pasolini: Between Enigma and Prophecy*. At the time of his death, he was at work on a biography of film director Norman Jewison.

Jay Scott died of AIDS in 1993.

Index

The titles of the movies reviewed, and the names of their directors, writers, and main actors, are included in the index. Page references are to the start of the relevant review.